Justine & Jesse

"2011"

the BRIDE & GROOM

FIRST AND FOREVER

COOKBOOK

the BRIDE & GROOM

FIRST AND FOREVER

COOKBOOK

by Mary Corpening Barber, and Sara Corpening Whiteford,

with Rebecca Chastenet de Géry

Photographs by Susie Cushner

CHRONICLE BOOKS

SAN FRANCISCO

ISBN 978-0-8118-6503-6

The Library of Congress has cataloged the previous edition as follows:
Barber, Mary Corpening, 1969–
 The bride & groom's first and forever cookbook : recipes, tips, and techniques to start you off right / by Mary Corpening Barber, Sara Corpening Whiteford, with Rebecca Chastenet de Gery ; photographs by Susie Cushner.
  p. cm.
Includes index.
 ISBN 0-8118-3493-X
 1. Cooking. I. Corpening Whiteford, Sara, 1969– II. De Gery, Rebecca W. Chastenet III. Title.
 TX714 .B36 2003
 641.5—dc 21
                    2002010089

Manufactured in China.

Prop styling by Aaron Hom / Zenobia
Food styling Amy Nathan
Designed by Sara Schneider

10 9 8 7 6 5 4 3 2 1

Chronicle Books LLC
680 Second Street
San Francisco, California 94107

www.chroniclebooks.com

Photographer Acknowledgment
THE RECIPE FOR EXECUTING A PROJECT OF THIS MAGNITUDE REQUIRES THE EXPERIENCE, TALENT, LOYALTY, COMMITMENT, AND GENEROSITY OF MANY PEOPLE. FOREMOST IS THE DESIGNER, AND MY DEAR FRIEND, SARA SCHNEIDER, WHO TOOK THIS PROJECT ON WITH A CLEAR GOAL TO DESIGN THE PERFECT ENVIRON-MENT. THE RESULT IS EXACTLY WHAT IT SHOULD BE FROM FRONT COVER TO BACK! I WISH TO EXPRESS GRATITUDE TO AMY NATHAN AND ELIZABET DERNEDERLANDEN, FOR OUTSTANDING FOOD STYLING, AARON HOM/ZENOBIA, FOR CONTRIBUTING PERFECT STYLE AND ART DIRECTION, ALONG WITH A CONNECTION TO THE MAGIC OF PAMELA FRITZ OF INTERIEUR PERDU, FOR ONE OF OUR LOCALES; AND PAUL HAMMOND, ROD MCLEAN, AND STEPHANIE SULSER FOR EXCELLENT ASSISTANCE. SPECIAL THANKS TO BILL LEBLOND FOR INTRODUCING ME TO THE WEISS FAMILY— LISA, DAN, AND JORDON GAVE US ACCESS TO THE WARMTH AND GENEROSITY OF THEIR NEST AND FAMILY, WHICH WAS PURE JOY FOR FIVE DAYS. OUR AUTHORS, SARA AND MARY, CONTRIBUTED THEIR UNIQUE ENERGY AND INSPIRATION. THEY WERE A PLEA-SURE TO WORK WITH. I ALSO WISH TO THANK MY STAFF, JUDY AND TERI, AND MY CHILDREN, JENNA AND KAYLA.

ACKNOWLEDGMENTS

To our beloved Mom and Dad, we could never thank you enough for passing on your love for cooking and entertaining. Our passion for cooking has made life so wonderful, and this opportunity to share our recipes has been so rewarding. Thank you, both, from the bottom of our hearts, for getting us started early in the kitchen and for providing us with our culinary foundation.

We are indebted to Bill LeBlond for convincing us to write this book. What an incredible journey! Thanks for your valuable insights and for keeping us on track along the way. A sincere thank you to Kris Balloun, Amy Treadwell, Sara Schneider, and to the crew at Chronicle Books who worked tirelessly on this project. Thanks to our fabulous agent, Doe Coover, for her genuine friendship and savvy guidance along the way, and to Susie Cushner and her creative entourage for her wonderful photographs.

We raise a glass to Rebecca Chastenet de Géry, who not only captured our voices and organized our thoughts into a cohesive body of work, but also provided a great deal of support along the way. Thanks for your calm approach and your cool sensibilities right on through the arduous editing phase. We are forever grateful for your contributions in the way of words.

To Molly Naughton, this book would never have made the deadline without your endless contributions. A lot of people did a lot of things, but Molly, you have done it all! Thanks for sticking with us—for schlepping groceries, for relentlessly testing recipes, for researching every query, and for being the referee during our intense culinary disputes. Your scholarly approach and your brilliant organizational skills gave us sanity and strength. You are the yin to our yang in our culinary world, our private 411 and 911 with regard to our computer incompetence. Thanks for putting up with us and for always being there. Most importantly, thanks for your wonderful friendship.

To Emily Feinstein, you made us believe that angels really do descend from the heavens! Thanks for rescuing us during the tedious editing phase, when we were exhausted and out of steam. You kept us grounded, focused, and sane during this shaky time, guiding us through the final stages of this project. Thanks a million, dear.

A heartfelt thanks to the amazing men in our lives, Jack and Erik, for their love and unwavering support on so many accounts. Without sacrifice on the part of our husbands, this project would never be. Thank you, boys, for being our truest and most honest recipe tasters and, more importantly, for being Mr. Moms when we had to work long hours and weekends. Most of all, thanks for encouraging our pursuit of culinary knowledge and our quest to share what we consider to be one of life's greatest pleasures—great-tasting food.

A big, warm, fuzzy hug to our devoted recipe testers (if they weren't already friends and family, they are now). As we approached the deadline for our book, we sent out every single recipe to be retested (for the fifth, sixth, or even tenth time!). Thanks for your honesty, your culinary insights, and your final stamp of approval—we can finally rest easy at night. Thanks to:

Carmen Ames, Ali Banks, Lucy Bowen and Bruce Taylor, Wizzie Broach, Chris and Robin Bulger, Amy Burlaga, Katherine Cobbs, John Corpening, Susan Corpening, Carolyn Edwards, Jennifer Elam, Susannah Fassberg, Susan Feinstein, Carter Foster, Susannah Gaterud-Mack, Greta Hamm, Deli Haynes, Catherine Kot, Andrea and Daniel Madruga, Katrina Martelino, Veronia Minas and her family, Mary Nell Naughton, Haley and John Nolde, Julie Panger and Alois Crowell, Fairley Pilaro, Tori Ritchie, Tracy Salamon, Libit Schoch, Mandy Schoch, Gabby Skurnick, Sally Smith, Lila Steinle, Susan Stuart, Katie Sullivan, Patricia Willets, Cammy Davis, Martha Chamberlin, and Katarzyna Zmudzinska.

Finally, thanks to Jackson, Lucy, and William, our precious li'l pun'kins who, without even knowing it, provide us with so much love and support. You all are our everythings.

TABLE OF CONTENTS

10 *INTRODUCTION*

CHAPTER 1: KITCHEN BASICS

14 Essential Cutlery

14 Essential Pots and Pans

15 Basic Baking Equipment

16 Basic Cooking Utensils

16 Basic Appliances

17 Kitchen Extras (Not Essential but Great Add-ons)

17 Basic Glassware and Bar Accessories

CHAPTER 2: THE GLOBAL PANTRY

20 Pantry Essentials

26 A Guide to Herbs and Spices

27 Stocking the Home Bar

CHAPTER 3: BASICS *&* BEYOND

30 Chicken Stock

31 Vegetable Stock

32 Mayonnaise

33 Our "Can't-Do-Without" Marinade

34 Roasted Garlic Two Ways

36 "Gussied-Up" Marinara Sauce

37 Summertime Marinara Sauce

39 Flaky Piecrust

41 Pizza Dough

43 Croutons

44 Caesar Dressing

45 Balsamic Vinaigrette

45 Mighty Mint Vinaigrette

46 Peanut Sauce

47 Tahini-Ginger Dipping Sauce

48 Pesto

49 Cranberry Relish

50 Caramelized Onions

51 Pimiento Cheese Spread

CHAPTER 4: APPETIZERS, FINGER FOODS *&* SNACKS

54 Warm Artichoke and Green Onion Dip

55 Lemony-Tarragon Crab Dip with Salt-and-Vinegar Potato Chips

57 Crudités with Green Onion–Mint Dip

58 Guacamole

59 1-2-3 Mexican Dip

60 Artichokes with Lemon-Garlic Butter

61 Caramelized Onion, Gruyère, and Olive Tarts

62 Goat Cheese, Sun-Dried Tomato, and Pesto Torta

64 Chicken Satay

65 Herbed Buttermilk Popcorn

66 Smoked Salmon Platter

68 Marinated Olives and Feta Cheese

69 Party Pecans

CHAPTER 5: SOUPS *&* SALADS

72 Chicken Soup for Your Soul Mate

73 Creamy Mushroom Soup with Brie Crostini

74 Summer Garden Gazpacho

76 Mrs. Birdsong's Cabbage Soup

79 Roasted Butternut Squash Soup with Crème Heart Swirls

81 Thai-Style Corn Soup with Shrimp and Green Curry

82 Sherry-Spiked French Onion Soup

83 Butter Lettuce with Mango, Goat Cheese, and Mighty Mint Vinaigrette

86 Red Leaf Lettuce with Grapes, Blue Cheese, Pecans, and Balsamic Vinaigrette

88 Green Beans, Beets, and Goat Cheese with Sherry Vinaigrette

89 Arugula with Cranberries, Cambozola, Walnuts, and Raspberry Vinaigrette

91 Summer Tomato Stack

92 Confetti Coleslaw

93 Asian Spinach Salad with Hoisin-Glazed Salmon

94 Orzo Salad with Lemon, Feta, and Pine Nuts

96 Caesar Salad with Lemon-Pepper Shrimp

97 Mexican Chicken Salad with Taco-Ranch Dressing

CHAPTER 6: CLASSICS & ALL-TIME FAVORITES

101 Brie and Champagne Fondue

102 Individual Four-Cheese Pizzas

103 Classic Lasagna

105 Roast Chicken and Vegetables for Two

107 Pan-Fried Pork Chops with Glazed Apples

109 Personalized Chicken Potpies

111 Beef Burgundy

112 "Oh-Baby!" Baby Back Ribs

113 Sweet-and-Sour Brisket

114 Texas Chili with All the Fixin's

116 Stovetop Macaroni and Cheese

117 Better Than Grandma's Meat Loaf

CHAPTER 7: ENTRÉES

121 Wild Mushroom Risotto

122 Bow Tie Pasta with Asparagus, Sun-Dried Tomatoes, and Boursin

124 Linguine with Scallops, Spinach, and Bacon in Champagne-Cream Sauce

126 Pasta with Pesto, Shrimp, and Sweet 100s

128 Salmon with Honey-Mustard Glaze

129 Corn Chip–Crusted Halibut with Creamy Salsa and Cilantro

131 Grilled Tuna with Soy-Ginger Glaze and Pickled Cucumbers

132 Chicken with Prosciutto, Fontina, and Mushroom Sauce

133 Chicken "Divine"

135 Grilled Chicken with Roasted Red Pepper Salsa

137 Holiday Turkey

139 Prime Rib with Red Wine Gravy

141 Pork Tenderloin with Mango Salsa and Blackberry Syrup

142 Lamb Chops with Mint-Mustard Sauce

145 Grilled Butterflied Leg of Lamb with Lemon and Rosemary

147 Grilled London Broil Fajitas

149 Filets Mignon with Green Peppercorns and Brandy-Cream Sauce

CHAPTER 8: SIDE DISHES

152 Roasted Asparagus

153 Spinach with Raisins and Pine Nuts

155 Sweet Corn with Jalapeño Essence

156 Broccoli with Sun-Dried Tomatoes and Parmesan

157 Maple-Glazed Spiced Carrots

158 Sweet Peas with Red Onion and Mint

160 Roasted Tomato Pie

161 Sausage and Roasted Garlic Stuffing

162 Spicy Chipotle Black Beans

163 Creamy-Dreamy Mashed Potatoes

164 Potato Pancakes with Sour Cream and Chives

166 Killer Roasted Potatoes

167 Sweet Potatoes with Praline Topping

169 Wild Rice with Dried Cranberries, Green Onions, and Pecans

170 Coconut Rice

171 Couscous with Melted Leeks and Thyme

CHAPTER 9: BREAKFAST & BRUNCH

175 Eggs Benedict

177 Frittata with Sun-Dried Tomatoes, Cream Cheese, and Basil

178 Sausage and Cheddar Cheese Strata

180 French Toast with Hot Buttered Rum–Maple Syrup

181 Peanut Butter Toast with Icy-Cold Banana Milk

183 Mom's "Flyaway" Pancakes with Melted Berries

185 Quick-and-Easy Drop Biscuits

186 Yogurt-Granola Parfaits

188 Unbelievable Banana Bread

189 Rise-and-Shine Smoothie

CHAPTER 10: SWEETS

193 Spiced Carrot Cake with Fluffy Cream Cheese Icing

195 Shhh, Don't Tell—Chocolate Fudge Birthday Cake!

197 Strawberry Shortcakes d'Amour

200 Very Vanilla Cheesecake

202 Peanut Butter Pie Sealed with Kisses

203 Silken Chocolate Tart

204 Pumpkin Pie with Bourbon-Spiked Whipped Cream

207 Nectarine Tarts for Two

208 Harvest Apple Crisp

210 Shortbread Sweethearts

211 Daddy's Oatmeal Cookies

212 Our Favorite Chocolate Chip Cookies (Mary vs. Sara)

214 Ooooey-Gooey Caramel Candy Brownies

215 Raspberry-Almond Dream Cream

217 Puckery Lemon Parfaits with Summer Berries

219 "Hidden-Treasure" Bread Pudding

CHAPTER 11: THE GLOBAL BAR

222 Sauza Margaritas

222 Raspberry Champagne Sparklers

223 Strawberry Daiquiris

225 Mojitos

225 Cosmopolitans

226 Vodka-Spiked Lemonade with Red Rocks

226 Classic Martinis

227 Great Robert's Whiskey Sour Slush

228 Citrusy Sangria

229 Mary's Bloody Marys

CHAPTER 12: COOKING SIDE-BY-SIDE

232 Breakfast in Bed

233 Elegant Supper for two

234 Romantic picnic

CHAPTER 13: INSPIRATIONAL MENUS FOR
HOLIDAYS *&* SPECIAL OCCASIONS

238 Super Bowl Party

239 Valentine's Day

240 Easter Brunch

241 Fourth of July

242 Thanksgiving

243 Hanukkah

244 Christmas

245 Picnic Lunch

246 Cocktail Party

247 Summer Seated Dinner

248 Fireside Gathering

249 First Anniversary

CHAPTER 14: DINNERS *&* DESSERTS
IN A DASH

252 Linguini Alfredo with Clams

252 Stuffed Chicken Parmesan

253 Tuna with White Beans, Artichokes, and Black
Olive Tapenade

253 Cumin-Crusted Halibut with Salsa Verde

254 Pasta with Roasted Red Bell Pepper Sauce

254 Chicken, Chipotle, and Tortilla Soup

256 Pork, Bell Pepper, and Snow Pea Stir-Fry

256 Green Curry with Shrimp

257 Chinese Chicken Salad

257 Chicken with Tarragon Mustard and Pretzels

258 Chocolate Fondue

258 Triple-Decker Pound Cake with Raspberries
and Lemon Glaze

260 Hazelnut Hot Chocolate

260 Rum-Spiked Coconut Tapioca

261 Cherry Potpies

262 *DEFINITIONS OF COMMONLY USED
COOKING TERMS*

263 *GUIDE TO SEASONAL FRUITS AND VEGETABLES*

266 *INDEX*

272 *TABLE OF EQUIVALENTS*

INTRODUCTION

TO HAVE AND TO HOLD, IN SICKNESS AND IN HEALTH, TO LOVE AND TO CHERISH . . .

CONGRATULATIONS!

As women who have said "I do," we know you're in for a thrilling ride. We remember so vividly coming home from our honeymoons to settle into our new homes. What a giddy time—full of romance, joy, and great promise! There was decorating to do, new routines to create together, compromises to be made, and, most of all, a desire to nest and nurture. One of the most satisfying ways for us to nurture and to show affection during this special time in our lives was to provide and share great-tasting food.

In a lot of ways, nurturing is the foundation of this book. Food is, and has always been, our love line—it's in our blood. We have had a love affair with food since we were five years old; we honestly cooked before we could read. Oh, how we cherish our childhood memories back in North Carolina, picking blackberries from the bramble to make preserves, and plucking green tomatoes off the vines and frying them up in bacon grease for the best fried green tomatoes our side of the Mason-Dixon line. We fondly reminisce about filleting fresh-caught bream from our pond (Dad taught us to scale the fish with a grapefruit spoon when we were too young to handle a sharp knife), collecting eggs from our chicken coop for Sunday omelettes, and gathering persimmons from under the tree for Thanksgiving pudding.

Looking back now, it is clear that our direction was mapped out early on. Our passion for food (and two cute boys in New York City) led us to Peter Kump's New York Cooking School (now called The Institute of Culinary Education), followed by stints at La Varenne in Paris and in four-star New York restaurant kitchens. Our love of food (and of one of those two boys, now Mary's husband) led us out to San Francisco, where we continued our restaurant pursuits. San Francisco is home to Thymes Two, Inc., which was originally founded as home-base for our catering company, and is now a culinary consulting and cookbook writing partnership.

Although we cook professionally, we are also wives and mothers, and understand that getting a meal on the table after a busy workday or hosting a dinner party can be overwhelming. We wrote this book, keeping in mind the multiple demands on today's busy couples. We share with you a collection of user-friendly recipes, emphasizing our do-ahead philosophy wherever possible. After all, our primary goal is for you to create *great*-tasting food fast, so you'll have more time to spend with your mate. You'll find everything from modern twists on the classics and comfort foods that feed your soul to quick pantry-inspired meals. More than anything, we want to pass on our repertoire of great-tasting, simple-to-follow recipes that you'll turn to time and again—recipes you'll use as you build the foundation for your lives together and will treasure in the years to come.

Whether you and your spouse are beginning cooks or seasoned players in the kitchen, we want to make it easy and enjoyable for you to cook and entertain. With that in mind, we take you through the basics and beyond. Throughout the book, we've stripped down what you need to the bare essentials—the must-have knives, pots and pans, and basic equipment. We provide you with insights into stocking your pantry, so you'll have flavor-packed staples at your fingertips, at all times. We give you our tried-and-true formulas for made-from-scratch staples, such as piecrust, chicken stock, and mayonnaise, and provide recipes for our zesty, can't-live-without sauces, vinaigrettes, dips, and dunks that spruce up an array of foods.

Entertaining is our love, and cocktail fare—along with great cocktails—has always been of special interest. After all, we're grazers at heart. We share our secrets learned from years of catering, including no-brainer recipes for appetizers, finger foods, and snacks that are sure to satisfy. Part of entertaining during the first year of marriage includes the fear factor of holidays and special occasions. Trust us, we've been there. In our quest to simplify our lives, we always try to plan ahead . . . don't make it hard on yourselves. We've created planning guides, complete with detailed do-ahead tips so you can throw a special party with ease and confidence (and a guaranteed bubble bath before your guests arrive).

When it comes to the "main event," we offer you a cross section of entrées, from modern flavors to timeless favorites. Who can't relate to the comforts of macaroni and cheese, lasagna, chili, or chicken pot-pie? These are some of the homiest, coziest dishes we know of, and they never go out of style. For more sophisticated fare, we walk you through everything from romantic dinners for two to showstopping recipes for your first dinner party. And we haven't forgotten casual weeknight dining. Savoring a yummy casserole or a rich soup-and-salad duo will have you both feeling satisfied.

We've said it before and we'll say it again—brunch is underrated, whether you're newlyweds or not. We'll take you beyond basic eggs, giving you the confidence to make no-fail Eggs Benedict for an amorous breakfast in bed. And, for a healthful "breakfast on the fly," we've created our Rise-and-Shine Smoothie and Yogurt-Granola Parfaits.

Then, when it comes to desserts, we'll help you indulge every sweet tooth and sweetheart with our array of cakes, pies, tarts, brownies, crisps, and creams. Give your sugar some *sugar!*

Although humbly positioned at the back of the book, Dinners & Desserts in a Dash is the chapter nearest and dearest to our hearts. Here we share pantry-inspired dishes that can be turned out lightning-quick, using products already on hand. We live by these recipes during the week, when we're fiercely overprogrammed, or our husbands work late. We also love these recipes because our husbands use them to prepare impressive, delicious weeknight dinners for us. (If you knew our husbands, you'd know that's a really big deal!) We hope all of these recipes will inspire you to cook side-by-side with your spouse. There is nothing more fun than creating incredible food together. Pour two glasses of wine, turn on some great music, and stir that risotto.

When it comes to cooking side-by-side and nurturing with food, we had great role models. Our parents cooked for and with each other all the time—they truly spoiled each other. We kid you not, Mom brought Dad breakfast in bed *every* day of his life, on a silver tray, no less. Part of this was her Southern heritage (and we certainly don't live up to this standard), but it nonetheless set an example for us about keeping romance alive through food. While we wouldn't dare expect you to undertake daily breakfast delivery, we do know how rewarding it can be to nourish your relationship by feeding each other. The best part of every day is sharing a meal together. Well, almost the best part of every day . . .

If y'all have half as much fun cooking with these recipes as we did creating them, we'll feel as if we've succeeded. So get in there together and have some fun!

Maybe it's your *first* attempt in the kitchen (maybe not), but we hope cooking these recipes will become a part of your life . . . *forever.*

Mary   Sara

P. S. To *love* and to cherish = to nurture and to cook!

CHAPTER 1

KITCHEN BASICS

SKIING WITH OLD WOODEN SKIS, mountainbiking on a skinny-tired 10-speed, or trying to download a big JPEG file on an ancient Mac SE—all seem ridiculous and outdated now. The same is true when it comes to basic kitchenware and appliances. Honestly, there is nothing more frustrating than chopping an onion with a dull knife (as the tears stream down your face) or ruining soup in an uninsulated pot. We can't emphasize enough how important it is to invest in good-quality cooking equipment. As trite as it sounds, you do get what you pay for. Poor-quality, outdated equipment takes the fun right out of cooking. Quality pots, pans, knives, and equipment make cooking effortless and enjoyable—they will last for years and years, and are worth every penny.

Consider this chapter our kitchen and bar primer, where we'll help you and your mate create a home that works when it comes to food and drink. We'll show you how to stock your kitchen with no-nonsense pots and pans, utensils, and small appliances, and fill your bar (or a kitchen cupboard) with all the necessary libations and cooking wines.

If you've recently tied the knot, we suggest you take stock of what you already have. Spend a half-hour in the kitchen and compare the contents of your cupboards to our handy lists. Note something missing? Use leftover registry credit to fill in the gaps, or make it a tradition to mark each holiday with a new piece of kitchenware that you give to each other as a shared family gift. Then pull out those shiny new pots, pans, and glasses; select a couple of our food and drink recipes; and initiate your kitchen and bar!

If you're not yet married, this chapter will come in handy to you and your future mate. Bring photocopies of our equipment lists with you as you begin the wedding registry process. Suggest that shower hosts pick a party theme that focuses on equipping a particular section of your kitchen or bar.

Equipped with the right basic tools, cooking becomes a pleasure—a creative pastime you share with your spouse—and a great way to turn up the heat.

ESSENTIAL CUTLERY

No need for the $500 knife block, as wonderful as it is. The starter kitchen can get by famously with four types of knives and a reliable knife sharpener. We like Chef's Choice electric sharpener for sharpening and honing. For manual sharpening, we like a diamond steel to sharpen and realign the edge of the knife blade. Pair the selection we've listed below with a couple of cutting boards. (We recommend you have both a wooden and a dishwasher-safe acrylic board.) Add a two-pronged fork, and you'll be well equipped for all manner of chopping, dicing, slicing, and carving.

CHEF'S KNIFE (6 INCH AND 8 INCH): Intimidating at first, the chef's knife will soon become your best friend in the kitchen. Ideal for cutting vegetables and large fruits, the knife has a wide blade that also works as a pie, pizza, or quiche cutter and server. We prefer the smaller sizes because they are lighter and easier to manage than the 10 inch knife.

CARVING OR SLICING KNIFE: This all-purpose meat and poultry knife is great for slicing servings of boneless meats like pork tenderloin and carving cooked meats off the bone. The carving knife is also a sure bet for slicing or filleting fish.

SERRATED KNIFE: The serrated edge of this knife practically guarantees clean slices of bread. A bread knife doubles as a cake knife in a pinch, and its serrated edge also does a surprisingly precise job of slicing tomatoes without squashing them.

PARING KNIVES: We suggest you keep two or three of these little knives in different sizes (3 inch and 4 inch) sharp and ready for action. Paring knives peel, chop, slice, and dice, and are ideal for the detailed cuts that a chef's knife is too big to handle.

ESSENTIAL POTS AND PANS

A number of the pots and pans we consider essential are included in the 8- and 10-piece cookware sets many manufacturers make available. Purchasing pots and pans (or registering for them) this way does offer considerable savings, but there are several pots and pans we just can't live without—the Dutch oven, for example—that aren't typically included in these multi-piece sets. Make sure you have a vegetable steamer and a roasting pan with a V-shaped rack, too. We use these almost daily in our kitchens.

NONSTICK SKILLET (8 INCH AND 10 INCH): This is the all-purpose sauté, stir-fry, and omelette pan.

SAUCEPANS WITH LIDS (2 QUART AND 4 QUART): These "can-do" pans are ideal for myriad cooking tasks: melting butter, simmering sauces, heating canned foods, cooking fresh or frozen vegetables, making small batches of soup, steaming rice, preparing hot cereals, and reheating leftovers.

LARGE STOCKPOT WITH LID (8 QUART): This is a must-have for boiling pasta and simmering stews, chilies, and soups as well as preparing homemade stocks.

DUTCH OVEN WITH LID: This pan does it all: It goes from the stovetop to the oven and, if you wish, even to the table for serving. The pan's versatility makes it a great choice for stews, baked rice pilafs, casseroles, and oven-roasted vegetables. It is also ideal for slow-cooking pot roasts and braising meats. Le Creuset is a reliable brand that offers an extensive selection of attractive enameled cooking vessels.

ROASTING PAN WITH V-SHAPED RACK: You've gotta have it for oven-roasting meats and collecting their tasty juices. We prefer a large nonstick roasting pan (16 1/2 by 14 by 3 1/2 inches). The rack elevates the meat so heat circulates around it, and prevents skins from sticking or burning. Without the rack, the pan can be used for roasting vegetables and potatoes. It also makes a good vessel for marinating meats.

VEGETABLE STEAMER: While blanching vegetables in a pot of salted boiling water produces more flavorful results, steaming is a healthier alternative. We prefer a stainless steel insert, but a bamboo steamer works just fine.

BASIC BAKING EQUIPMENT

If the cook is a painter, the baker is a sculptor—both kitchen artists in their own right, but each relying on a different set of tools to create a masterpiece. Most home cooks wear both hats, baking desserts, breakfast breads, and other treats as often as they roast potatoes or chicken. Below you'll find our list of essential baking equipment—everything you'll need for great cakes and pies, killer cookies and breads, and delicious muffins, custards, tarts, and pastries.

BAKING SHEETS
    (FOUR RIMMED SHEET PANS/JELLY-ROLL PANS)
BUNDT PAN
CAKE PANS
    (TWO 9-INCH PANS)
COOKIE CUTTERS
GLASS BAKING DISHES
    (8-INCH SQUARE, 7-BY-10-INCH, AND 8-BY-12-
    INCH PANS)
LOAF PANS
    (TWO 4-BY-9-INCH PANS)
MUFFIN TINS
PARCHMENT PAPER
PASTRY BRUSH
PIE DISH
PIE RING
PIE WEIGHTS
RAMEKINS
    (EARTHENWARE, OF VARYING SIZES)
ROLLING PIN
SPRINGFORM PAN
    (9 INCH, MAKE SURE IT IS DURABLE!)
TART PAN
    (10 INCH)
WIRE RACK

BASIC COOKING UTENSILS

These are the small kitchen details we'd simply be lost without. No professional-quality oven or cookware set is complete without the support of these "little guys." If you're not yet married, a utensil shower is a great way to collect these kitchen necessities. If you've already said, "I do," take note of what's missing in your kitchen, and make a point to acquire a new item each month. And the next time you're wondering what to give the prospective bride and groom as a wedding gift, wrap up a "kitchen bouquet"—a terra-cotta pot "blooming" with these odds 'n' ends that make cooking so much more pleasurable.

BASTING BRUSH OR BULB BASTER

BOWLS

   (GRADUATED SET)

CANISTERS

   (THREE LARGE ONES FOR FLOUR, BROWN
    SUGAR, AND GRANULATED SUGAR)

CITRUS PRESS

CITRUS REAMER

COLANDER

CUTTING BOARDS

   (ONE FOR RAW MEATS, DISHWASHER-SAFE
    ACRYLIC; ONE FOR COOKED MEATS AND
    VEGETABLES, WOODEN)

GARLIC PRESS

GINGER GRATER

HAND GRATER

KITCHEN SHEARS

KITCHEN TWINE

LADLE

MEASURING CUPS

MEASURING SPOONS

MEAT MALLET

MEAT THERMOMETER

MICROPLANE GRATER

   (BOTH COARSE AND FINE GRATER)

OPENERS

   (CAN, BOTTLE, AND CORKSCREW)

PEPPER MILL

PLASTIC STORAGE CONTAINERS

POTATO RICER

POT HOLDERS

SALAD SPINNER

SPATULAS

   (SILICONE) IN VARIOUS SIZES AND COLORS

SPATULA

   (NONSTICK; SLOTTED)

SPOON, SLOTTED

SPOON, SOLID

   (LARGE METAL)

STRAINER

TIMER

TONGS

   (12-INCH UTILITY TONGS WITH
    LOCKING MECHANISM)

VEGETABLE PEELER

WHISK

WOODEN SPOONS

BASIC APPLIANCES

With these electric appliances make a great purée, create your own spice blends, chop and grate with perfection, and whip up easy meals in a flash.

BLENDER

COFFEEMAKER

CROCK-POT OR SLOW COOKER

ELECTRIC COFFEE BEAN/SPICE GRINDER

ELECTRIC HAND MIXER AND/OR STAND MIXER

FOOD PROCESSOR

GRILL

   (CHARCOAL OR GAS)

MICROWAVE

RICE COOKER

TOASTER

KITCHEN EXTRAS (NOT ESSENTIAL BUT GREAT ADD-ONS)

DOUBLE BOILER

EGG POACHING SET

FLOUR SACK TOWELS

GRILL PAN

KITCHEN TWEEZERS
  (FOR DEBONING FISH)

SCALES

BASIC GLASSWARE AND BAR ACCESSORIES

Here we've tried to pare down the myriad selection of glass- and stemware available, so you'll have multi-purpose glassware that not only works for you but won't take up valuable space if your storage is limited. We think everyone needs medium-sized all-purpose juice glasses and slightly larger all-purpose tumblers or coolers in their glass repertoire. When it comes to wineglasses, there are dozens of different bowls and stems, each created for different wine varietals. For simplicity, we suggest 12- to 15-ounce wineglasses with an open bowl, which are fine for serving both red and white wines. If storage and price are not an issue, it's great to have glasses for both. If you are serving only red wine, you can use the white wine glasses for water, and vice versa. For festive barware, we think martini glasses and Champagne flutes are a must. We use martini glasses both for high-octane cocktails and as an elegant way to present desserts.

CHAMPAGNE FLUTES: Tall, elegant flutes are a must for serving Champagne, sparkling wines, and Champagne-based cocktails.

DOUBLE OLD-FASHIONED GLASSES: 10- to 15-ounce tumblers (sometimes referred to as "coolers") are durable, multipurpose glasses for beer, soda, alcohol–soft drink combinations, milk, water, and juice.

JUICE GLASSES: 6- to 8-ounce straight-sided glasses are designed for serving fruit juices and alcohol–soft drink combinations as well as whiskey on the rocks. If you drink large quantities of juice, you may want to skip this glass size, and substitute double old-fashioned glasses or tumblers.

MARTINI GLASSES: With their wide-rimmed top and triangular glass shape, these glasses make great all-purpose cocktail stems.

WINEGLASSES: We recommend you keep it practical, stocking a 12- to 15-ounce wineglass with a relatively open rim and a long stem. Note that glasses with extra-long stems and large bowls (typically the prettiest) may not fit in the dishwasher.

BLENDER

BOTTLE OPENER

COCKTAIL NAPKINS

COCKTAIL PICKS
  (FOR GARNISHES)

COCKTAIL SHAKER WITH STRAINER

CORKSCREW

JIGGER

PITCHER

SMALL BOWLS FOR GARNISHES

SWIZZLE STICKS
  (GLASS, DISPOSABLE)

WINE-BOTTLE COOLER AND/OR
  CHAMPAGNE BUCKET

CHAPTER 2

THE GLOBAL PANTRY

OUR PANTRY MANTRA IS "USE, ROTATE, AND REPLACE." Why stock a cupboard with canned goods and other staples that never get used? The pantry exists to add zip and flair to everything you cook. It should be your primary source of culinary inspiration, assuring quick, interesting meals that never taste like afterthoughts—even though they sometimes might be. In this chapter we outline our version of the practical cook's pantry. Here you'll find tried-and-true ingredients as well as specialty items for those times when you want your cooking to be extra special, with minimum effort.

In our own homes, we turn to the pantry every night, sometimes in search of an added flavor kick, other times for stylish, simple dishes like our Dinners & Desserts in a Dash (see page 251). In fact, we have to admit that, as much as we thrill in creating elaborate entrées using all fresh ingredients, we sometimes get even more satisfaction out of assembling a jaw-droppingly delicious meal from our pantry products. And we really love it when our husbands treat us to a surprise pantry meal!

Take the time to familiarize yourselves with your pantry. That way, using those products becomes as automatic to both of you as, say, grabbing a chunk of cheese from the refrigerator. At mealtimes—and especially on those busy evenings when you find yourselves cooking off the cuff—move beyond what we call "refrigerator stare" and open that pantry. Having an enticing food stash on hand is one household luxury neither of you should live without.

Because the goal is to use, rotate, and replace your pantry's contents often, pay attention to the usage notes we've included after each entry. Some pantry items may need refrigerating after opening, so read product labels carefully. Transfer any leftover foods from their original aluminum cans and store in sealable glass or plastic containers.

Be sure to check out our pantry-inspired Dinners in a Dash. All of these recipes can be quickly assembled using one or two pantry products as a foundation. This is truly one of our favorite chapters in the book, and we hope it will become yours, too.

ALFREDO SAUCE (REGULAR AND ROASTED GARLIC): This cheesy sauce, originally created for all the pasta lovers in Rome, has a smooth, creamy texture that is rich and decadent. We keep both the regular and roasted-garlic sauces on hand for on-the-fly pasta dishes and casseroles.

ARTICHOKES: Although we prefer marinated, oil-packed artichokes in a jar to the canned, water-packed variety, we stock both kinds.

BAKING POWDER: A leavening agent, baking powder is a common ingredient in cakes and cookies. Always check the expiration date; if baking powder is old, baked goods won't rise.

BAKING SODA: A standard ingredient in baking recipes, baking soda doubles as a super kitchen cleaner for removing baked-on foods and stains from utensils, appliances, and ceramic and laminate countertops. Always check the expiration date before using.

BALSAMIC VINEGAR: Splash this sweet elixir over salad greens, or reduce it to create a mellow glaze for roasted meats and grilled vegetables. Or get adventurous and toss a pint of halved fresh strawberries in a tablespoon of it—fantastic!

BARBECUE SAUCE: A ready-made sauce that adds pizzazz to oven-baked or grilled chicken, pork, beef, ribs, and even pizza crust. Look for high-quality specialty barbecue sauces and buy several different ones, then conduct a taste test to find your favorite brand.

BEANS AND LEGUMES (BLACK, CANNELLINI, GARBANZO OR CHICKPEAS, GREAT NORTHERN, KIDNEY, PINTO, LENTILS): Perfect sources of protein, beans and legumes make a meal feel "meaty" even when it's not. Wrap black beans in a tortilla with avocado, grated cheese, and salsa. For a quick hummus, purée garbanzos with garlic, lemon, and a dollop of plain yogurt. Toss great Northern or cannellini beans with fresh tomatoes and basil over pasta, and serve lentils at room temperature, dressed with a curry-spiked vinaigrette. Keep an array of both dried and canned beans on hand. Soak dried beans overnight in water before cooking. We like to rinse and drain canned beans before using (except for baked beans or flavored beans).

BLACK OLIVE TAPENADE: This puréed olive product from the south of France typically includes garlic, lemon juice, and, when authentic, anchovies. For a sophisticated hors d'oeuvre, spread on a crostini that has been slathered with goat cheese or dollop onto a grilled tuna steak for an unexpected burst of flavor.

BREAD STICKS (GRISSINI): Prop them up in a colorful tumbler and display as an accent to your meals. Serve instead of croutons with a salad or alongside a steaming bowl of soup. Paired with assorted crackers, they add variety to cheese platters.

BROTH/BOUILLON: Chicken, vegetable, or beef broth is used as a base for soups, sauces, and stews. We cook rice and couscous in broth rather than water for enhanced flavor. Buy low-sodium broth when available and look out for flavored broths with added garlic, mushroom, or herbs. We love the "tetra-brick" cartons of stock because they are resealable, but there are powder and cube forms as well.

BUTTERMILK (POWDERED): Powdered buttermilk is a brilliant substitute for fresh buttermilk when you don't have a quart in the refrigerator. Honestly, you'd never know the difference. We also keep the powdered version on hand so we won't have to buy an entire carton of buttermilk when we may need only a cup for a recipe.

It is great for impromptu pancakes, biscuits, and other baked goods—it gives them a fine crumb and light texture. This powder is made from real sweet cream and churned Wisconsin buttermilk, whereas dairy-case buttermilk is actually a cultured skim-milk product. Powdered buttermilk keeps for at least 1 year in the refrigerator. SACO brand is most widely available.

CANNED TOMATOES: There are many styles of canned tomatoes and tomato sauces. Many companies offer Italian-, Mexican-, and Cajun-style stewed tomatoes and even fire-roasted ones, which add variety to your pantry. We stock diced, crushed (with and without purée), and stewed tomatoes in addition to tomato paste. We prefer tomato paste in a tube because we can squeeze out just the amount we need, and it's easy to store. Whenever possible, we like to buy organic brands, such as Muir Glen.

CANOLA OIL: The perfect all-purpose cooking oil, canola oil is low in saturated fat, with plenty of those heart-healthy monounsaturated fats and even beneficial omega-3 fatty acids.

CAPERS: The buds of a Mediterranean bush, capers are sold in brine or layered in salt. If packed in salt, be sure to rinse them. Capers have a distinctive sour "punch" that adds dimension to mayonnaise and brightens lightly sauced pasta and broiled fish dishes.

CHOCOLATE CAKE MIX: We always keep a box on hand for instant gratification. See our Shhh, Don't Tell—Chocolate Fudge Birthday Cake (page 195). Just remember, you can get away with using a cake mix, if you make the icing from scratch.

CHOCOLATE CHIPS: A must for baking, chocolate chips can be melted to create an instant fondue to coat fresh and dried fruit. Seek the highest quality available.

COCOA: Cocoa has multiple uses in baking. When blended with equal parts cinnamon and chili powder, it is also excellent as an exotic dry rub for chicken. We prefer Dutch cocoa for its rich, mellow flavor.

COCONUT EXTRACT: A drop of coconut extract imparts a tropical flavor punch to smoothies, tapioca, and custards. Coconut extract often bears the label "imitation" and, though we usually balk at anything imitation, we make an exception here. Remember that just a little dab will do. Add too much and your dish will taste more of suntan lotion than real coconut!

COCONUT MILK: Coconut milk is made from equal parts water and shredded fresh coconut that is simmered until foamy, then strained through cheesecloth. Do not confuse with coconut cream, which is thicker and usually sweetened, or "cream of coconut," which is used in desserts and tropical drinks. Use coconut milk as a base for soups, curries, and creamy desserts, such as rice pudding. We've even been known to add it to smoothies for a voluptuous tropical touch.

CORNBREAD MIX: Spiff up your favorite cornbread mix with some chopped jalapeño chile, a dollop of bacon grease, or some fresh corn kernels.

CORNSTARCH: Most often used for thickening sauces, soups, and puddings, this powdery flour is usually mixed with a small amount of cold liquid before being added to a hot mixture.

COUSCOUS: A staple of North African cuisine, couscous is often mistaken for a grain, but it is actually a tiny pasta made from semolina flour. Few side dishes can be prepared faster than couscous. Just add boiling broth or water and . . . voilà! Mild in flavor, couscous adopts the taste of the food it is paired with, so be creative with flavor combinations. It's best served warm or at room temperature.

CRACKERS (CARR'S TABLE WATER CRACKERS, WHEAT THINS, TRISCUITS, RITZ): Crackers are the essential hors d'oeuvre base for dipping, spreading, and topping. We also crumble them with dried herbs to create a simple topping for poultry, fish, and casseroles.

DRIED FRUITS (RAISINS, APRICOTS, CRANBERRIES, CHERRIES, PRUNES): Beyond healthful snacking, dried fruits are an important ingredient in many bread and cookie recipes. We also add dried fruits to savory dishes—raisins to sautéed greens, and cranberries to rice pilafs and green salads, for example.

FLOUR (ALL-PURPOSE AND CAKE): All-purpose flour is a blend of hard and soft wheat flours and, like its name suggests, is the most commonly used cooking flour. Cake flour is made solely from soft wheat, ensuring light, tender cakes. Do not use cake flour for baking bread. For accurate measuring, spoon flour into the measuring cup and level it with a knife. Do not scoop flour directly from the bag into your measuring cup and level it against the side of the sack.

GREEN CURRY PASTE: Commonly used in Thai cooking, green curry paste is a blend of green chiles, garlic, onion, and spices. It is potent, so be conservative.

HOISIN SAUCE: Also known as Peking sauce, hoisin sauce is a slightly sweet Asian sauce made from soybeans, dried chiles, and spices. We like to "doctor" hoisin with a squeeze of lime juice and a splash of chili oil for a gutsy glaze on broiled salmon, grilled pork tenderloin, or roast chicken breast.

HONEY: Great spread on warm biscuits and toast, of course, honey also makes an excellent glaze for oven-roasted pork and root vegetables. For a simple appetizer, drizzle a "designer honey," such as lavender or orange blossom, over a log of goat cheese garnished with toasted walnuts, and serve with warm breads.

HORSERADISH (PREPARED): This condiment enlivens meats, stews, potato salads, and smoked deli products. Blend prepared horseradish with sour cream, add a touch of lemon juice and salt and pepper, and serve with roast beef.

JAM: The beloved accompaniment to a Continental breakfast and often the finishing touch on fruit tarts, jam also has a place in savory preparations. Melt it down for an instant glaze for meats, such as duck, pork, or lamb.

KETCHUP: No pantry is complete without this all-American condiment. Look out for a variety of "specialty" ketchups accented with sundried tomatoes, ginger, chiles, or roasted garlic.

MAPLE SYRUP: Be sure to buy "pure" maple syrup, not the artificial maple-flavored, pancake syrups sold in most grocery stores. These consist of corn syrup flavored with artificial maple extract. Real maple syrup ranges in grades and color from light amber to very dark and molasses-like in flavor. Think outside the box . . . maple syrup is perfect for sweet potatoes and holiday hams, and naturally sweetens plain yogurt and fruit.

MARINARA SAUCE: Use it over pasta, as a topping for store-bought or homemade pizza crusts, as a dipping sauce for breadsticks, or even in place of mayonnaise on a hearty sandwich of Italian cold cuts. We like Muir Glen brand. Tomato sauce in a jar takes on a new dimension in our "Gussied-Up" Marinara Sauce (see page 36).

MAYONNAISE: We prefer homemade but always keep prepared mayonnaise on hand. Add chopped herbs, minced shallots, and a squeeze of fresh lemon juice to this pantry staple, and you've created a specialty mayonnaise.

MUSTARD: Stock several kinds—Dijon, honey, tarragon, grainy—for a regular change of taste. Add grainy mustard and a big dollop of sour cream to the pan juices of a skillet-seared steak, then serve the creamy blend as a sinful steak sauce. Tarragon mustard is a feisty French Dijon flecked with aromatic tarragon leaves, which have a subtle anise flavor. It goes great with fish and poultry.

NUTELLA: This Italian hazelnut and chocolate spread tastes amazing on toast, croissants, crackers, and cookies. Or stir into hot milk for a new twist on hot chocolate. To satisfy a sweet tooth, we often dip strawberries and bananas into this unique spread.

NUTS (CASHEWS, HAZELNUTS, MACADAMIA NUTS, PEANUTS, PECANS, PINE NUTS, WALNUTS): Toasted nuts transform plain dishes into something special. We store raw nuts in the freezer to preserve their freshness. Toast nuts in the oven to release their flavor before incorporating them into your recipes.

OATMEAL: We're talking about natural rolled oats, regular or quick cook—not the instant sweetened oatmeal sold in single-serve packages. Oatmeal is great to have on hand for cookies and streusel, and of course, it makes a hearty, warming breakfast. But oatmeal needn't be bland or boring (so often it's prepared with just water and oats). Oatmeal is a perfect vehicle for creativity. Try adding fresh or dried fruits, toasted nuts, vanilla, maple syrup, warm milk, or cinnamon. Our favorite preparation consists of oats cooked with whole milk, and topped with warm sautéed Comice pears, toasted walnuts, and maple syrup.

OLIVE OIL: Olive oil has myriad uses: dressing salads, drizzling on vegetables, making marinades—you name it. Extra-virgin, virgin (also labeled as simply olive oil), and light olive oil have different uses. Extra-virgin olive oil comes from the first cold pressing of the olives. It is the most full flavored of the olive oil grades and should be reserved as a finishing oil. Do not use extra-virgin olive oil for high-heat cooking because of its low smoke point. Virgin olive oil is less fruity than extra-virgin and should be used for cooking, not as a finishing oil. Light olive oil has little of the classic olive oil flavor due to its extremely fine filtration, but, despite its name, it is not any lower in calories. Because of its high smoke point, it is ideal for high-heat cooking, such as pan-frying, sautéing, and deep-frying. Light olive oil may also be used in baking since it has a mild flavor.

OLIVES: Although best bought fresh from the bulk section, olives in jars are a great staple for an easy hors d'oeuvre or for adding to recipes. Stock several different varieties (Kalamata, sun-dried black, Spanish, pitted green, tiny Niçoise).

PANCAKE MIX (SUCH AS BISQUICK): The all-purpose pancake and waffle wizard is a lifesaver when you don't have time to make them from scratch. Enliven this store-bought product with fresh fruit, such as blueberries, bananas, or raspberries . . . or even chocolate chips.

PASTA: Stock different shapes and flavors for variety. Try rice vermicelli or soba (buckwheat) noodles in place of rice with Asian-inspired recipes. Look for fresh pastas in the refrigerated section of your supermarket.

PEANUT BUTTER: Hard to beat in a sandwich with a glass of milk, peanut butter is also excellent in baking and as a flavoring for Asian noodle dishes and sauces. We refrigerate it to preserve its flavor.

PEANUT SAUCE: A smooth bottled sauce found in the Asian section of most supermarkets, peanut sauce typically accompanies soft spring rolls or satay served in Asian restaurants. It has a distinctive peanut flavor, accentuated by an assortment of Asian spices.

PEPPERCORNS: Using freshly ground peppercorns rather than preground pepper will contribute considerably more flavor to your food. Consider owning two pepper mills—one filled with black peppercorns for cooking and the other a transparent mill filled with a colorful peppercorn blend for use at the table. We also keep green peppercorns in brine on hand for making steak *au poivre*. (Our version of this classic dish is called Filets Mignon with Green Peppercorns and Brandy-Cream Sauce; page 149.) These soft, underripe pepper berries have a distinctly different flavor from regular peppercorns. They are not as spicy yet have a delightful complexity.

PICKLES: Pickles are often best when bought from the deli section of the supermarket. Always taste them before buying to be sure they have a crisp texture and bright flavor. We recommend storing classic kosher dills, bread and butter pickles, and the diminutive French pickled gherkins known as cornichons.

RICE: Think beyond Uncle Ben's and round out your selection with fragrant basmati or jasmine rice, earthy brown rice, and the distinctively nutty American wild rice, which is actually not a rice but a long-grained marsh grass. And keep plenty of Italian Arborio rice on hand for making tasty risottos.

ROASTED RED BELL PEPPERS: These sweet, soft red bell peppers have been roasted before being packed in jars. Available both red and yellow, roasted peppers are used frequently in Mediterranean cooking. When using jarred peppers as a substitute for home-roasted peppers, we rinse the peppers, pat them dry, and season with high quality extra-virgin olive oil and salt and pepper.

SALSA: Stock a standard tomato-based red salsa; a smoky, fire-roasted red version; and a tart tomatillo, or green salsa. Look for tomatillo salsa in the Mexican section of your supermarket or in ethnic groceries. Herdez makes a wonderful canned salsa verde. Oftentimes we'll fold in freshly chopped avocado and cilantro to the store-bought salsa verde to impact freshness.

SALT: We call for kosher salt in all of our recipes because we like its bright, clean flavor. Kosher salt is free of additives and has a wonderfully coarse texture that makes it ideal for adding to food in pinches. If you prefer plain table salt or iodized salt (which is table salt with added iodine), simply use half the amount called for in our recipes. Sea salt, which costs a bit more, has become the rage of the food world. It packs great flavor and is available in a variety of textures, from the finest *fleur de sel*, used as a final seasoning, to the coarser *sel gris*. Because of the range of textures available, sea salt equivalents are difficult to provide.

SOY SAUCE: A key ingredient in Asian cuisine, soy sauce is an excellent salt substitute and all-purpose seasoning. Add it to marinades and pan juices for enhanced flavor. Tamari, also known as Japanese soy, is similar in flavor but considerably less salty.

SPIRITS (MADEIRA, SHERRY, BRANDY, PORT, MARSALA): Added to braising liquids and sauces, spirits supply depth and flavor. Their alcohol content is drastically diminished (if not entirely removed) during cooking. Try to stay away from "cooking" spirits, often found in grocery stores. As a rule of thumb, we buy moderately priced spirits, but buy according to your budget.

SUGAR: Keep white, brown, and powdered sugars on hand for cooking and baking. Stock sugar cubes—European "rough-cut" cubes and whimsically colored rock crystals—to add a special touch when serving coffee and tea.

SUN-DRIED TOMATOES: We prefer sun-dried tomatoes packed in oil to the ones sold dry in the produce section. If you're purchasing dried tomatoes, hydrate in very hot water until soft. Be sure to drain tomatoes thoroughly before using.

TABASCO SAUCE (OR OTHER BOTTLED HOT SAUCE): A dash jazzes up soups, dips, dressings, marinades, dipping sauces, and even eggs.

TAPIOCA: Extracted from the tropical cassava plant, this starchy substance is sold in many forms, including quick-cooking tapioca and tapioca flour. The quick-cooking variety is the most readily available and can be made in a jiff. Just don't overcook it or it will become gluey. We love tapioca both warm and chilled as a soothing dessert.

TUNA: We prefer the solid white albacore tuna that is packed in water. It has a milder, less fishy flavor than tuna packed in oil. However, if you can find imported tuna packed in extra-virgin olive oil, it's a delicious departure from standard oil-packed brands and is well worth purchasing. To take canned tuna a step beyond the ordinary, use it to create a salade Niçoise, with hard-boiled eggs, black olives, tomatoes, red onion, potatoes, and green beans.

VANILLA BEANS: The vanilla bean is actually the pod of an orchid flower. When the pod is slit open lengthwise, the black specks can be scraped from the inside using the tip of a sharp knife. Because the vanilla beans that are available commercially are often thin, brittle, and overly expensive, we order high-quality vanilla beans in bulk from Penzey's Spice (800) 741-7787 or www.penzeys.com. We store them, refrigerated, in a glass jar submerged with vodka, brandy, or bourbon. They keep indefinitely. The steeping of the pods in alcohol becomes pure vanilla extract.

VANILLA EXTRACT: A key ingredient in baking, vanilla extract also perks up coffee, hot chocolate, yogurt, and creamed puddings. Be sure to purchase "pure" vanilla extract, not "imitation."

WINE VINEGAR (RED AND WHITE): White wine vinegar's subtle flavor best complements white meats, seafood, and delicate sauces. With its more pronounced astringency, red wine vinegar is ideal for dressing salads. Both act as a tenderizing agent in marinades.

WORCESTERSHIRE SAUCE: This soy-based condiment typically contains vinegar, molasses, anchovy paste, shallots, and sugar. In small doses, Worcestershire adds flavor to soups as well as marinades for grilled meats, poultry, and fish. Add a dash to horseradish sauce or to vegetable dips. It's also great in Bloody Marys and on hamburgers.

YEAST: Used for ages as a leavening agent, baker's yeast comes in three basic forms—active dry yeast, compressed fresh yeast, and yeast starters. Active dry yeast is the easiest to find. These tiny dehydrated granules are available in two forms, regular and quick rising. The latter takes about half as long to leaven. Pay attention to expiration dates. Baked goods made with old yeast won't rise.

A GUIDE TO HERBS AND SPICES

Herbs and spices add an extra-special touch to your foods by accentuating flavors. Understanding how to use these seasonings provides a key to great cooking. In general, herbs come from the green, leafy parts of plants, while spices are derived from the aromatic pods, roots, and seeds.

BUYING AND STORING

Herbs are available fresh and dried, the latter sold primarily in flaked form. Spices are sold both whole and ground. Whole spices will retain their flavor considerably longer than ground ones. Fresh herbs typically must be refrigerated, while dried herbs and spices should be kept in the pantry or in an enclosed spice rack. Continued exposure to light and heat will diminish their flavor.

To ensure that your herbs and spices do what they are supposed to do—add flavor to your food—do not store dried herbs and spices for more than a year (6 months if spices are preground). Buying them in small, as-needed amounts from the bulk section of your supermarket is a great way to follow our pantry mantra to "use, rotate, and replace."

FRESH HERBS

Because fresh herbs have a less intense flavor than dried ones, add them at the end of cooking for optimum impact. Exceptions include rosemary, sage, bay leaf, oregano, and savory, all of which can withstand simmering even when fresh. Generally, fresh herbs are two to three times less potent than dried herbs, so when substituting fresh herbs in a recipe that calls for dried ones, use proportionately more fresh.

We recommend that you use the following herbs only in their fresh form, as their dried versions are dull by comparison: basil, chervil, chives, cilantro, and parsley.

DRIED HERBS

Many dried herbs provide the foundation for long-simmered dishes. To increase their flavor power, crush or "pinch-grind" dried herb flakes as you add them.

We suggest that you keep these dried herbs on hand: bay leaf, dill weed, marjoram, oregano, rosemary, sage, tarragon, and thyme. Dried herb blends, such as French herbes de Provence, are great to stock as well.

SPICES

Whenever possible, buy whole spices and grind them at home in a coffee-bean grinder (reserved just for spices) or by hand, using a mortar and pestle. If your supermarket doesn't sell bulk spices, affix a mailing label or other sticker to your spice jars, noting the date of purchase.

BASIC SPICES WE ALWAYS STOCK:

Whole—black peppercorns, nutmeg, red pepper flakes, sesame seeds

Ground—cayenne, chili powder, coriander, cumin, curry powder, mustard, onion powder, garlic powder

Whole and Ground—allspice, cinnamon, cloves

STOCKING THE HOME BAR

Every home bar should be stocked according to your taste preferences—and those of your friends. How you stock your bar will depend upon the type of event you are hosting and your budget. There are times when top-shelf alcohols are important (when making a gin or vodka martini) and other times when a lesser-quality brand will do (buying vodka for a pitcher of Bloody Marys). Keep this in mind as you stock your bar. Following is a list of what we consider the most common alcohols, mixers, and liqueurs to keep on hand.

ALCOHOLS
Beer
Bourbon
Champagne
Gin
Rum (light and/or dark)
Scotch
Tequila
Vermouth
Vodka
Wine (red and white)

MIXERS
Bottled water
Club soda
Juices (cranberry, grapefruit, and orange)
Soft drinks
Tonic

BRANDY AND LIQUEURS

It used to be that brandy and liqueurs were a regular part of post-dinner bar service. Today, they crop up more often in cooking than at the bar. We recommend that you stock the following in your bar for after-dinner drinks, or in your pantry for cooking.

Brandy
Flavored liqueurs: Amaretto (almond), crème de menthe, framboise (raspberry), Frangelico (hazelnut), Grand Marnier (orange), Tia Maria (coffee)
Port
Sherry

CHAPTER 3

BASICS & BEYOND

IN THIS CHAPTER WE PROVIDE YOU WITH BASIC CULINARY BUILDING BLOCKS as well as recipes for simple yet sophisticated sauces, vinaigrettes, dips, and dunks. There is a time and a place for making things *completely* from scratch—sometimes you have it in you and sometimes you don't. We always keep jarred mayonnaise, frozen piecrusts, and roasted garlic on hand, just in case. By all means, take advantage of the high-quality prepared products out there—we certainly do. But when time allows, the extra effort required to create the homemade versions of The Basics is time well invested. After all, it's prepared with an extra dose of TLC. On a leisurely Sunday afternoon, we'll prepare Chicken Stock (page 30) to freeze or a double batch of Pizza Dough (page 41) for make-your-own-pizza nights during the week. When we crave BLTs, the only way to get a real fix is to make one with our homemade Mayonnaise (page 32). (We Southerners put mayonnaise on just about everything!)

When you're stepping Beyond the Basics we urge you to keep a stash of our signature sauces and vinaigrettes on hand to dress up your dish in a flash, or add another layer of flavor to ordinary recipes. Most of the time all you need is one little thing—that pull-it-out-of-the-fridge-fast touch—to create a winning meal. We always keep a few of our zippy Beyond Basics items in our fridge, such as Mighty Mint Vinaigrette (page 45), Peanut Sauce (page 46), or Caramelized Onions (page 50), to top, dollop, or smother, and douse to our hearts' and tummies' content. With easy access to these in-the-fridge creations, you'll be amazed at how quickly culinary rock stars are born. All of these recipes were our catering standbys for years. We hope you'll develop a crush on them, too.

CHICKEN STOCK

Makes about 10 cups

Homemade chicken stock can't be beat for adding a wealth of flavor to dishes in which you would usually use canned broth. Freeze in sealable bags and fill an ice tray with homemade stock, so you'll have large and small amounts on hand for all your cooking needs. | We want to share one of our little secrets: Don't throw out the chicken fat that rises to the top after the stock cools. Melt the fat and drizzle it—in lieu of olive oil or butter—over vegetables before roasting them. Yes, it's decadent, but it adds unbeatable flavor. There is a reason why vegetables taste oh-so-good when you roast them alongside a chicken!

5	POUNDS CHICKEN BONES (BACKS, NECKS, CARCASSES, AND/OR WING TIPS)
10	CUPS WATER, PLUS MORE AS NEEDED
1	LARGE YELLOW ONION, UNPEELED, COARSELY CHOPPED
2	CELERY STALKS, INCLUDING LEAVES, COARSELY CHOPPED
2	MEDIUM CARROTS, COARSELY CHOPPED
2	CLOVES GARLIC, UNPEELED, SMASHED
8	FRESH FLAT-LEAF OR CURLY PARSLEY SPRIGS (STEMS INCLUDED)
8	FRESH THYME SPRIGS
1	BAY LEAF
1	TEASPOON PEPPERCORNS
	KOSHER SALT

Combine the chicken bones, the 10 cups water, the onion, celery, carrots, garlic, parsley, thyme, bay leaf, peppercorns, and salt to taste in an 8-quart stockpot. Add more water as needed to cover the ingredients. Bring to a boil over high heat, reduce the heat to low, and simmer gently for 30 minutes, skimming the foam frequently. Continue simmering for about 3 hours more.

Strain the stock through a colander into a large bowl, pressing on the solids. Strain the stock again through a fine-mesh sieve into another large bowl. Let cool slightly, then refrigerate, uncovered. Remove the fat that solidifies on top of the chilled stock.

The stock will keep, covered and refrigerated, for 1 week or frozen for 3 months.

VEGETABLE STOCK

Makes 6 cups

You don't have to be a vegetarian to appreciate an aromatic, great-tasting, chock-full-of-vegetables stock. Not only is it a terrific substitute for chicken or beef stock, vegetable stock also makes a wonderful base for soups and stews, and gives couscous, rice, and other grains a flavor boost. With just a small time investment, a homemade vegetable stock soars above and beyond its canned cousins.

2	TABLESPOONS VEGETABLE OIL
2	LARGE CARROTS, CUT INTO 1-INCH PIECES
2	LARGE CELERY STALKS, INCLUDING LEAVES, CUT INTO 1-INCH PIECES
2	MEDIUM YELLOW ONIONS, UNPEELED, COARSELY CHOPPED
2	LEEKS, BOTH WHITE AND PALE GREEN PARTS, WASHED WELL AND ROUGHLY CHOPPED
8	CLOVES GARLIC, UNPEELED, SMASHED
10	FRESH FLAT-LEAF PARSLEY SPRIGS
1	BAY LEAF
8	FRESH THYME SPRIGS
1	TEASPOON PEPPERCORNS
8	CUPS WATER
1	TEASPOON KOSHER SALT

Heat the oil in a 6-quart stockpot over medium-high heat. Add the carrots, celery, onions, leeks, garlic, parsley, bay leaf, thyme, and peppercorns. Cook, stirring frequently, for 5 to 10 minutes. (The longer you cook the vegetables, the richer the stock will be.)

Add the water and kosher salt and bring to a boil. Reduce the heat to low and simmer for 30 minutes.

Strain the stock through a colander into a large bowl, pressing on the solids. Strain the stock again through a fine-mesh sieve into another large bowl. Let cool slightly, then refrigerate.

The stock will keep, covered and refrigerated, for 1 week or frozen for 3 months.

MAYONNAISE

Makes 2 ¹/₂ cups

Homemade mayonnaise was a staple in our home—in part because our mother knew that serving it offered a direct path to our father's heart! If you've never experienced smooth, silky, homemade mayonnaise, set aside time to whip up a double batch. We're warning you, it's habit-forming!

2	EGG YOLKS AT ROOM TEMPERATURE
1	EGG AT ROOM TEMPERATURE
1	TABLESPOON DIJON MUSTARD
1	TABLESPOON WATER
2	TEASPOONS FRESH LEMON JUICE
2	TEASPOONS WHITE WINE VINEGAR
1	TEASPOON SUGAR
¹/₂	TEASPOON KOSHER SALT
	PINCH OF FRESHLY GROUND PEPPER
2	CUPS VEGETABLE OIL

IF USING A FOOD PROCESSOR: Fit with the steel blade. Combine the egg yolks, egg, mustard, water, lemon juice, vinegar, sugar, kosher salt, and pepper in the bowl and process until well mixed. With the motor running, add the oil through the feed tube drop by drop so the eggs and oil will combine smoothly. (Most feed tubes have a small hole in them specifically for this purpose. Fill the tube repeatedly with a portion of the oil, and it will drip slowly into the bowl.) After emulsification has begun and the mayonnaise starts to hold together, pour in the oil in a slow, steady stream. When all the oil has been added, shut off the motor and scrape down the sides of the bowl.

IF USING A BLENDER: Combine the egg yolks, egg, mustard, water, lemon juice, vinegar, sugar, kosher salt, and pepper in the blender and blend on medium until well mixed. With the blender running on high speed, add the oil drop by drop so the eggs and oil will combine smoothly. After emulsification has begun and the mayonnaise starts to hold together, pour in the oil in a slow, steady stream. (Halfway through, the mixture will become very thick. Thin with 2 to 3 tablespoons water if necessary before adding the remaining oil.)

Tips for perfect mayonnaise:

1. To fix mayonnaise that has separated, put 1 egg yolk (at room temperature) in a clean bowl. Slowly drizzle the "broken" mayonnaise into the egg yolk (as you would drizzle oil into mayonnaise) and whisk to incorporate. If it gets overly thick, add a little lukewarm water to the mixture before adding to the rest of the "broken" mayonnaise.

2. While classic mayonnaise recipes use raw eggs (we feel totally comfortable with this), if you are concerned about salmonella, use soft-cooked yolks (discard whites) in place of raw ones, but realize the texture will not be as smooth and light. It will also be thicker. Add more water if necessary. (For soft-cooked, bring eggs to a boil, cover, and remove from heat for 3 minutes.)

Our *"Can't-Do-Without"* MARINADE

Makes 1 heaping cup

We can't live without this powerfully flavorful marinade, and we don't think you'll want to either. It truly doesn't get any easier than this—no excessive chopping or futzin'. Just throw everything in the blender and away you go. Pureeing the garlic and rosemary together imparts such amazing flavor to this can't-do-without creation. It is versatile enough to use on beef and lamb, as well as on chicken, pork, and fish. For smaller cuts of meats, we marinate for up to an hour (30 minutes outside of the refrigerator). If you have more time, marinate larger cuts in the refrigerator for up to 24 hours. This recipe makes enough to marinate two pounds of meat.

MARINADE FOR RED MEATS

1/4	CUP OLIVE OIL, PLUS MORE AS NEEDED
1	TABLESPOON SOY SAUCE
1/2	CUP RED WINE
1/2	SMALL YELLOW ONION, QUARTERED
1/4	CUP FRESH ROSEMARY LEAVES
3	LARGE CLOVES GARLIC, PEELED

MARINADE FOR PORK, POULTRY, AND FISH

1/4	CUP OLIVE OIL, PLUS MORE AS NEEDED
1/2	CUP WHITE WINE
1/2	SMALL YELLOW ONION, QUARTERED
3	TABLESPOONS CUP FRESH ROSEMARY LEAVES
3	LARGE CLOVES GARLIC, PEELED
1	TEASPOON KOSHER SALT

TO MAKE THE MARINADE: Combine all the ingredients in a blender and blend until smooth.

Pour the marinade over the meat, massaging the meat on both sides with your fingers. This helps jump-start the marinating process. Let stand at room temperature for up to 30 minutes or refrigerate for up to 24 hours. (Refrigerating the marinade for long periods of time works best for larger cuts of meat.)

Remove the meat from the marinade and pat dry with paper towels. Brush with oil and season lightly with kosher salt and pepper to taste and cook as desired.

Note: If using the marinade for fish, you don't need to massage the flesh, nor do you marinate it for more than 1/2 hour.

ROASTED GARLIC *Two Ways*

ROASTED GARLIC PURÉE

Makes ³/4 cup

Prepeeled garlic cloves from your produce section make this recipe even simpler. Whip the heady purée into mashed potatoes, sauces, soups, and pasta for added depth of flavor. The garlic purée and garlic oil keep for at least 2 weeks refrigerated.

2   CUPS PEELED CLOVES GARLIC (SEE NOTE)

1   CUP OLIVE OIL, PLUS MORE AS NEEDED

Preheat the oven to 275 degrees F.

Put the garlic in a small glass baking dish or ovenproof saucepan. Add enough olive oil to cover the cloves. Bake until the cloves are soft and tender, about 1 hour. Let cool slightly. Using a slotted spoon, transfer the cloves to the bowl of a food processor fitted with a steel blade and purée until smooth, adding the olive oil from the baking dish as needed. Reserve the remaining oil for other uses. Refrigerate the purée and oil until ready to use.

Note: For hassle-free peeling, soak the garlic cloves in a bowl of cold water for 20 to 30 minutes. The papery skin should slip off easily.

WHOLE ROASTED GARLIC

Makes about ¹/3 cup

We're huge fans of garlic . . . especially when it's enjoyed as a twosome. Cozy up together fireside on a crisp fall evening with whole roasted garlic, crostini, and fresh goat cheese. Add a couple of glasses of red wine and a green salad, and smooch—after all, you'll both have garlic breath!

2   WHOLE HEADS OF GARLIC

1   TABLESPOON OLIVE OIL

Preheat the oven to 350 degrees F.

Cut the top off each head of garlic, making a horizontal cut about 1 inch below the top. Place the bottom halves on a large piece of aluminum foil and drizzle with the olive oil. Place the tops on the bottom halves and fold the foil to seal the garlic inside. Bake until the garlic is light brown and very soft, 1 to 1¹/2 hours. Let cool slightly and serve.

To reserve the garlic for later use, remove the cloves from the skins by squeezing the bottom of each clove. Place in a bowl and mash with the back of a spoon. The roasted garlic will keep, covered and refrigerated, for at least 2 weeks.

"Gussied-Up" MARINARA SAUCE

Makes 3 cups

Begin with basic jarred spaghetti sauce—we like Newman's Own and Muir Glen brands—and, within minutes, sit down to the taste of homemade. It's amazing what sautéed onion and garlic, a dash of sugar, and a handful of herbs can do. In just a few simple steps, we've turned something very ordinary into a sauce you won't soon forget. Mamma mia! Use this sauce in lasagnas and tossed over pastas of various shapes and sizes.

1	TABLESPOON OLIVE OIL
1	CUP CHOPPED YELLOW ONION
1	TABLESPOON CHOPPED GARLIC
1/4	TEASPOON KOSHER SALT
1/8	TEASPOON FRESHLY GROUND PEPPER
1	JAR (26 OUNCES) SPAGHETTI OR MARINARA SAUCE
3/4	TEASPOON SUGAR
1/4	TEASPOON DRIED OREGANO
1	TABLESPOON UNSALTED BUTTER OR EXTRA-VIRGIN OLIVE OIL
2	TABLESPOONS CHOPPED FRESH BASIL

Heat the olive oil in a medium heavy-bottomed saucepan over medium heat. Add the onion, garlic, kosher salt, and pepper. Cook, stirring frequently, until the onion is soft and translucent, 5 to 7 minutes. Add the prepared spaghetti sauce, sugar, and oregano and simmer for 10 to 15 minutes. Stir in the butter and basil. Taste and adjust the seasonings. The sauce will keep, covered and refrigerated, for 1 week. The flavor improves over time.

Tips:

Try adding one or more of the following ingredients to the marinara sauce prior to simmering:

1/3 CUP DRAINED ROUGHLY CHOPPED SUN-DRIED TOMATOES PACKED IN OIL

1/3 CUP PITTED ROUGHLY CHOPPED KALAMATA (BLACK) OR PICHOLINE (GREEN) OLIVES

2 TABLESPOONS RINSED CAPERS

1/4 CUP HEAVY CREAM

12 OUNCES SAUSAGE, COOKED AND ROUGHLY CHOPPED

1/4 CUP RAISINS (ALONG WITH THE SUN-DRIED TOMATOES, OLIVES, OR CAPERS)

1/2 CUP CARAMELIZED ONIONS (FYI: YES, IT'S FINE TO ADD THE CARAMELIZED ONIONS BEFORE SIMMERING.)

Summertime MARINARA SAUCE

Makes 2^1/2 cups

Fresh, fresh, fresh! We love this rustic summertime marinara for its bright color, chunky texture, and sweet flavor—and its ease of preparation (We don't even blanch the tomatoes to remove the skin, or bother with removing the seeds). Nothing beats a summery fresh tomato sauce, but only if the tomatoes are perfectly ripe, rich, and perfumed. Don't even bother making this sauce unless your tomatoes are at the peak of their season. At other times of the year, when great tomatoes are hard to find, try our "Gussied Up" Marinara Sauce (facing page) for a tasty alternative. | We like to make extra batches of this marinara sauce and freeze if to enjoy in the wintertime. Ladle the sauce into sealable freezer bags and defrost in the dead of winter for a perfect kick of summer warmth.

2	TABLESPOONS OLIVE OIL
1	MEDIUM YELLOW ONION, CHOPPED
3	LARGE CLOVES GARLIC, FINELY CHOPPED
	KOSHER SALT AS NEEDED, PLUS 1 TEASPOON
	FRESHLY GROUND PEPPER
3	POUNDS RIPE TOMATOES, COARSELY CHOPPED
2	TEASPOONS BALSAMIC VINEGAR
	PINCH OF SUGAR (OPTIONAL)
^{1}/3	CUP CHOPPED FRESH BASIL

Heat the olive oil in a large skillet over medium heat. Add the onion and garlic and season with kosher salt and pepper to taste. Cook, stirring frequently, until the onion is soft and translucent, 5 to 7 minutes. Add the tomatoes, vinegar, the 1 teaspoon kosher salt, and pepper to taste.

Increase the heat to high and cook until the tomatoes have softened slightly but have not broken down, 5 to 7 minutes. Season with a pinch of sugar if necessary (the amount of sugar depends on the ripeness and quality of the tomatoes). Remove from the heat and stir in the basil.

Flaky PIECRUST

Makes one 9-inch deep-dish (2 inches deep) piecrust

We have vivid memories of helping our grandmother roll out piecrust. This recipe is an adaptation of Nanny's recipe. Though she used all lard (Crisco), which produced an incredibly "short" and crumbly piecrust, we prefer a combination of butter and Crisco because of the flavor the butter adds to the crust. This piecrust is the perfect nest for sweet fruit tarts, mile-high cream pies, and savory quiches. When you have the time to make crust from scratch, you'll find it's extra special—we promise!

1 1/2	CUPS BLEACHED ALL-PURPOSE FLOUR
1	TABLESPOON SUGAR (IF USING THE PIECRUST FOR DESSERTS)
1	TEASPOON KOSHER SALT
5	TABLESPOONS COLD UNSALTED BUTTER, CUT INTO 1/4-INCH PIECES
4	TABLESPOONS COLD SOLID VEGETABLE SHORTENING, SUCH AS CRISCO
3 1/2 TO 4 1/2	TABLESPOONS ICE WATER

Put the flour, sugar (for dessert piecrusts only), and kosher salt in the bowl of a food processor fitted with the steel blade and pulse briefly to mix. Scatter the butter over the flour mixture and, using a spoon, toss lightly to coat. Pulse 5 times at 1-second intervals. Add the shortening in small pieces and pulse about 4 more times at 1-second intervals. The texture should resemble coarse meal, with the butter and shortening bits no bigger than peas. Sprinkle 3 1/2 tablespoons of the water over the mixture, and pulse until the dough begins to hold together, about 6 times. Pinch a small amount of the dough between your fingers. If it doesn't hold together, add 1/2 tablespoon of the water and pulse 3 times. Pinch the dough again. If necessary, add the remaining 1/2 table-spoon water and pulse 3 more times. When the dough holds together when pinched, it is ready. Do not allow it to form a ball in the processor.

Transfer the dough to a large sheet of plastic wrap. Pressing gently, form the dough into a 5-inch disk. Wrap in plastic wrap and refrigerate for at least 45 minutes, preferably overnight. At this point, the dough may be refrigerated for up to 2 days or frozen for up to 3 months.

Let the chilled dough soften at room temperature for 10 to 15 minutes (longer if frozen). Using the rolling pin, tap the dough firmly to flatten it. Place the dough between 2 large pieces of plastic wrap and roll out the dough to 1/8-inch thickness.

To transfer the dough to the pie dish or tart pan, fold the dough in half and then in half again. Place the point of the wedge in the center of the pan and unfold. If using a pie dish, use scissors to trim the excess dough, leaving a 1/2-inch overhang. Tuck the overhang under itself so that the folded edge is about 1/4 inch beyond the edge of the dish. Crimp decoratively. If using a tart pan, use your fingers to press the dough against the edges of the pan, or use a rolling pin to press firmly over the edges of the pan, releasing any excess dough.

Proceed according to your master recipe.

If the recipe calls for prebaking (blind baking) the crust: Refrigerate the pie shell or tart pan for at least 1 hour. Position the rack in the center of the oven, place baking sheet on rack, and preheat oven to 375 degrees F.

CONTINUED

Press two 12-inch squares of aluminum foil into the pie shell so that the foil covers the edge of the crust. Add raw beans, rice, or metal pie weights. (Position the weights as far up the sides as possible to prevent the crust from shrinking.) Set the pie dish or tart pan on the baking sheet and bake for about 17 minutes. Carefully remove the foil and weights and continue baking until the crust is light brown, about 8 minutes. If a fully baked crust is desired (if the filling requires no further cooking), bake until golden brown, about 15 minutes more. Transfer the pie dish to a wire rack and let cool, then proceed with the master recipe.

After adding the filling and before baking the pie again, we recommend using foil or a disposable pie ring (available in baking stores) to protect the edges from overbrowning.

Tips for perfect piecrust:

1. Start with cold butter and shortening.
2. Do not use unbleached flour.
3. To measure flour accurately, spoon it into your measuring cup and level it with a knife. Do not scoop flour directly from the bag into your measuring cup and level it against the side of the sack.

PIZZA DOUGH

Makes four 8- to 10-inch pizza crusts

There's always a friendly family competition involved when we whip up pizza dough. In the Barber household, the crust of choice is thin, while the Whitefords prefer a thicker, chewier crust. We make the rapid-rise version of this recipe when we want a thin, well-browned crust and use the traditional recipe for a chewier crust. We like to prepare the dough in advance and freeze it. The night before serving, transfer the dough to the fridge. With minimal planning, you can get a pizza on the table in less than 30 minutes.

1	CUP WARM WATER (110 DEGREES TO 115 DEGREES F)
1	PACKET ACTIVE DRY YEAST (2 1/4 TEASPOONS)
1 1/4	TEASPOONS SUGAR
3 1/4	CUPS ALL-PURPOSE FLOUR, PLUS MORE AS NEEDED
1 3/4	TEASPOONS KOSHER SALT
1/4	CUP OLIVE OIL, PLUS MORE AS NEEDED

Pour the warm water into a bowl. Sprinkle the yeast and sugar over the water and stir. Let stand until the yeast dissolves or swells, about 5 minutes.

IF USING A FOOD PROCESSOR: Fit with the steel blade. Put 3 cups of the flour and the kosher salt in the bowl and pulse to combine. While pulsing, pour the yeast mixture and the 1/4 cup olive oil through the feed tube. Pulse until the dough forms a ball. Continue to process for 30 seconds more. If the dough is sticky, add the remaining flour 1 table-spoon at a time until the dough is no longer sticky.

Put the dough in an oiled bowl and turn it at least once to cover all sides with the oil. Cover with plastic wrap or a kitchen towel and let rise in a warm place for 1 1/2 hours.

After the dough has risen, it is ready to be rolled out and baked. Be sure to press out all the air with the palms of your hands before rolling out the dough with a rolling pin (kneading the dough will release any bubbles). It can also be wrapped with plastic wrap and refrigerated for up to 4 hours or frozen for up to 3 months.

IF USING A STAND MIXER: Fit with the paddle attachment. Combine 3 cups of the flour and the kosher salt in the bowl of the mixer. Add the yeast mixture and the 1/4 cup olive oil. Mix on low speed for 10 seconds. Replace the paddle attachment with the dough hook and knead on medium speed until the dough is smooth, about 3 minutes. Feel the dough. If it is sticky, add the remaining flour 1 tablespoon at a time and knead until the dough is no longer sticky. Follow the preceding directions.

IF MAKING THE DOUGH BY HAND: Combine 3 cups of the flour and the kosher salt in a large bowl. Add the yeast mixture and olive oil. Stir with a wooden spoon until the dough comes together. Turn the dough out onto a floured surface and knead for 15 minutes. If the dough is sticky, add the remaining flour 1 tablespoon at a time until the dough is no longer sticky. Follow the preceding instructions.

Variation: Add about 1 tablespoon finely chopped fresh rosemary or 1 1/2 teaspoons crumbled dried rosemary while kneading the dough.

CONTINUED

QUICK RAPID-RISE METHOD

Preheat the oven to 200 degrees F for 10 minutes, then turn off the oven. Substitute 1 package rapid-rise yeast for the active dry yeast and use 2 1/2 teaspoons sugar.

IF USING A FOOD PROCESSOR: Fit with the steel blade. Put the warm water, yeast, and sugar in the bowl and pulse twice. Add 3 cups of the flour, the kosher salt, and 1/4 cup olive oil and pulse until the dough forms a ball. Continue to process for 30 seconds more. If the dough is sticky, add the remaining flour 1 tablespoon at a time until the dough is no longer sticky.

Put the dough in an oiled bowl and turn it at least once to cover all sides with the oil. Cover with plastic wrap and place in the oven until the dough is doubled in volume, about 40 minutes. The dough is ready to be rolled out and baked, or refrigerated or frozen for later use. Be sure to press out all the air with the palms of your hands before rolling out the dough with a rolling pin (kneading the dough will release any bubbles).

IF USING A STAND MIXER: Fit with the paddle attachment. Combine the warm water, rapid-rise yeast, and sugar in the bowl of the mixer and mix on low speed for 10 seconds. Add 3 cups of the flour, the kosher salt, and 1/4 cup olive oil and mix on low speed until the dough comes together, about 15 seconds. Replace the paddle attachment with the dough hook and knead on medium speed until the dough is smooth, about 3 minutes. Feel the dough. If it is sticky, add the remaining flour 1 tablespoon at a time and knead until the dough is no longer sticky. Then follow the preceding directions.

IF MAKING BY HAND: Combine the warm water, rapid-rise yeast, and sugar in a large bowl and whisk together for about 10 seconds. Add 3 cups of the flour, the kosher salt, and 1/4 cup olive oil and stir with a wooden spoon until the dough comes together. Turn the dough out onto a floured surface and knead for 15 minutes. If the dough is sticky, add the remaining flour 1 tablespoon at a time until the dough is no longer sticky. Then follow the preceding directions.

CROUTONS

The perfect way to use up that leftover baguette or stale loaf of bread, homemade croutons beat the boxed ones, hands-down. We grew up eating these jazzy little numbers as an after-school snack, right out of the cookie jar, and have followed in our mother's footsteps by storing them the same way. You'll see how quickly these morsels disappear when you're hungry for a snack. Just make sure to save some for garnishing soups and salads.

4   CUPS 3/4-INCH BREAD CUBES (PREFERABLY MADE
    FROM DAY-OLD BREAD)

1   TABLESPOON UNSALTED BUTTER, MELTED

1   TABLESPOON OLIVE OIL

1/2   TEASPOON ONION POWDER

1/2   TEASPOON GARLIC POWDER

1/4   TEASPOON SEASONED SALT, SUCH AS LAWRY'S

1/8   TEASPOON FRESHLY GROUND PEPPER

Preheat the oven to 300 degrees F.

Toss the bread cubes with the butter, olive oil, onion powder, garlic powder, seasoned salt, and pepper in a medium bowl. Spread the cubes in a single layer on a baking sheet and bake until lightly browned, about 20 minutes. Let cool. Store in an airtight container at room temperature for up to 1 week.

CAESAR DRESSING

Makes scant 1¹/₂ cups

This timeless dressing from Tijuana has been reinvented so often, it's become nearly as universal as bottled French or Thousand Island. It's a shame most people don't think to prepare Caesar dressing from scratch because it makes a world of difference. This lemony, garlicky, homemade dressing is dy-no-mite on salads and is a killer dunk for veggies, shrimp, and chicken. Don't omit the anchovies! They give the dressing body and enhance its flavor with a kiss of salt (we promise you won't taste anything "fishy"). Our husbands honestly despise anchovies but oddly enough, they can't get enough of this dressing.

1 CUP MAYONNAISE

1/4 CUP PARMESAN CHEESE, PREFERABLY PARMIGIANO-REGGIANO

1 TABLESPOON PLUS 1 TEASPOON FRESH LEMON JUICE

1 TABLESPOON DIJON MUSTARD

2 TEASPOONS WORCESTERSHIRE SAUCE

2 TEASPOONS MINCED GARLIC

2 ANCHOVY FILLETS, FINELY CHOPPED

1/8 TEASPOON FRESHLY GROUND PEPPER

2 TABLESPOONS WATER, PLUS MORE AS NEEDED

Whisk together the mayonnaise, cheese, lemon juice, mustard, Worcestershire sauce, garlic, anchovy, and pepper in a small bowl until well incorporated. Whisk in the 2 tablespoons water.

Refrigerate until chilled. The dressing will keep, covered and refrigerated, for 5 days. Thin with more water and adjust the seasonings if necessary before serving.

BALSAMIC VINAIGRETTE

Makes about 1¹/₂ cups

Master this basic vinaigrette and you'll never want to buy those shake 'n' serve dressing bottles again. The delightfully bright dressing kisses green salads with the perfect hint of sugar. Experiment with other vinegars and flavored oils for a change of pace.

¹/₄ CUP BALSAMIC VINEGAR

1 TABLESPOON GRAINY MUSTARD

1 TEASPOON FINELY MINCED GARLIC

¹/₂ TEASPOON SUGAR

¹/₂ TEASPOON KOSHER SALT

FRESHLY GROUND PEPPER

1 ¹/₄ CUPS BEST-QUALITY OLIVE OIL

Whisk together the vinegar, mustard, garlic, sugar, kosher salt, and pepper to taste in a medium bowl. Drizzle in the olive oil, whisking to incorporate. Alternatively, combine all the ingredients in a jar, cover tightly, and shake until thoroughly blended. Adjust the seasonings to taste. The vinaigrette will keep, covered and refrigerated, for up to 1 week.

Mighty MINT VINAIGRETTE

Makes about 1 cup

This vinaigrette is great on mixed greens, fabulous on fruit salads, and dreamy swirled into room-temperature couscous or drizzled onto salmon. Lamb is one of our favorite mates for this sassy sauce! The green vinaigrette looks prettier on the platter than the traditional mint jelly and tastes far brighter.

³/₄ CUP OLIVE OIL

¹/₂ CUP FIRMLY PACKED FRESH MINT LEAVES

¹/₄ CUP WHITE WINE VINEGAR

1 TABLESPOON PLUS 1 TEASPOON DIJON MUSTARD

1 TABLESPOON PLUS 1 TEASPOON HONEY

¹/₄ TEASPOON KOSHER SALT

FRESHLY GROUND PEPPER

Combine the olive oil and mint in a blender and blend until puréed, about 15 seconds. Add the vinegar, mustard, honey, kosher salt, and pepper to taste and blend until just incorporated, about 5 seconds. Do not overblend or the vinaigrette will be too thick. The vinaigrette will keep, covered and refrigerated, for up to 1 week.

PEANUT SAUCE

Makes 1 1/4 cups

Peanut butter all grown up, this versatile sauce is excellent with Asian noodles and cabbage salads. Or, serve it "satay style" with grilled skewered chicken and meats. We've been obsessed with peanut sauce after discovering it in a Thai restaurant when we first moved to San Francisco. Just one taste and you'll understand our love affair.

1/2	CUP CREAMY PEANUT BUTTER
1/3	CUP WATER
2	TABLESPOONS SOY SAUCE
2	TABLESPOONS RICE VINEGAR
1	TABLESPOON HONEY
1	TABLESPOON ASIAN SESAME OIL
1 1/2	TEASPOONS PEELED AND GRATED FRESH GINGER
1	TEASPOON MINCED GARLIC
	PINCH OF CAYENNE PEPPER OR DASH OF CHILI SAUCE

Combine the peanut butter, water, soy sauce, vinegar, honey, sesame oil, ginger, and garlic in the bowl of a food processor fitted with the steel blade and process until smooth. Season with the cayenne pepper or chili sauce. The sauce will keep, covered and refrigerated, for 1 month.

TAHINI-GINGER DIPPING SAUCE

Makes 1 heaping cup

Ordinary foods take on the exotic flavors of Asia when paired with our multipurpose sauce. Spread it over salmon, chicken, grilled pork, tuna, and even shrimp. Or, retire the ranch dip and serve this sauce as the centerpiece for your veggie platters. The possibilities are endless! We discovered that some brands of tahini are thicker than others, so add more water if needed to achieve the desired consistency.

3/4   CUP MAYONNAISE

1/4   CUP TAHINI (STIR TOGETHER IF OIL AND NUT BUTTER
        HAVE SEPARATED)

1   TEASPOON SOY SAUCE, PLUS MORE AS NEEDED

1   TABLESPOON RICE VINEGAR

1   TABLESPOON ASIAN SESAME OIL

1 1/2 TEASPOONS PEELED AND FINELY CHOPPED FRESH GINGER

2   TEASPOONS HONEY

2   TABLESPOONS WATER, PLUS MORE AS NEEDED

1/2   TEASPOON FRESH LIME JUICE, PLUS MORE AS NEEDED

Combine the mayonnaise, tahini, the 1 teaspoon soy sauce, the vinegar, sesame oil, ginger, honey, the 2 tablespoons water, and the 1/2 teaspoon lime juice in the bowl of a food processor fitted with the steel blade and process until smooth. Add more water if necessary. Season with more soy sauce and lime juice to taste. Refrigerate in an airtight container until ready to use. The sauce will keep, covered and refrigerated, for 2 to 3 weeks. (The sauce will thicken over time, so adjust the consistency with more water if necessary. The flavor will also mellow over time, so adjust the seasonings if necessary.)

PESTO

This perfect pesto has never failed us. In fact, we credit it for bringing Mary's eldest son, Jackson, into the world. Nine months pregnant, Mary made a huge batch of this flavor-packed paste and tossed it with a pound of angel hair pasta, thinking she and her husband, Jack, would enjoy plenty of leftovers. After serving up two normal-sized portions for dinner, Mary set aside the rest for leftovers. Jack was completely satisfied with the meal, but Mary just couldn't get enough. She sneaked back into the kitchen for an extra bite or two, and, before she knew it, she'd eaten it all! Mortified, she slipped into bed, embarrassed that she didn't feel the least bit uncomfortable, and, within hours, baby Jackson was born. Pesto may not bring on labor for you, but it certainly inspires gluttony. Enjoy!

1/2 CUP PINE NUTS

4   CUPS LIGHTLY PACKED FRESH BASIL LEAVES

1 1/2 TEASPOONS CHOPPED GARLIC

1   TEASPOON FRESH LEMON JUICE

1/2 TEASPOON KOSHER SALT

1/4 TEASPOON FRESHLY GROUND PEPPER

1/2 CUP EXTRA-VIRGIN OLIVE OIL, PLUS MORE
   FOR DRIZZLING

3/4 CUP (1 1/2 OUNCES) GRATED PARMESAN, PREFERABLY
   PARMIGIANO-REGGIANO

Preheat the oven to 325 degrees F. Spread the pine nuts on a baking sheet and cook until aromatic and golden brown, 8 to 10 munitues. Stir the nuts frequently to ensure even cooking. Remove from oven and let cool.

Combine the basil, pine nuts, garlic, lemon juice, kosher salt, and pepper in the bowl of a food processor fitted with a steel blade and process until the ingredients are well incorporated, about 15 seconds. Shut off the motor and scrape down the sides of the bowl. With the motor running, slowly add the 1/2 cup olive oil through the feed tube. Shut off the motor and scrape down the sides of the bowl. Add the cheese and pulse until the mixture comes together and looks like a thick paste. Use immediately or transfer to a container, drizzle with a thin layer of olive oil, cover tightly, and refrigerate. This pesto will keep for 2 weeks.

Note: The herbal base of this pesto, minus the cheese, can be frozen for 2 months. Add the cheese after defrosting the pesto, and stir well to combine.

CRANBERRY RELISH

Makes 1 3/4 cups

Bring the taste of Thanksgiving to your turkey sandwiches all year 'round with this super-simple relish. We purchase several extra bags of frozen cranberries during the holidays and pop them in our freezer so that we can prepare this zesty condiment any time. The relish keeps beautifully in the refrigerator for several weeks and works wonders on pork tenderloin, lamb, duck, and chicken.

2	*TEASPOONS VEGETABLE OIL*
1/2	*CUP CHOPPED SHALLOT*
1	*CINNAMON STICK*
3/4	*CUP APPLE JUICE*
1	*BAG (12 OUNCES) CRANBERRIES (ABOUT 3 CUPS)*
1/4	*CUP SUGAR*
1/4	*TEASPOON KOSHER SALT, PLUS MORE AS NEEDED*
1/8	*TEASPOON GROUND ALLSPICE*
2	*TABLESPOONS GRAND MARNIER*
	FRESHLY GROUND PEPPER

Heat the oil in a medium saucepan over medium heat. Add the shallot and cinnamon stick and cook, stirring frequently, until the shallot is soft, about 5 minutes. Add the apple juice, cranberries, sugar, the 1/4 teaspoon kosher salt, and the all-spice. Increase the heat to high and bring to a boil. Reduce the heat to low and simmer for about 5 minutes. Remove from the heat and immediately add the Grand Marnier. Transfer the relish to a bowl and let cool. Season with more kosher salt and freshly ground pepper to taste. Cover and refrigerate until ready to use. Remove and discard the cinnamon stick before serving. The relish will keep, covered and refrigerated, for 2 weeks.

CARAMELIZED ONIONS

Makes about 1 cup

The perfect pick-me-up, caramelized onions add spirit and flair to balsamic vinaigrettes, spinach salads, and marinara sauces. We love them. As our friend and fellow cookbook author Frances Schultz says, "They'd make boiled tennis shoes taste good!" Serve the onions as a condiment for meats and poultry or as an accompaniment to grilled vegetables or rice dishes. And don't forget to pile 'em high on burgers and sandwiches. One of our favorite suppers-in-a-snap is pita bread smothered with these onions, then topped with Cambozola cheese and chopped black olives. We just have to exercise patience while the flavors melt together in the toaster oven.

2	TABLESPOONS OLIVE OIL
2	MEDIUM YELLOW ONIONS, HALVED AND THINLY SLICED (ABOUT 4 CUPS)
$1/2$	TEASPOON KOSHER SALT, PLUS MORE AS NEEDED
$1/8$	TEASPOON FRESHLY GROUND PEPPER, PLUS MORE AS NEEDED
$1/2$	CUP FULL-BODIED RED WINE, SUCH AS MERLOT OR CABERNET SAUVIGNON
$1/4$	CUP RED WINE VINEGAR
2	TEASPOONS SUGAR
1	TEASPOON HERBES DE PROVENCE

Heat the olive oil in a large nonstick sauté pan over medium-high heat. When the oil is very hot but not smoking, add the onions, the $1/2$ teaspoon kosher salt, and the $1/8$ teaspoon pepper. Cook, stirring occasionally, until the onions are soft and lightly brown, 10 to 15 minutes. Add the wine, vinegar, sugar, and herbes de Provence. Reduce the heat to low and cook, stirring occasionally, until the onions are very soft and the liquid has evaporated, about 30 minutes. Remove from the heat and let cool. Season with more kosher salt and pepper if necessary. The onions will keep, covered and refrigerated, for at least 2 weeks.

PIMIENTO CHEESE SPREAD

Makes about 3 cups

One bite of this all-American sandwich spread and you'll feel like you've died and gone to heaven. Create open-faced sandwiches on soft potato bread, crowned with slices of summer tomato or picante sauce if tomatoes are not in season. Pimiento cheese also magically boosts the appeal of a basic grilled cheese sandwich and makes an amazing addition to a frittata. Slather the spread onto a celery stick for a quick, satisfying snack, or serve it as a downright delicious dip for corn chips.

8   OUNCES EXTRA-SHARP WHITE CHEDDAR CHEESE

8   OUNCES EXTRA-SHARP AGED YELLOW CHEDDAR CHEESE

1/2 CUP MAYONNAISE

1   JAR (4 OUNCES) PIMIENTOS, DRAINED AND
     FINELY CHOPPED

2   TEASPOONS FINELY GRATED YELLOW ONION

1/2 TEASPOON SUGAR

1/4 TEASPOON FRESHLY GROUND PEPPER

3   TABLESPOONS HOT PICANTE SAUCE

2   TABLESPOONS FINELY CHOPPED FRESH FLAT-LEAF PARSLEY

1/4 CUP CHOPPED PITTED GREEN OLIVES (OPTIONAL)

Finely grate the cheeses into a medium bowl. Add the mayonnaise, pimientos, onion, sugar, pepper, picante sauce, parsley, and olives if desired and stir until well incorporated.

Refrigerate, covered, for at least 2 hours to allow the flavors to develop. The pimiento cheese spread will keep, tightly covered and refrigerated, for up to 1 week.

CHAPTER 4

APPETIZERS
FINGER FOODS & SNACKS

LET'S GET IT OUT IN THE OPEN: We love a good party! We grew up in the South, and our earliest memories as little girls ("knee-high to grasshoppers" as we say) are of being a part of our parents' lives as they entertained. Most Friday and Saturday nights, we passed Mom and Dad's homemade hors d'oeuvres to family and friends, sharing in the excitement as their guests enjoyed the food (of course, we sneaked and savored tastes of the goodies). Ever since, we've been in love with finger foods and entertaining—so much so that, in 1999, we wrote a book entitled *Cocktail Food.* Thankfully, we've been able to make a career out of entertaining and love nothing more than to share some of our Southern hospitality with friends.

For eight years as caterers at Thymes Two, our catering company, we watched all kinds of appetizers being passed and learned what guests love to nibble on—what the reach-out-and-grab-ya' foods really are. The recipes in this chapter are easy to make and will help you establish your home as a warm, lively gathering spot for friends and family.

Whether you're looking for appetizers to serve a crowd or simply to enjoy with your mate, you'll find them here. For a seductive start to a romantic dinner for two, try our easy, elegant Artichokes with Lemon-Garlic Butter (page 60), a sensual, eat-with-your-fingers treat. Want to impress the in-laws with a show-stopping buffet centerpiece? Look no further than our Smoked Salmon Platter (page 66), a luxurious creation that really wows and requires no cooking, just simple assembly.

And, because we're dedicated to gourmet grazing, this chapter is packed with recipes for fabulous dips and snacks, what we consider "fun foods." As we like to say, it's all about "finger foods with attitude." We gladly share our addictive Herbed Buttermilk Popcorn (page 65) for stay-at-home movie nights and rowdy game days, as well as our stylish Party Pecans (page 69) for nibbling with high-octane cocktails. Whatever you're craving to nosh and nibble, this chapter will deliver!

Warm ARTICHOKE AND GREEN ONION DIP

Makes 4 cups; serves 8 to 12

We've brightened up the popular artichoke, mayonnaise, and cheese dip with garlic and thyme, then added to the dip's eye-appeal with a handful of green onions. The real secret to this updated favorite comes in the form of freshly grated Parmesan. Buy a wedge of Parmigiano-Reggiano and grate it just before using to ensure freshness. If your loved one loves this dip as much as ours do, we suggest you routinely make an extra half-batch. Thinned with a little milk or water, this dip romances the humblest of weeknight fare. Try it over a basic chicken breast, fish fillet, or bowl of pasta. It's to die for.

2   CANS (14 OUNCES EACH) WATER-PACKED ARTICHOKE
      HEARTS, WELL DRAINED, CHOPPED

1 1/2 CUPS MAYONNAISE

1 1/2 CUPS FINELY GRATED HIGH-QUALITY PARMESAN CHEESE,
      SUCH AS PARMIGIANO-REGGIANO

1/3   CUP, PLUS 2 TABLESPOONS SLICED GREEN ONIONS,
      GREEN PART ONLY

2   TEASPOONS MINCED GARLIC

1 1/2 TEASPOONS CHOPPED FRESH THYME, OR 3/4 TEASPOON
      DRIED THYME

1/4   TEASPOON KOSHER SALT, PLUS MORE AS NEEDED

1/4   TEASPOON FRESHLY GROUND PEPPER, PLUS MORE AS NEEDED

      BAGEL CHIPS, FRENCH BREAD SLICES, OR CRACKERS (SUCH AS
      WHEAT THINS AND TRISKETS) FOR SERVING

Preheat the oven to 400 degrees F.

Combine the artichoke hearts, mayonnaise, 1 cup of the cheese, the 1/3 cup green onions, the garlic, thyme, the 1/4 teaspoon kosher salt, and 1/4 teaspoon pepper in a large bowl. Adjust the seasonings with more kosher salt and pepper if necessary.

Transfer the mixture to an 8-inch square glass baking dish or an attractive ceramic dish that is similar in size. Sprinkle with the remaining 1/2 cup cheese. Cover and bake until heated through,

10 to 15 minutes. Increase the heat to broil and cook until the top is bubbly and golden brown, 2 to 3 minutes more. Garnish with the 2 tablespoons green onions just before serving.

Serve warm with bagel chips, French bread slices, or crackers.

Do-Ahead: The dip can be assembled 1 day ahead but not cooked. Cover and refrigerate until ready to bake.

LEMONY-TARRAGON CRAB DIP WITH SALT-AND-VINEGAR POTATO CHIPS

Makes about 2 cups; serves 8 to 10

During our summers spent on Figure 8 Island in North Carolina, we anxiously awaited low tide on Saturdays so Dad could take us to the marshes for crabbin'. We'd pick the crabs and sauté the fresh meat with a little butter, salt, and pepper chased with a capful of vinegar. This family tradition inspired this spirited hors d'oeuvre—a perfect marriage of crab and vinegar (chips). Given the explosion of designer potato chips in the market, finding a match made in heaven was easy. You'll gobble up every bite of this gentle herbal dip atop these feisty, salty, surprisingly tangy chips.

$1/4$ CUP (1 OUNCE) CREAM CHEESE AT ROOM TEMPERATURE

3 TABLESPOONS FINELY CHOPPED RED ONION

2 TABLESPOONS MAYONNAISE

1 TABLESPOON PLUS $1^1/2$ TEASPOONS FRESH LEMON JUICE, PLUS MORE AS NEEDED

2 TEASPOONS CHOPPED FRESH TARRAGON, OR $3/4$ TEASPOON DRIED TARRAGON

2 TEASPOONS CHOPPED FRESH DILL, OR $1/2$ TEASPOON DRIED DILL WEED

$1/2$ TEASPOON LEMON ZEST

8 OUNCES FRESH CRABMEAT, PICKED OVER FOR SHELLS, WELL DRAINED

$1/4$ CUP FINELY CHOPPED CUCUMBER

KOSHER SALT AND FRESHLY GROUND PEPPER

SALT-AND-VINEGAR POTATO CHIPS FOR SERVING

Combine the cream cheese, red onion, mayonnaise, the 1 tablespoon plus $1^1/2$ teaspoons lemon juice, the tarragon, dill, and lemon zest in a small bowl. Stir in the crabmeat and cucumber. Season with kosher salt, pepper, and more lemon juice to taste. Refrigerate until chilled, at least 30 minutes. Serve with potato chips.

Do-Ahead: The crab dip can be prepared up to 1 day in advance and refrigerated.

CRUDITÉS WITH GREEN ONION–MINT DIP

Serves 8 to 10

Trust us. The key to successful crudités is to blanch the vegetables (plunge them into boiling water briefly and refresh in cold water) before arranging them on a platter. Blanching requires only a few minutes and transforms the vegetables, giving them vibrant color and enhancing their natural sweetness. Once you've tried blanched veggies, you'll never go back to the standard raw platter. This dip is wonderfully fresh tasting and works equally well with basil in place of the mint. It will keep, refrigerated, up to 1 week and is delicious spooned on fish topped with sliced cucumbers.

DIP

3/4	CUP MAYONNAISE
1/3	CUP PLAIN YOGURT
1/3	CUP ROUGHLY CHOPPED FRESH MINT
1/4	CUP ROUGHLY CHOPPED GREEN ONIONS, GREEN PART ONLY
1/2	TEASPOON WHITE WINE VINEGAR, PLUS MORE AS NEEDED
	PINCH OF SUGAR
	KOSHER SALT AND FRESHLY GROUND PEPPER

CRUDITÉS

2	MEDIUM CARROTS, PEELED AND CUT INTO 3-INCH-LONG STRIPS
12	BITE-SIZED BROCCOLI FLORETS
20	ASPARAGUS SPEARS, PEELED (SEE NOTE, PAGE 152)
1	MEDIUM RED BELL PEPPER, CUT INTO 1-INCH-WIDE STRIPS
1	SMALL CUCUMBER, HALVED LENGTHWISE, SEEDED, AND CUT INTO 1/2-INCH-THICK HALF-MOONS (SEE NOTE)

TO MAKE THE DIP: Combine the mayonnaise, yogurt, mint, green onions, the 1/2 teaspoon vinegar, and sugar in a blender. Blend until bright green and well incorporated. Season with kosher salt, pepper, and more vinegar to taste. (Yogurts vary in acidity, so add more vinegar if necessary.) Refrigerate until chilled, at least 45 minutes.

TO PREPARE THE CRUDITÉS: Fill a medium pot three fourths full of water. Bring to a boil over high heat and add kosher salt. (We add 1 1/2 teaspoons kosher salt per quart of water.) Add the carrots and blanch until tender-crisp, about 2 minutes. Using a strainer, transfer the carrots to a large bowl of salted ice water. We use the same ratio of kosher salt and water. When the carrots are cool, transfer to a colander and drain. Return the water in the pot to a boil. Add the broccoli and blanch until tender-crisp, 1 to 2 minutes. Using a strainer, transfer the broccoli to the bowl of salted ice water and drain. Repeat the process with the asparagus spears, blanching for 2 minutes. Blot all the vegetables with paper towels to remove excess moisture. Place a bowl with the green onion–mint dip on a platter. Artfully arrange the blanched vegetables along with the raw bell pepper and cucumber on the platter.

Note: If the cucumber has a wax coating, peel it.

GUACAMOLE

Makes 1 1/2 cups; *serves* 4 to 6

Good guacamole requires perfectly ripe avocados, which give slightly when touched. (Hass avocados are our favorite.) This recipe provides the guidelines for basic guacamole with lime juice, garlic, jalapeño, and salt. We always add a pinch of cumin for more flavor. Adjust the ingredients and include others, such as chopped onion, corn, or black beans, to suit your taste. The jalapeño's heat is concentrated in its ribs and seeds, so add the seeds to the guacamole at your own risk.

2 *MEDIUM RIPE AVOCADOS (ABOUT 1 POUND TOTAL), HALVED*

1 *PLUM TOMATO, SEEDED AND CHOPPED*

1/4 *CUP CHOPPED FRESH CILANTRO*

1 *TABLESPOON FRESH LIME JUICE, PLUS MORE AS NEEDED*

2 *TEASPOONS MINCED GARLIC*

1 *TEASPOON FINELY MINCED JALAPEÑO CHILE,
PLUS MORE AS NEEDED*

1/2 *TEASPOON KOSHER SALT, PLUS MORE AS NEEDED*

1/8 *TEASPOON GROUND CUMIN*

 TORTILLA CHIPS FOR SERVING

Using a metal spoon, scoop out the avocado flesh, releasing it from the peel. Remove the pit. Put the flesh in a medium bowl and lightly mash with a fork. Add the tomato, cilantro, the 1 tablespoon lime juice, the garlic, the 1 teaspoon jalapeño, 1/2 teaspoon kosher salt, and the cumin and stir to combine. Taste and season with more lime juice, jalapeño, and kosher salt if necessary. Serve with tortilla chips.

Do-Ahead: Guacamole is best made and served immediately, but you may refrigerate it, covered with plastic wrap pressed directly onto the top of the guacamole, for 4 to 6 hours. Taste and adjust the seasonings just before serving, as the flavor dulls over time.

1-2-3 MEXICAN DIP

Serves 10 to 12

Don't think of this dip as old hat. We've updated the Mexican dip we knew and loved as children, eliminating the canned olives and taco mix. And you can prepare it in 3 easy steps. When Mary entertained a big crowd at her in-laws' mountain home in Roaring Gap, North Carolina, she set this dip out on a card table, far from the elaborate buffet she had created. The buffet was essentially ignored, as the guests huddled around the card table and gobbled up the dip. A double batch of dip and 4 bags of corn chips later, the guests had little room left for the buffet, beef tenderloin and all. Enough said?

1	CAN (16 OUNCES) REFRIED BEANS
1 1/2	CUPS MEDIUM SALSA
1	TEASPOON CHILI POWDER
1	TEASPOON GROUND CUMIN
3/4	TEASPOON DRIED OREGANO
3/4	CUP SOUR CREAM
1/2	CUP MAYONNAISE
1/4	CUP FINELY CHOPPED RED ONION
1/3	CUP CHOPPED FRESH CILANTRO
1	TEASPOON ONION POWDER
1	SMALL RED BELL PEPPER, SEEDED, DERIBBED, AND CHOPPED
1	CUP (2 OUNCES) GRATED EXTRA-SHARP CHEDDAR CHEESE
1	FRESH JALAPEÑO CHILE, CUT INTO ROUNDS (ABOUT 20)
	TORTILLA CHIPS FOR SERVING

Combine the refried beans, 1/4 cup of the salsa, the chili powder, cumin, and oregano in a medium bowl. Spread evenly over the bottom of a 9-inch round ceramic casserole dish (at least 2 inches deep) or an 8-by-8-by-2 1/4-inch glass baking dish.

Combine the sour cream, mayonnaise, red onion, cilantro, and onion powder in a small bowl. Spread over the top of the beans mixture.

Combine the bell pepper and the remaining 1 1/4 cups salsa in a small bowl. Gently spread over the sour cream mixture, being careful to not mix the layers. Top with the cheese and jalapeño and refrigerate until chilled, at least 1 hour. Serve with tortilla chips.

Do Ahead: The dip can be made 1 day in advance and refrigerated.

ARTICHOKES WITH LEMON-GARLIC BUTTER

Serves 2

Truly "finger-licking good," artichokes aren't considered aphrodisiacs for nothing. Take a stab at preparing this sensuous vegetable, and settle in for a sensational evening at home. We prefer steamed artichokes to boiled ones, which take on too much water. If you don't have a steamer, simply boil the artichokes in salted water, then place them upside down on a towel-lined plate to drain. Squeeze firmly before serving to remove excess water.

2	LARGE ARTICHOKES
1/2	LEMON
4	TABLESPOONS UNSALTED BUTTER
1	TEASPOON MINCED GARLIC
1/2	TEASPOON MINCED FRESH THYME, OR 1/4 TEASPOON DRIED THYME
1/8	TEASPOON KOSHER SALT, PLUS MORE AS NEEDED
	FRESHLY GROUND PEPPER
1	TABLESPOON FRESH LEMON JUICE

Fill a large pot with enough water to come 1/2 inch below the bottom of a steamer rack and set the rack in place. Cover the pot and bring the water to a boil. Meanwhile, using a serrated knife, cut off the top one-third of each artichoke. Rub the cut surfaces with the lemon half. Trim the stem, removing as little as possible. Pull off the tough outer leaves at the base. Using scissors, cut off the pointed tips of the leaves. Arrange the artichokes on the rack. Cover the pot and steam the artichokes until a knife pierces the base easily, 30 to 40 minutes, depending on their size. Add more water if necessary.

Meanwhile, melt the butter in a small heavy saucepan over medium heat. Add the garlic, thyme, the 1/8 teaspoon kosher salt, and pepper to taste. Cook for about 1 minute. Add the lemon juice and remove from the heat. Season with more kosher salt and pepper if necessary. Transfer the seasoned butter to a small serving bowl. Serve the artichokes warm with the seasoned butter.

HOW TO EAT AN ARTICHOKE

If someone tells you that he or she wasn't daunted when first presented with an artichoke, then someone is trying to put one over on you. If you haven't yet had the pleasure of eating a whole artichoke, we offer this primer.

Beginning with the outer leaves, pull a leaf off the base of the artichoke and dip the meaty end into the sauce of your choice. Pull the leaf between your teeth, scraping the artichoke flesh into your mouth. Discard the leaf. Don't stop once you've worked your way through all the leaves—the best is yet to come.

Remove the thin, purple-tipped leaves from the center of the artichoke. Using a spoon, gently scrape off the prickly fuzz. What remains is the heart. Slice it into chunks, dip, and savor.

CARAMELIZED ONION, GRUYÈRE, AND OLIVE TARTS

Serves 2

The first time we made these tarts, we pulled them out of the oven 15 minutes before we were due at a Bikram yoga class—a workout way too challenging to endure with a full belly. On our way out the door, we agreed to have one little sample. But after a single bite of the tasty trio of onions, cheese, and olives, our willpower was gone. (Needless to say, we never made it to class that day.) On days when we do exercise self-control and the tarts actually make it to the table, we serve them with a salad of spicy arugula and fresh figs. The tarts are also superb set out fireside along with warm bowls of comforting Creamy Mushroom Soup (page 73)—perfect for a cozy meal for two.

1   *SHEET FROZEN PUFF PASTRY (10 INCH SQUARE), SUCH AS PEPPERIDGE FARM*

1   *EGG, LIGHTLY BEATEN WITH 1 TABLESPOON WATER*

2   *TABLESPOONS GRATED GRUYÈRE CHEESE*

1/4   *TEASPOON CHOPPED FRESH ROSEMARY, OR 1/8 TEASPOON DRIED ROSEMARY, CRUMBLED*

3   *TABLESPOONS CARAMELIZED ONIONS (PAGE 50)*

2   *TEASPOONS SOUR CREAM OR CRÈME FRAÎCHE*

4   *NIÇOISE OLIVES, PITTED AND ROUGHLY CHOPPED*

Preheat the oven to 400 degrees F. Line a baking sheet with aluminum foil and coat lightly with vegetable oil.

Remove the sheet of puff pastry from the freezer. Using a heavy knife, cut the pastry in half crosswise and return the remaining half to the freezer for later use. Let thaw slightly and lay the pastry flat. Cut it in half again crosswise, creating two 5-inch squares. Place the squares on the prepared baking sheet.

Fold the sides of each pastry square about 1/2 inch toward the center. Use your index finger to make indentions and lightly squeeze the dough around your finger, creating a fluted effect around the edge. (This forms a "little boat" for the cheese and caramelized onions.) Brush the edges of the tarts with the beaten egg mixture.

Sprinkle 1 tablespoon of the cheese and a pinch of the rosemary in the center of each tart. Mix the onions and sour cream in a small bowl. Divide the onion mixture between the tarts and spread evenly. Top with the olives.

Bake until the crust is golden brown, 25 to 35 minutes. Let cool slightly before serving.

Do-Ahead: The tarts can be baked 4 to 6 hours in advance and left at room temperature. Warm them just before serving. Brush the edges with extra-virgin olive oil and heat in a 400-degree F oven for about 3 minutes.

GOAT CHEESE, SUN-DRIED TOMATO, AND PESTO TORTA

Serves 8 to 12

We have served hors d'oeuvres to thousands of folks during our years of catering. When we're entertaining, we strive for three things: dishes that can be made ahead of time, those that are beautifully displayed, and, most importantly, ones that pack a punch in the flavor department. This torta, a modern take on the traditional cheese platter, is a triple hitter. When we have leftovers, we toss the torta with pasta (you may need to thin with water or vegetable stock), dollop on baked potatoes, or spread onto focaccia and top with grilled vegetables.

4   OUNCES GOAT CHEESE AT ROOM TEMPERATURE

1   PACKAGE (8 OUNCES) CREAM CHEESE AT ROOM TEMPERATURE

     KOSHER SALT AND FRESHLY GROUND PEPPER

3/4   CUP DRAINED OIL-PACKED SUN-DRIED TOMATOES, FINELY CHOPPED

3   TABLESPOONS TOMATO PASTE

1/2   TEASPOON BALSAMIC VINEGAR

2/3   CUP HOMEMADE PESTO (PAGE 48) OR PURCHASED PESTO (SEE NOTE)

     FRESH BASIL LEAVES OR PARSLEY SPRIGS FOR GARNISHING

     TOASTED BAGUETTE SLICES OR ASSORTED CRACKERS FOR SERVING

Stir together the goat cheese and cream cheese in a medium bowl. Season with kosher salt and pepper to taste.

Combine 1/4 cup of the goat–cream cheese mixture with the sun-dried tomatoes, tomato paste, and vinegar in a separate bowl. Season with kosher salt and pepper to taste.

Line a 2-cup ramekin or a small bowl with plastic wrap, extending the plastic over the sides. Spray the plastic wrap with vegetable-oil cooking spray. Spread half of the goat–cream cheese mixture evenly over the bottom of the ramekin. Cover with the pesto, then with the cheese-tomato mixture. Top with the remaining goat–cream cheese mixture. Fold the plastic wrap over the final cheese layer and refrigerate until chilled, at least 1 1/2 hours.

Invert the torta onto a platter and peel off the plastic wrap. Garnish with basil leaves and serve with baguette slices or crackers.

Do-Ahead: The torta can be made 2 days ahead and refrigerated.

Note: All pestos were not created equal. Some are nearly solid and others can be downright soupy. This recipe requires a pesto that can hold its shape. If yours is a little thin, add grated Parmesan cheese until you reach a thick consistency.

Tip: This torta is a real beauty if you pay careful attention to making clean, well-defined layers. After spreading each layer, make certain that the plastic wrap that adheres to the inside of the ramekin above each layer is perfectly clean to ensure clear delineation between the colors.

CHICKEN SATAY

Serves 4

This Thai appetizer is universally loved and has been one of our most popular Thymes Two catering dishes. It makes for an explosive taste sensation as a first course for sit-down dinner parties, and also gets rave reviews when we set it out as stylish cocktail fare. Don't forget to put out a container for used skewers—a Champagne glass serves the purpose well. Flank steak, beef tenderloin, and shrimp are wonderful alternatives for the chicken.

1	TABLESPOON PEANUT OIL
2	MEDIUM CLOVES GARLIC, THINLY SLICED
2	SKINLESS, BONELESS CHICKEN BREAST HALVES (ABOUT 8 OUNCES EACH)
12	EIGHT-INCH WOODEN SKEWERS
	KOSHER SALT AND FRESHLY GROUND PEPPER
2	CUPS THINLY SLICED RED CABBAGE
1	CUP PEANUT SAUCE (SEE PAGE 46)
2	TEASPOONS CHOPPED FRESH CILANTRO, PLUS SPRIGS FOR GARNISHING
	RED PEPPER FLAKES FOR GARNISHING

Combine the peanut oil and garlic in a small bowl. Cut the tenderloin from the bottom of each chicken breast half, in one piece if possible. Cut each breast lengthwise into five 1/2-inch-thick strips (see note.) Add the chicken strips and the tenderloins to the garlic oil, stir until the oil is evenly distributed, and cover with plastic wrap. Let marinate for 30 minutes and up to 24 hours. Refrigerate if marinating for more than 30 minutes.

Soak the skewers in water for at least 30 minutes to prevent splintering and burning.

Prepare a medium-hot charcoal fire, or preheat a gas grill to medium-high. Oil the grill rack.

Thread 1 piece of chicken onto each skewer, bunching the meat tightly at the end of the skewer. Season with kosher salt and pepper to taste. Grill the chicken until cooked through, about 3 minutes on each side.

Divide the cabbage among 4 plates. Arrange 3 skewers on each plate along with a small ramekin of peanut sauce. Sprinkle the chicken with the chopped cilantro and red pepper flakes. Garnish with cilantro sprigs.

Note: When serving the skewers as a passed finger food without a knife and fork, we cut the five 1/2-inch-thick strips in half horizontally, creating more manageable mouthfuls.

Do-Ahead: The peanut sauce can be made up to 3 days in advance. Refrigerate until ready to use. Marinate the chicken and skewer the strips up to 1 day in advance. The chicken can be grilled 8 hours in advance and refrigerated. Be careful not to overcook the meat. Just before serving, cover the skewered chicken with aluminum foil and reheat in a 350-degree F oven for about 5 minutes.

Herbed BUTTERMILK POPCORN

Makes 8 cups; *serves* 4

Friday night is movie night in the Barber household, and it is one of the most anticipated nights of the week. Mary, Jack, and their little fellas pile onto the king-sized bed with a bowl of homemade popcorn. One batch is rarely enough. Eldest son Jackson loves the ritual of making the popcorn almost as much as he loves watching the movie. Pop your corn on the stovetop the old-fashioned way and sprinkle on the flavor; microwave popcorn just can't measure up. Trust us, you'll want to smuggle this lively herbed popcorn into the movie theater.

1	TABLESPOON POWDERED BUTTERMILK (SEE NOTE)
1	TEASPOON GARLIC POWDER
1	TEASPOON ONION POWDER
1	TEASPOON LEMON PEPPER
1/2	TEASPOON DRIED DILL WEED
1/2	TEASPOON POWDERED CHICKEN BOUILLON OR KOSHER SALT
1	TABLESPOON CORN OIL
1/3	CUP POPCORN KERNELS
2	TABLESPOONS UNSALTED BUTTER

Combine the buttermilk, garlic powder, onion powder, lemon pepper, dill weed, and chicken bouillon in a small bowl.

Heat the oil in a large saucepan over medium heat. Add the popcorn and cover with a lid. Shake the pan frequently. Remove from the heat when the popping subsides. Pour the popcorn into a bowl. Wipe the pan clean with a paper towel. Melt the butter in the pan. Pour the butter over the popcorn, tossing to distribute evenly. Sprinkle with the flavoring mixture and toss to coat.

Do-ahead: For convenience, we multiply the recipe for the flavoring mixture 6 or 8 times. It keeps in the refrigerator for several months. Use 2 heaping tablespoons per batch of popcorn.

Note: SACO offers a cultured buttermilk powder that can be found in the baking section of most grocery stores or can be ordered at www.sacofoods.com. It is one of our favorite products. Wonderful to have on hand for baking, this powder makes last-minute buttermilk pancakes a reality and enlivens mashed potatoes. You can also use it to create great salad dressings and dips. Try it!

SMOKED SALMON PLATTER

Serves 8 to 10

This attractive platter will fool your guests into thinking that you have been in the kitchen for hours. It is impressive yet requires no cooking, only assembly. When we were young chefs in New York City, we discovered pastrami-cured salmon through David Burke of the acclaimed Park Avenue Café. We've never forgotten his exceptionally peppery version. Look for pastrami-cured salmon in the deli section of your grocery store. Its peppery flavor is dynamite and adds unforgettable flair to the traditional smoked salmon platter.

1/4	CUP HONEY MUSTARD
1/4	CUP SOUR CREAM
1	TEASPOON CHOPPED FRESH DILL, OR 1/2 TEASPOON DRIED DILL WEED
1/2	CUP DRAINED CAPERS
1/2	CUP FINELY CHOPPED RED ONION
1	POUND PRESLICED SMOKED SALMON, PREFERABLY PASTRAMI-CURED, CUT INTO 2-INCH PIECES
16	COCKTAIL-SIZED PUMPERNICKEL BREAD SLICES
1	LEMON, CUT INTO WEDGES, SEEDS REMOVED
	FRESH FLAT-LEAF PARSLEY SPRIGS FOR GARNISHING

Mix together the mustard, sour cream, and dill in a small bowl.

Select 3 demitasse cups or small ramekins. Fill 1 cup with the capers, another with the red onion, and the other with the mustard-dill sauce. Place the cups on a medium platter and arrange the smoked salmon around them.

Stack the pumpernickel slices and cut on the diagonal, creating triangles. Artfully arrange the bread slices and the lemon wedges on the outer edge of the platter. Garnish with parsley sprigs.

Place a small spoon in each of the condiments and present the salmon with a small serving fork, preferably a 3-pronged one.

Presentation Tip: Cut a lemon in half horizontally, creating either a straight or a zigzag edge. Then cut a thin slice off the bottom of each half so that the halves sit upright on a flat surface without tipping. Use each lemon half as the base for a small flower arrangement, inserting the stems of sturdy, attractive herbs and flowers. We like to use rosemary, thyme, lavender, parsley, and any small flowers we have on hand such as nasturtiums, baby roses, and pansies. Avoid using toxic flower varieties and garden flowers that have been sprayed with insecticides or fertilizers.

MARINATED OLIVES AND FETA CHEESE

Serves 6

Each fall, we head up to our friend Sloat Vanwinkle's country home in Sonoma County, for an olive-picking extravaganza. We look forward to the invitation year after year for a spirited celebration of the harvest season, not to mention all the great food and wine. Each time we make this dish, Sonoma comes to our table. We typically serve the olives and cheese with slices of French bread, and a great bottle of Sonoma Chardonnay.

$1/2$ *CUP HIGH-QUALITY EXTRA-VIRGIN OLIVE OIL*

2   *TEASPOONS GRATED LEMON ZEST*

2   *TABLESPOONS FRESH LEMON JUICE*

5   *MEDIUM CLOVES GARLIC, SLICED*

$1/4$ *CUP CHOPPED FRESH FLAT-LEAF PARSLEY*

1   *TABLESPOON HERBES DE PROVENCE*

$3/4$ *TEASPOON DRIED CHILI FLAKES*

1   *CUP KALAMATA OR OTHER BRINE-CURED BLACK OLIVES*

1   *CUP GREEN OLIVES, SUCH AS PICHOLINES OR MANZANILLAS*

10   *OUNCES FETA CHEESE, CUT INTO $1/2$-INCH-THICK SLICES*

     FRENCH BREAD SLICES (ABOUT 24) FOR SERVING

Place a sealable plastic bag in a medium bowl. Combine the olive oil, lemon zest, lemon juice, garlic, parsley, herbes de Provence, and chili flakes in the bag and stir. Transfer 3 tablespoons of the marinade to a small glass or plastic container. Add the olives to the bag and seal. Refrigerate the olives and the 3 tablespoons reserved marinade for at least 24 hours and up to 1 week.

About 30 minutes before serving, remove the olives and the reserved marinade from the refrigerator so the oil will become fluid. Place feta on a plate and drizzle with the reserved marinade. Just before serving, transfer the olives to a serving bowl. Put the bread in a napkin-lined basket and serve alongside.

Presentation Tip: Garnish with whole rosemary sprigs, lavender sprigs, or lengthy curls of lemon peel.

Party PECANS

Makes 2 cups

Our friends go absolutely "nuts" for these nuts! So over the years, these little numbers have become a holiday gift-giving tradition for us. The scrumptious tidbits are a perfect balance of sweet, salt, smoke, and heat—delightful on salads or for snacking (and especially tasty with a martini). One of the best things about this recipe is that the pecans will taste fresh and flavorful, even weeks after they were made. That is, if they last that long.

1	TABLESPOON WORCESTERSHIRE SAUCE
1	TABLESPOON UNSALTED BUTTER, MELTED
1/2	TEASPOON LIQUID SMOKE
2	CUPS (6 OUNCES) PECAN HALVES
2	TEASPOONS ONION POWDER
2	TEASPOONS GARLIC POWDER
1	TEASPOON SEASONING SALT, SUCH AS LAWRY'S
1	TEASPOON SUGAR
1/8	TEASPOON CAYENNE PEPPER

Preheat the oven to 250 degrees F. Line a baking sheet with aluminum foil.

Combine the Worcestershire sauce, butter, and liquid smoke in a medium bowl. Add the pecans and stir to coat. In a small bowl, combine the onion powder, garlic powder, seasoning salt, sugar, and cayenne. Sprinkle half the spice mixture over the nuts and stir well. Add the remaining spice mixture and stir again.

Spread the nuts in a single layer on the prepared baking sheet and bake until the nuts are dry and toasted, 30 to 40 minutes. Let cool completely before serving.

CHAPTER 5

SOUPS *&* SALADS

SOUP IS FOR ALL SEASONS. Warm, rich, and decadent in the fall and winter, it becomes pleasantly cool and refreshing in the warmer months. We've loaded this chapter with everything from exhilarating broths to comforting rich creams. The wide variety of colors, textures, and consistencies gives you a soup selection for every occasion. Most of our soups can be prepared in less than an hour, and all of them benefit on the flavor front when made ahead. Great for entertaining and ideal for casual suppers at home, soup satisfies.

Chicken Soup for Your Soul Mate (page 72) will be just what the doctor ordered when your loved one gets sick—it's a cure-all you'll sip side-by-side. Summer Garden Gazpacho (page 74) is a staple in our homes; we keep a pitcher of it ready for pouring the minute the mercury begins to rise. And for dinner parties, we've found it's hard to beat our Creamy Mushroom Soup with Brie Crostini (page 73) drizzled with aromatic truffle oil. Make extra and enjoy stylish leftovers snuggled up fireside together.

When it comes to salads, our mantra is "fruit, cheese, nuts . . . fruit, cheese, nuts." We guarantee you'll make spectacular salads if you follow this simple formula when combining ingredients. See page 85 for a chart with our favorite fruit, cheese, and nut combinations. Add some thinly sliced onion and one of our "extras" for dimension, and watch the flavors explode. Main-course salads are a mainstay in our households. Salads can quickly and creatively be converted into protein-packed entrées with the simple additions of chicken, pork, beef, or seafood.

Soup and salad have always been an inseparable pair. The two go hand in hand and are the perfect complement to each other. Pair our Roasted Butternut Squash Soup with Crème Heart Swirls (page 79) with Arugula with Cranberries, Cambozola, Walnuts, and Raspberry Vinaigrette (page 89). While such well-balanced combos will wow you, almost all of our soups and salads make great stand-alone appetizers or entrees as well. Try a small cup of Sherry-Spiked French Onion Soup (page 82) as an opener to a dinner party. Or create an entire meal around this soul-warming soup, coupling it with any of our salads, some crusty French bread, and a glass of wine.

CHICKEN SOUP *for Your Soul Mate*

Serves 4

"In sickness and in health ..." The definitive homespun flu remedy, this invigorating chicken soup boasts all the necessary health benefits without costing you precious hours in the kitchen. In less than an hour, you can dole out a rejuvenating bowl. As with any soup, this one's flavor will improve over time. Roasted garlic is our secret to this yummy soup. If you don't have any store-bought roasted garlic on hand, pop a bulb in the oven (see page 34); it will be roasted just in time to add to the finished soup. Be prepared for your mate to extend his or her sick leave, though. The last time Sara served her ailing Erik a bowl of this, he told her the soup was good enough to keep him home sick forever! We like to season the soup with chicken bouillon rather than with kosher salt as it adds depth of flavor along with a kiss of salt.

1   TABLESPOON VEGETABLE OIL

1   MEDIUM YELLOW ONION, COARSELY CHOPPED

1   TABLESPOON MINCED GARLIC

1/2   TEASPOON POWDERED CHICKEN BOUILLON, OR 1 SMALL CHICKEN BOUILLON CUBE, PLUS MORE AS NEEDED

1   TEASPOON CHOPPED FRESH THYME, OR 1/4 TEASPOON DRIED THYME

1/2   CUP DRY WHITE WINE

6   CUPS CHICKEN STOCK (PAGE 30) OR CANNED LOW-SODIUM CHICKEN BROTH

2   CUPS SHREDDED PURCHASED ROAST CHICKEN

2   MEDIUM CARROTS, PEELED AND ROUGHLY CHOPPED

1   CELERY STALK, ROUGHLY CHOPPED

2   OUNCES EGG NOODLES

1   TABLESPOON ROASTED GARLIC, HOMEMADE (PAGE 34) OR PURCHASED, PLUS MORE AS NEEDED

1/4   CUP CHOPPED FRESH FLAT-LEAF PARSLEY
     FRESHLY GROUND PEPPER

Heat the oil in a large heavy pot over medium heat. Add the onion and garlic. Add the 1/2 teaspoon powdered bouillon (if using a cube, add after the stock) and the thyme and cook, stirring frequently, until the onion is translucent, 5 to 7 minutes. Add the wine and cook for 2 minutes. Add the stock, the bouillon cube, if using, the chicken, carrots, and celery. Simmer until the vegetables are tender, 25 to 30 minutes. Add the egg noodles and cook until tender, about 5 minutes. Stir in the 1 tablespoon roasted garlic and the parsley. Just before serving, season with pepper to taste, and add more powdered bouillon and roasted garlic if necessary.

Do-Ahead: This soup is best made at least 1 day in advance. It will keep, refrigerated, for 3 days and freezes beautifully. Allow the flavors to marry in the refrigerator for 1 day before freezing.

Variation: For the egg noodles, substitute tortellini, or precooked rice (a combination of white and wild is delicious), or barley.

Creamy MUSHROOM SOUP WITH BRIE CROSTINI

Opposites attract, and creamy clings to chunky in a heavenly embrace in this soup. Blend half of the soup until smooth and leave the remaining portion chunky. The result is an earthy, rustic, yet elegant creation that suits any occasion, from formal to snuggle-up-to-the-fire casual. Experiment with exotic mushrooms, such as shiitakes, chanterelles, or oysters, when available. If you don't have Marsala on hand, sherry, Madeira, brandy, or even red or white wine will make an excellent substitute.

4	TABLESPOONS UNSALTED BUTTER
12	OUNCES CREMINI OR SHIITAKE MUSHROOMS, SLICED (IF USING SHIITAKES, DISCARD STEMS)
$1/4$	TEASPOON KOSHER SALT, PLUS MORE AS NEEDED
$1/8$	TEASPOON FRESHLY GROUND PEPPER, PLUS MORE AS NEEDED
1	SMALL YELLOW ONION, CHOPPED
1	TABLESPOON CHOPPED GARLIC
$1/4$	CUP DRY MARSALA
2	TABLESPOONS ALL-PURPOSE FLOUR
$3^1/2$	CUPS HOMEMADE VEGETABLE STOCK (PAGE 31) OR 2 CANS ($14^1/2$ OUNCES) VEGETABLE BROTH
$1/2$	CUP HEAVY CREAM
1	TEASPOON CHOPPED FRESH THYME, OR $1/2$ TEASPOON DRIED THYME
1	TEASPOON FRESH LEMON JUICE

CROSTINI

4 TO 6 FRENCH BAGUETTE SLICES, CUT ON THE DIAGONAL (EACH $1/2$ INCH THICK)

1 TO 2 OUNCES BRIE CHEESE, RIND REMOVED, CUT INTO SLICES OR SMALL PIECES

Preheat the oven to 350 degrees F.

Melt the butter in a large heavy-bottomed saucepan over medium-high heat. Add the mushrooms, the $1/4$ teaspoon kosher salt, and the $1/8$ teaspoon pepper. Cook, stirring occasionally with a wooden spoon, until the mushrooms are tender, about 5 minutes. Reduce the heat to medium and add the onion and garlic. Cook, stirring frequently, until the onion is tender, about 5 minutes. Add the Marsala and cook, stirring frequently, until most of the liquid evaporates. Add the flour and cook, stirring, for 2 minutes. Gradually stir in the stock, cream, thyme, and lemon juice. Remove from the heat.

Transfer 2 cups of the soup to a blender and blend, starting at low speed and slowly increasing to high, until well puréed. (Be careful that the hot mixture does not splatter.) Return the purée to the pot with the chunky mixture. Simmer over medium heat, stirring occasionally, until the soup is slightly thickened, 10 to 15 minutes. Season with more kosher salt and pepper if necessary.

Meanwhile, make the crostini: Place the baguette slices on a baking sheet, top with the cheese, and bake until the cheese melts, 10 to 12 minutes. Serve alongside the warm soup.

Do-Ahead: This soup is best made at least 1 day in advance. It will keep, refrigerated, for 3 to 4 days and freezes beautifully. Allow the flavors to marry in the refrigerator for 1 day before freezing.

Summer Garden GAZPACHO

Serves 6

Back when Mary and Jack were dating, Jack spent a summer in Spain and fell in love with gazpacho. He raved about it so much when he returned home that Mary, despite her culinary background, was intimidated to prepare it. In an attempt to win his heart and prove her prowess in the kitchen, she developed this big, bold gazpacho. Jack proclaimed it better than anything he'd tasted in Spain, and it has been our basic recipe ever since. We start with this gazpacho and make all sorts of variations, depending on what looks good at the market. Sometimes we toss in a handful of chopped parsley, basil, cilantro, or jalapeño after blending the soup. Other times, we add a dollop of sour cream and blend for a creamy variation. When preparing gazpacho, use summer tomatoes whenever possible and plum tomatoes during the off-season.

4	CUPS ROUGHLY CHOPPED RIPE SUMMER TOMATOES OR PLUM TOMATOES (ABOUT 1 ^{1}/$_2$ POUNDS)
1 ^{1}/$_2$	CUPS ROUGHLY CHOPPED ENGLISH CUCUMBER (ABOUT ^{1}/$_2$ A MEDIUM CUCUMBER) (SEE NOTE)
1	CUP PEELED AND ROUGHLY CHOPPED CARROT (ABOUT 1 CARROT)
1	SMALL RED BELL PEPPER, SEEDED, DERIBBED, AND ROUGHLY CHOPPED
^{1}/$_2$	CUP ROUGHLY CHOPPED RED ONION
4	CUPS TOMATO JUICE, PLUS MORE AS NEEDED
^{1}/$_4$	CUP RED WINE VINEGAR, PLUS MORE AS NEEDED
^{1}/$_4$	CUP EXTRA-VIRGIN OLIVE OIL
2	TEASPOONS KOSHER SALT, PLUS MORE AS NEEDED
2	TEASPOONS FINELY CHOPPED GARLIC
	FRESHLY GROUND PEPPER
	TABASCO OR CHILI SAUCE AS NEEDED (OPTIONAL)
	PINCH OR 2 OF SUGAR (OPTIONAL)

Combine the tomatoes, cucumber, carrot, bell pepper, and red onion in a large bowl. In the bowl of a food processor fitted with the steel blade, pulse the vegetables in two batches until coarsely chopped. Do not overprocess; the vegetables should retain some of their crunch. Transfer the vegetables to a large bowl. Add the 4 cups tomato juice, the ^{1}/$_4$ cup vinegar, the olive oil, the 2 teaspoons kosher salt, the garlic, and pepper to taste, and the Tabasco sauce and sugar, if desired. Stir to combine. Add more tomato juice as necessary to achieve the desired thickness. Cover and refrigerate for at least 4 hours or preferably overnight.

Just before serving, adjust the seasonings by adding more vinegar, kosher salt, pepper, or Tabasco as necessary.

Note: If English (or hothouse) cucumbers are not available, use conventional cucumbers and be sure to peel them. If the seeds are big, remove them by cutting the cucumber in half lengthwise and scraping out the seeds with a spoon.

Mrs. Birdsong's CABBAGE SOUP

Serves 8

All small-town cooks have their claim to fame, and our mom, Mrs. Birdsong Corpening, earned her culinary notoriety with this soup. She always roasts prime-rib bones (leftovers from Christmas Eve dinner), but we have adapted the recipe to suit our time-challenged lifestyles. To enrich the flavor, we've added some chopped garlic, and serve the soup with a dash of Tabasco and a dollop of sour cream. Though the folks back in High Point, North Carolina, know and love Mom's all-day-in-the-kitchen cabbage soup, thickened with slightly sweet gingersnaps, our friends in San Francisco rave about our sweet-and-sour rendition. Who says you have to roast bones to make soup that rates two thumbs up?

3	TABLESPOONS VEGETABLE OIL
1³/4	POUNDS CHUCK STEW MEAT, TRIMMED AND CUT INTO ¹/2-INCH PIECES
1	TEASPOON KOSHER SALT, PLUS MORE AS NEEDED
¹/2	TEASPOON FRESHLY GROUND PEPPER
2	SMALL YELLOW ONIONS, THINLY SLICED
2	CARROTS, ROUGHLY CHOPPED
2	PARSNIPS, ROUGHLY CHOPPED
4	LARGE CLOVES GARLIC, ROUGHLY CHOPPED
4	CANS (14 OUNCES EACH) BEEF BROTH (NOT DOUBLE STRENGTH)
4	CUPS WATER
1	CAN (28 OUNCES) CRUSHED TOMATOES (NOT IN PURÉE)
4	CUPS ROUGHLY CHOPPED GREEN CABBAGE
1	PACKAGE (10 OUNCES) FROZEN BUTTER BEANS OR BABY LIMAS
8	GINGERSNAPS, FINELY CRUSHED IN FOOD PROCESSOR (SCANT ¹/2 CUP)
3	TABLESPOONS FRESH LEMON JUICE, PLUS MORE AS NEEDED
3	TABLESPOONS FIRMLY PACKED DARK BROWN SUGAR, PLUS MORE AS NEEDED
1	BAY LEAF
	TABASCO SAUCE FOR SERVING
	SOUR CREAM FOR SERVING

Heat 1 tablespoon of the oil in an 8-quart heavy-bottomed stockpot over medium-high heat. Season the meat with ¹/2 teaspoon of the kosher salt and ¹/4 teaspoon of the pepper. Add the meat and cook until browned, 3 to 5 minutes. Transfer the meat to a large plate.

Add the remaining 2 tablespoons vegetable oil to the pot. Add the onions, carrots, parsnips, the remaining ¹/2 teaspoon kosher salt, and the remaining ¹/4 teaspoon pepper. Cook, stirring occasionally, until the vegetables begin to caramelize, about 5 minutes. Add the garlic and cook, stirring constantly, for 1 minute. Add the broth and the beef, then the water, tomatoes, cabbage, butter beans, gingersnaps, the 3 tablespoons lemon juice, 3 tablespoons brown sugar, and the bay leaf. Whisk vigorously to dissolve the gingersnaps. (They may clump at first, but will disintegrate as you stir.) Bring to a boil, then reduce the heat to low. Skim the surface with a ladle to remove excess foam. Simmer, stirring occasionally, for 1^1/$_2$ hours.

Season with more kosher salt, lemon juice, and brown sugar if necessary. Remove the bay leaf. Ladle into bowls and top each with a dash of Tabasco sauce and a dollop of sour cream.

Note: This makes an extra-large pot of soup. Eat what you can and freeze the rest for later.

Do-Ahead: This soup is best made at least 1 day in advance. It will keep, refrigerated, for several days and freezes beautifully. Allow the flavors to marry in the refrigerator for 1 day before freezing.

ROASTED BUTTERNUT SQUASH SOUP
WITH CRÈME HEART SWIRLS

Serves 4

As Mary's son Jackson says, "This soup is sweet like candy." Our autumns revolve around hard-shelled squashes, especially the smooth and shapely butternut variety. After all, who doesn't love smooth and shapely? Butternut squash makes for a hardy soup, sure to spread warmth on a brisk, wind-whirring, teeth-chattering night. Swirl small hearts ♥ on top of this soup for your sweetheart, and away you'll go . . .

1   2¹/₂-POUND BUTTERNUT SQUASH (3 CUPS, COOKED)

1   TABLESPOON OLIVE OIL, PLUS EXTRA FOR BRUSHING

1   TABLESPOON UNSALTED BUTTER

1   MEDIUM YELLOW ONION, CHOPPED

¹/₂   TEASPOON KOSHER SALT, PLUS MORE TO TASTE
    FRESHLY GROUND PEPPER

3   TABLESPOONS CALVADOS OR BRANDY

3¹/₂ CUPS HOMEMADE CHICKEN STOCK (PAGE 30), VEGETABLE
    STOCK (PAGE 31), OR TWO 14-OUNCE CANS CHICKEN OR
    VEGETABLE BROTH, PLUS MORE AS NEEDED

³/₄   CUP EVAPORATED MILK
    FRESH GRATED NUTMEG, OR PINCH OF GROUND NUTMEG

2   TABLESPOONS SOUR CREAM

Preheat the oven to 375 degrees F.

Cut the squash in half, lengthwise. Brush the squash flesh with olive oil, and place face-down on a roasting pan. Check the squash after 35 to 45 minutes, though it could take over an hour. When the squash is very soft and yields to the touch, remove from the oven and let cool enough to handle, about 20 minutes.

Meanwhile, add the olive oil and butter to a medium skillet over medium heat. Add the onion and cook until soft and translucent, about 10 minutes, stirring frequently. Be careful that the onion does not color at all. Sprinkle with kosher salt and freshly ground pepper. Add the Calvados and cook until the liquid evaporates. Remove from heat.

Once the squash has cooled, remove the seeds, and scoop out the squash flesh, discarding the skin. Place in a small bowl. You will need 3 cups of butternut squash for this recipe. Reserve any extra for later use.

Combine half of the cooked squash, half of the onion, half of the chicken stock, and half of the evaporated milk in a blender, and blend until smooth. Pour back into a medium heavy-bottomed pot. Repeat, blending the second half of the squash, onion, chicken broth, and evaporated milk. Once blended, pour into the pot with the first batch. Season with kosher salt, pepper, and nutmeg to taste. Bring to a simmer over medium-low heat. (Adjust consistency, if necessary, with more chicken stock or water.)

Place the sour cream in a small bowl and stir using a spoon, until silky smooth. Thin slightly by stirring in 2 teaspoons of warm water. Divide the soup among the number of bowls to be served. With a small spoon, drop 5 small, pea-size dots, in a circle, on top of the soup. Take a sharp knife, and run the knife straight through the dot, creating a heart shape. Serve immediately.

THAI-STYLE CORN SOUP WITH SHRIMP AND GREEN CURRY

Serves 3

We live a few blocks from Clement Street, an Asian neighborhood in San Francisco, where we seek out Thai coconut soup with lemongrass, galangal, Thai chile peppers, and lime leaves. Our rendition of this world-class soup spares you the trouble of tracking down hard-to-find ingredients. Green curry paste is a store-bought blend of green chiles, garlic, onion, and spices. It is potent, so watch out! While this spirited soup makes a great meal on its own, it is also a big hit served in demitasse or tea cups as an opener to an Asian-style dinner. Try it with our Grilled Tuna with Soy-Ginger Glaze and Pickled Cucumbers (page 131) and Coconut Rice (page 170).

1 TABLESPOON VEGETABLE OIL

1 SMALL YELLOW ONION, CHOPPED

2 SLICES FRESH GINGER (EACH $1/4$ INCH THICK)

$1/2$ TEASPOON KOSHER SALT

2 CUPS FRESH CORN KERNELS (CUT FROM 2 EARS OF CORN) OR FROZEN CORN KERNELS

$13/4$ CUPS HOMEMADE VEGETABLE STOCK (PAGE 31) OR 1 CAN ($14 1/2$ OUNCES) VEGETABLE BROTH

1 CAN ($14 1/2$ OUNCES) UNSWEETENED COCONUT MILK

3 TABLESPOONS FISH SAUCE

2 TABLESPOONS FRESH LIME JUICE, PLUS MORE AS NEEDED

1 TABLESPOON FIRMLY PACKED LIGHT BROWN SUGAR

1 TEASPOON GRATED LIME ZEST

$1/2$ TEASPOON GREEN CURRY PASTE, PLUS MORE AS NEEDED (SEE NOTE)

8 OUNCES MEDIUM SHRIMP, PEELED AND DEVEINED

3 TABLESPOONS CHOPPED FRESH BASIL OR CILANTRO, OR $1 1/2$ TABLESPOONS OF EACH

Heat the oil in a medium heavy-bottomed saucepan over medium heat. Add the onion, ginger, and kosher salt. Cook, stirring occasionally, until the onion is tender, 5 to 7 minutes. Add the corn, stock, coconut milk, fish sauce, the 2 tablespoons lime juice, the brown sugar, lime zest, and the 1/2 teaspoon curry paste and bring to a boil. Reduce the heat to low and simmer for about 10 minutes. Add the shrimp and cook until opaque in the center, 2 to 3 minutes. Remove the ginger with a slotted spoon and stir in the basil. Add more lime juice and curry paste if necessary.

Note: Thai Kitchen curry paste is widely available. Look for it in the Asian ingredient section of supermarkets, or visit their Web site at www.thaikitchen.com.

Tip: Fish Sauce, composed of salted, fermented fish and water, is a distinctive blend that lends great flavor to Asian-inspired dishes. Just remember that a little goes a long way! It can be found in the Asian section of the grocery stores or in Asian markets.

Sherry-Spiked FRENCH ONION SOUP

Serves 4

The secret to this simple yet delicious soup is to cook the onions with cream sherry, which enriches the soup, adding depth and sweetness. Our quick-and-easy method eliminates the time-consuming process of making beef stock and caramelizing the onions. This soup can be prepared in less than 30 minutes and is elegant enough to serve on any occasion. When we've not had Gruyère or French bread on hand, we've served the soup (minus the topping) alongside a smoked-mozzarella grilled cheese sandwich on white bread. Too good for words!

12   *FRENCH BAGUETTE SLICES, CUT ON THE DIAGONAL (EACH 1 INCH THICK)*

2   *TABLESPOONS UNSALTED BUTTER*

3   *CUPS SLICED YELLOW ONION (ABOUT 1 LARGE ONION)*

1/8   *TEASPOON KOSHER SALT*

FRESHLY GROUND PEPPER

3/4   *CUP CREAM SHERRY, SUCH AS HARVEY'S BRISTOL CREAM*

3   *CANS (10 1/2 OUNCES EACH) PREPARED FRENCH ONION SOUP, SUCH AS CAMPBELL'S*

2   *CUPS WATER*

1 1/2   *TEASPOONS CHOPPED FRESH THYME, OR 1/2 TEASPOON DRIED THYME*

2   *CUPS (4 OUNCES) GRATED GRUYÈRE OR OTHER SWISS CHEESE*

Preheat the oven to 350 degrees F.

Place the baguette slices on a baking sheet and bake, turning once, until lightly toasted on both sides, 10 to 12 minutes. Set aside. Turn the oven to broil.

Melt the butter in a medium saucepan over medium heat. Add the onion and salt and season with pepper to taste. Cook, stirring occasionally, until the onion is very soft and translucent, about 10 minutes. Add the sherry and continue to cook until most of the liquid has evaporated, 3 to 5 minutes. Add the canned French onion soup, water, and thyme and bring just to a boil. Simmer for 15 minutes.

Ladle 1 1/2 cups of soup into each of four 2-cup ovenproof bowls. Top each with 3 pieces of toasted bread (or less, depending on the size of your baguette) and 1/2 cup of the cheese. Broil until the cheese is melted and bubbling, 3 to 4 minutes. Serve immediately.

Note: Baguettes come in a multitude of sizes. Because the bread differs in width, the number of slices you will need for topping the soup will vary.

BUTTER LETTUCE WITH MANGO, GOAT CHEESE, AND MIGHTY MINT VINAIGRETTE

Serves 2

Perfect for a ladies' lunch, this salad puts the light, bright feel of the tropics on the plate. We like this side salad so much that we transform it into an entrée by adding grilled skewered shrimp, a fillet of grilled red snapper, or a piece of broiled halibut. If you're in the mood for a bunch of "crunch," top with a handful of banana chips for a whimsical, great-tasting garnish.

4	*CUPS LIGHTLY PACKED TORN BUTTER LETTUCE LEAVES*
	KOSHER SALT AND FRESHLY GROUND PEPPER
1/2	*CUP ROUGHLY CHOPPED MANGO*
	SCANT 1/4 CUP MACADAMIA NUTS, ROASTED AND SALTED, ROUGHLY CHOPPED
2	*TABLESPOONS CRUMBLED GOAT CHEESE*
2	*TABLESPOONS FINELY CHOPPED GREEN ONIONS, BOTH WHITE AND GREEN PARTS*
3	*TABLESPOONS MIGHTY MINT VINAIGRETTE, OR AS NEEDED (PAGE 45)*

Put the lettuce in a large bowl and season lightly with kosher salt and pepper to taste. Add the mango, macadamia nuts, goat cheese, and green onions and toss with enough vinaigrette to coat. Serve immediately.

TOP-10 TIPS FOR TERRIFIC SALADS

1. Wash, wash, wash your greens! Nothing ruins a salad faster than something unexpected on the greens, whether it's dirt or an uninvited insect. For a thorough cleaning, fill a large bowl or the sink with cold water, add the greens, and plunge them up and down. Lift the greens out of the water, leaving the dirt behind, and spin them in a salad spinner to dry.

2. Fresh, crisp, cold greens make the best salads. Quite simply, fresh dry greens are the answer to crisp greens. The dryer the greens, the longer they will keep fresh in the refrigerator. Store greens in a sealable bag with a paper towel or two (to absorb excess moisture) and refrigerate in the crisper section for up to 3 days. Keep greens refrigerated until ready to serve.

3. Cheese, on the other hand, will be at its best served at room temperature. Pull it out of the fridge 20 minutes before the greens.

4. To guarantee a delicious salad, all the components should be delicious on their own. To nudge your lettuce into the delicious category, season it lightly with kosher salt and freshly ground pepper before adding any additional ingredients. Use a variety of greens in your salad for added color and dimension—mix and match with ingredients, such as arugula, watercress, frisée, endive, and the like.

5. So now you have delicious ingredients. Let them shine! Don't overcrowd your salad with too many items that will compete for your attention. Keep it simple.

6. Do add fresh herbs. Fresh basil, mint, cilantro, chervil, parsley, dill, and tarragon leaves add brightness of flavor to lettuce.

7. We often find that vinaigrette "bites," or tastes strongly acidic, when you dip your finger in to sample it. Don't be so quick to alter the acidity. It will be diluted when tossed with the other ingredients.

8. Dressing flavors mingle over time—even a brief time. We've found that dressings taste best when freshly made and refrigerated for at least 15 minutes.

9. Think of the perfect salad: It's light, crisp, and fresh, right? Protect your perfection by properly dressing your salads. Too much dressing burdens the greens and can quickly transform a refreshing salad into a heavy, soggy mess, while underdressed greens are scant on flavor. Use a light hand, adding more dressing as needed. Greens are tricky to measure, but we've found that, for most salads, a ratio of 1 tablespoon dressing to 2 cups greens works well.

10. That said, when making vinaigrettes, we like to make some for immediate use and some extra to have on hand for lunch or dinner the next day. You can marinate chicken with it, drizzle it over grilled fish, or toss it with steamed vegetables.

"OFF THE CHART" SALAD COMBINATIONS

FRUIT +	CHEESE +	NUTS (TOASTED)	EXTRAS
Apples	Feta	Pine nuts	Fresh dill or lemon zest
Dried apricots	Goat Cheese	Pistachios	Fresh mint or basil
Dried cherries	Gorgonzola	Hazelnuts	Shaved radicchio or crisp pancetta
Figs	Cambozola	Walnuts	Orange zest, walnut oil, or prosciutto
Grapefruit	English Stilton	Pecans	Avocado
Nectarines	Manchego	Macadamia nuts	Fresh mint
Pears	Shaved Parmesan curls	Walnuts	Crumbled bacon or shaved endive
Persimmons	Goat cheese or blue cheese	Pecans (optional: caramelized) or toasted pumpkin seeds	Cayenne pepper or freshly grated nutmeg
Strawberries	Pepper-flavored Boursin cheese	Hazelnuts	Fresh basil or hazelnut oil
Sun-dried tomatoes	Fresh mozzarella (preferably Boccocini)	Pine nuts	Fresh basil

RED LEAF LETTUCE WITH GRAPES, BLUE CHEESE, PECANS, AND BALSAMIC VINAIGRETTE

Serves 2

We think this is the perfect "wine-country" salad, as it stands as a veritable tribute to wine, with its sweet grapes, red wine–loving blue cheese, and sweet balsamic vinegar. This lovely combination is reminiscent of a salad Sara and Erik shared on their first anniversary dinner at Tra Vigne, Michael Chiarello's celebrated restaurant in St. Helena, in the Napa Valley. Every time they taste the salad, they remember that romantic night and the sweetness of their first year of marriage. We love to transform this first-course salad into a full meal by adding deli-roasted chicken to the mix.

$^1/_4$	CUP PECANS
4	CUPS LIGHTLY PACKED TORN RED LEAF LETTUCE LEAVES
	KOSHER SALT AND FRESHLY GROUND PEPPER
$^1/_2$	CUP HALVED RED SEEDLESS GRAPES
$^1/_4$	CUP CRUMBLED BLUE CHEESE
	SCANT $^1/_4$ CUP PAPER-THIN RED ONION SLICES
3	TABLESPOONS BALSAMIC VINAIGRETTE, OR AS NEEDED (SEE NOTE)

Preheat the oven to 350 degrees F.

Put the pecans on a baking sheet and roast until aromatic and lightly browned, about 10 minutes. (After 6 to 8 minutes, shake the pan and rotate if necessary to ensure even browning.) Let cool, then roughly chop the pecans or break into pieces by hand.

Put the lettuce in a large bowl and season lightly with kosher salt and pepper to taste. Add the grapes, blue cheese, pecans, and red onion and toss with enough vinaigrette to coat. Serve immediately.

Note: The balsamic vinaigrette recipe (page 45) yields 1 1/2 cups. Use as a staple dressing for salads, steamed vegetables, and grains throughout the week.

GREEN BEANS, BEETS, AND GOAT
CHEESE WITH SHERRY VINAIGRETTE

Serves 2

This salad requires a bit more effort than your average plate of mixed greens with vinai-grette, but it is well worth it. An adaptation of a recipe Mary made during her days at Montrachet, one of Drew Nieporent's popular New York City restaurants, this green bean-beet-chèvre trio tastes as good as any salad served at a white-tablecloth restaurant. Go the extra mile to find the highest-quality ingredients, as the salad is at its best when you use tender, ultrathin French green beans, high-quality goat cheese (such as Montrachet or Boucheron), and freshly toasted walnuts. Beyond its incredible taste, this salad is visually exquisite—and all the ingredients can be prepared 1 day in advance and refrigerated, then assembled just before serving. It's a surefire bet when entertaining.

1	LARGE RED BEET (ABOUT 8 OUNCES), PEELED AND CUT INTO $1/2$-INCH PIECES
	KOSHER SALT
$1/4$	CUP WALNUTS
1	TABLESPOON OLIVE OIL
2	LARGE SHALLOTS, MINCED (ABOUT 1/3 CUP)
3	TABLESPOONS SHERRY VINEGAR
1	TEASPOON SUGAR
$1/2$	TEASPOON CHOPPED FRESH THYME
	FRESHLY GROUND PEPPER
3	TABLESPOONS WALNUT OIL
8	OUNCES THIN FRENCH GREEN BEANS, TRIMMED
$1^1/2$	OUNCES GOAT CHEESE, CRUMBLED

Preheat the oven to 350 degrees F.

Fill a small saucepan half full of water. Add the cut beet and kosher salt. (We add $1^1/2$ teaspoons kosher salt per quart of water.) Bring to a boil over high heat, reduce the heat to low, and simmer until the beet is tender, about 5 minutes. Drain the beet, transfer to a small bowl, and refrigerate.

Put the walnuts on a baking sheet and roast until aromatic and lightly browned, about 10 minutes. After 6 to 8 minutes, shake the pan and rotate if necessary to ensure even browning. Let cool, then roughly chop the walnuts or break into pieces by hand.

Heat the olive oil in a small saucepan over medium heat. Add the shallots and cook, stirring frequently, until soft and translucent, about 2 minutes. Add the vinegar, bring to a boil, and boil

for about 20 seconds. Transfer to a small bowl. Add the sugar, thyme, and kosher salt and pepper to taste. Add the walnut oil and whisk until well combined. Set aside.

Fill a medium saucepan three fourths full of water. Bring to a boil over high heat and add kosher salt. (We add $1^1/2$ teaspoons kosher salt per quart of water.) Add the green beans and cook until very tender, 3 to 5 minutes. Drain the beans and refresh in a bowl of ice water to stop the cooking. Pat the beans dry with paper towels.

Put the beans in a medium bowl and add the beet and walnuts. Season with kosher salt and pepper to taste. Add the vinaigrette and toss gently. Divide among 2 salad plates. Top with the goat cheese.

ARUGULA WITH CRANBERRIES, CAMBOZOLA, WALNUTS, AND RASPBERRY VINAIGRETTE

Serves 2

Sweet raspberry vinaigrette tames spicy arugula in this enticing autumnal salad. Cambozola is one of our favorite cheeses; it combines the best of Camembert's creaminess with Gorgonzola's punch. If you cannot find Cambozola, substitute any blue-veined cheese. We often replace the 2 tablespoons olive oil with the same amount of walnut oil for a wonderful variation.

RASPBERRY VINAIGRETTE

1   *TABLESPOON PLUS 2 TEASPOONS RASPBERRY VINEGAR*

2   *TEASPOONS RASPBERRY JAM*

    PINCH OF KOSHER SALT

    FRESHLY GROUND PEPPER

$^1/_4$ *CUP BEST-QUALITY OLIVE OIL*

SALAD

$^1/_4$ *CUP WALNUTS*

4   *CUPS LIGHTLY PACKED ARUGULA*

    KOSHER SALT AND FRESHLY GROUND PEPPER

3   *TABLESPOONS DRIED CRANBERRIES*

2   *OUNCES CAMBOZOLA CHEESE, RIND REMOVED, CUT INTO SMALL PIECES (ABOUT $^1/_4$ CUP)*

TO MAKE THE VINAIGRETTE: Whisk together the vinegar, jam, kosher salt, and pepper to taste in a small bowl. Drizzle in the olive oil, whisking to incorporate. Adjust the seasonings to taste. Refrigerate until ready to use.

Preheat the oven to 350 degrees F.

Put the walnuts on a baking sheet and roast until aromatic and lightly browned, about 10 minutes. (After 6 to 8 minutes, shake the pan and rotate if necessary to ensure even browning.) Let cool, then roughly chop the walnuts or break into pieces by hand.

Put the arugula in a large bowl and season lightly with kosher salt and pepper to taste. Add the dried cranberries, Cambozola, and walnuts and toss with enough dressing to coat, about 3 tablespoons. Serve immediately.

Summer TOMATO STACK

Serves 2

We go berserk when summer rolls around and tomatoes are at their absolute prime. When we were pregnant at the same time (we had the same unplanned due date, no joke!), we honestly ate 4 to 5 beef-steak tomatoes a piece each day. We craved tomatoes above all else and practically survived on this recipe all summer long. The sweet acidity of the tomatoes marries harmoniously with the rich, soft mozzarella, the pungency of fresh basil, and the sweet and sour balsamic syrup. Use the ripest, most picture-perfect tomatoes you can find, and purchase only fresh, preferably water-packed mozzarella. (If you're ever pregnant in the summertime, we recommend eating Summer Tomato Stacks . . . they're every bit as satisfying as ice cream and pickles . . . and healthier.)

4	OUNCES FRESH MOZZARELLA CHEESE
$^1/_2$	CUP BALSAMIC VINEGAR
	KOSHER SALT AND FRESHLY GROUND PEPPER
2	SMALL RIPE SUMMER TOMATOES (ABOUT 4 OUNCES EACH), STEMS ATTACHED
1	TEASPOON EXTRA-VIRGIN OLIVE OIL
8	LARGE FRESH BASIL LEAVES

Slice the mozzarella into four $^1/_2$-inch-thick slices and set them on a paper towel–lined plate to drain. Blot the cheese with paper towels to remove excess moisture.

Heat the balsamic vinegar with a pinch of kosher salt and a pinch of pepper in a small heavy-bottomed saucepan over medium-high heat. Cook at a moderate boil until reduced to 1 tablespoon, about 7 minutes. (Watch carefully to avoid overreducing. The reduction is complete when the vinegar coats the bottom of the pan yet still flows freely. It will thicken as it cools.) Immediately transfer the vinegar to a small bowl.

Cut a very thin slice from the bottom of each tomato to create a flat surface. Discard. Cut each tomato into 3 slices. Place the bottom slice of each tomato on a serving plate. Drizzle each slice with $^1/_4$ teaspoon of the olive oil. Season generously with kosher salt and pepper to taste. Top each slice with 2 basil leaves and a slice of mozzarella. Season the cheese generously with kosher salt and pepper to taste. Create another layer following the same process, using the middle slice of each tomato. Top the stacks with the remaining slices, stem-side up.

Just before serving, decoratively drizzle the balsamic syrup around the tomato stack.

Note: If you reduce the balsamic vinegar too much so that it is too thick to pour when cooled, simply stir in a few more drops of vinegar.

Confetti COLESLAW

Serves 6

Okay, here's the scoop! We have made coleslaw dozens of different ways—some with a vinegar base, some with mayo, and others with a combination of the two. All have been quite tasty, but thanks to our friend and fellow cookbook author Jamee Ruth, we've got a new coleslaw secret. Jamee swears by salting the cabbage and rinsing it before you add the dressing. This produces a coleslaw with a texture that is limp, yet pickle-crisp. Yes, we know that the salting means an added step for you—and if you're shy on time, it's okay to skip it. But boy, does it ever result in a coleslaw with a winning texture!

5	CUPS THINLY SLICED GREEN CABBAGE (ABOUT $1/2$ HEAD SMALL CABBAGE)
5	CUPS THINLY SLICED RED CABBAGE (ABOUT $1/2$ HEAD SMALL CABBAGE)
1	TABLESPOON PLUS $1/2$ TEASPOON KOSHER SALT, PLUS MORE AS NEEDED
$1/4$	CUP DISTILLED WHITE VINEGAR
3	TABLESPOONS SUGAR
3	TABLESPOONS VEGETABLE OIL
1	TEASPOON DRY MUSTARD
$1/4$	TEASPOON CELERY SEEDS
2	TABLESPOONS MAYONNAISE
2	TEASPOONS FRESH LEMON JUICE, PLUS MORE AS NEEDED
1	LARGE CARROT, PEELED AND GRATED
$1/3$	CUP THINLY SLICED GREEN ONIONS, WHITE AND GREEN PARTS
	FRESHLY GROUND PEPPER

Toss the cabbage with the 1 tablespoon kosher salt in the base of a salad spinner or colander and set over a medium bowl. Let stand at room temperature for at least 1 hour or up to 4 hours.

Meanwhile, combine the vinegar, sugar, oil, mustard, celery seeds, and the $1/2$ teaspoon kosher salt in a medium saucepan over medium heat, stirring until the sugar dissolves. Bring to a boil, then remove from the heat. Let cool completely. Whisk in the mayonnaise and the 2 teaspoons lemon juice.

Discard the salty cabbage water from the bowl and fill the bowl with cold water. Rinse the cabbage twice, return it to the salad spinner, and spin dry. Alternatively, pat dry with paper towels.

Combine the cabbage, carrot, and green onions in a medium bowl. Add the dressing and toss to coat. Refrigerate until chilled, at least 1 hour or up to 1 day. Season with pepper to taste and add more kosher salt and lemon juice if necessary before serving.

Do-Ahead: The cabbage can be salted, rinsed, dried, and stored in a sealable container in the refrigerator for up to 12 hours in advance.

ASIAN SPINACH SALAD WITH
HOISIN-GLAZED SALMON

Serves 2 as an entrée

     Entrée salads are big in our households—we serve them 2 to 3 times a week, varying the source of protein. There is something super-satisfying about nourishing your loved one with a salad that is as delicious as it is hearty and healthy. Not only does this recipe give you an essential fatty acid boost, it's chock full of age-defying antioxidants. One taste of this flavor-packed salmon-and-spinach duo, and you'll forget it's heart-wise!

DRESSING:

1¹/₂	TABLESPOONS UNSEASONED RICE VINEGAR
1¹/₂	TABLESPOONS SUGAR
1	TABLESPOON SOY SAUCE
1	TEASPOON ASIAN SESAME OIL
	DASH OF CHILI OIL OR CHILI SAUCE
3	TABLESPOONS VEGETABLE OIL

SALAD:

6	CUPS BABY SPINACH (PRE-WASHED)
1	CAN (11 OUNCES) MANDARIN ORANGES, CHILLED AND DRAINED
¹/₄	CUP CHOPPED GREEN ONION, BOTH WHITE AND GREEN PARTS
¹/₄	CUP TORN FRESH MINT
2	SKINLESS SALMON FILLETS (6 OUNCES EACH)
2	TABLESPOONS HOISIN SAUCE
¹/₃	CUP DRY ROASTED, SALTED PEANUTS, ROUGHLY CHOPPED
¹/₄	CUP CHOW MEIN NOODLES

Preheat the oven to 450 degrees F. Line a baking sheet with aluminum foil.

    TO MAKE THE DRESSING: Combine the vinegar, sugar, soy sauce, sesame oil, chili oil, and vegetable oil in a jar. Cover tightly and shake until the dressing is thoroughly blended. Alternatively, whisk the vinegar, sugar, soy sauce, sesame oil, and chili oil in a medium bowl, drizzle in the vegetable oil, whisking to incorporate. Refrigerate until ready to use.

    Combine the spinach, mandarin oranges, green onions, and mint in a large bowl.

    Put the salmon in the center of the foil-lined baking sheet. Spread the top of each fillet with 1 tablespoon hoisin sauce and wrap the foil loosely around the salmon, creating a sealed package. Cook until the salmon is just opaque in the center, 8 to 10 minutes. (Cooking time will vary according to the thickness of the salmon.)

    Toss the salad with enough dressing to coat, about 5 tablespoons. Divide between 2 rimmed bowls, top each with a salmon fillet, and garnish with the peanuts and chow mein noodles. Serve immediately.

ORZO SALAD WITH LEMON, FETA, AND PINE NUTS

Serves 4

Close your eyes with each forkful of this salad, and you will be transported to the Mediterranean seaside. Lemon, feta, and pine nuts come together in a trinity of sun-drenched Greek flavor, enhanced by intense black olives, sweet golden raisins, and bright fresh basil. A great accompaniment to grilled meats, the salad is also a fabulous addition to your picnic basket.

$^1/_4$	CUP OLIVE OIL
2	TABLESPOONS FRESH LEMON JUICE
$1^1/_2$	TEASPOONS MINCED GARLIC
$^1/_2$	TEASPOON DRIED OREGANO
$^1/_2$	TEASPOON KOSHER SALT, PLUS MORE AS NEEDED
$^1/_8$	TEASPOON FRESHLY GROUND PEPPER, PLUS MORE AS NEEDED
$^1/_2$	TEASPOON SUGAR
1	CUP ORZO
$^1/_4$	CUP PINE NUTS
$^1/_4$	CUP GOLDEN RAISINS
3	TABLESPOONS FINELY CHOPPED PITTED OIL-CURED BLACK OLIVES
3	TABLESPOONS FINELY CHOPPED RED ONION
$^1/_4$	CUP THINLY SLICED FRESH BASIL
2	OUNCES FETA CHEESE, DRAINED AND CRUMBLED

Whisk together the olive oil, lemon juice, garlic, oregano, the $^1/_2$ teaspoon kosher salt, the $^1/_8$ teaspoon pepper, and the sugar in a small bowl. Set aside.

Fill a large pot three fourths full of water. Bring to a boil over high heat and add kosher salt. We use $1^1/_2$ teaspoons kosher salt per quart of water. Add the orzo and cook, stirring occasionally, until just tender but still firm to the bite, 8 to 10 minutes.

Meanwhile, put the pine nuts in a dry small skillet over medium-low heat. Shake constantly until evenly toasted on all sides, about 5 minutes.

Drain the orzo and transfer to a medium bowl. Add the dressing to the hot pasta and toss to coat. Let cool to room temperature, stirring occasionally. Add the pine nuts, raisins, olives, red onion, and basil and stir to combine. Add the feta and toss lightly. Adjust the seasonings with more kosher salt and pepper as necessary.

Do-Ahead: This dish can be made 6 to 8 hours ahead. Cover and refrigerate. Bring to room temperature, taste, and adjust the seasonings before serving.

CAESAR SALAD WITH LEMON-PEPPER SHRIMP

Serves 2

Who knew that Caesar salad was a Mexican creation? The piquant shrimp skewers that top our version of the Caesar would make the salad's hometown of Tijuana proud. | We can't think of a salad more often ordered and adored than the Caesar. Look no further. . . this version offers the perfect balance of lemon, garlic, and Parmesan cheese.

4	*8- TO 10-INCH WOODEN SKEWERS*
16	*LARGE SHRIMP, PEELED AND DEVEINED (TAILS ON)*
1	*TABLESPOON OLIVE OIL*
1	*TEASPOON LEMON-PEPPER (NOT LOW SODIUM)*
1	*CUP CROUTONS (SEE PAGE 43)*
2	*TABLESPOONS, PLUS $^1/_4$ CUP CAESAR DRESSING (SEE NOTE)*
3	*CUPS LIGHTLY PACKED MIXED BABY GREENS*
3	*CUPS LIGHTLY PACKED CHOPPED HEARTS OF ROMAINE*
	KOSHER SALT AND FRESHLY GROUND PEPPER
2	*TABLESPOONS GRATED PARMESAN CHEESE, PREFERABLY PARMIGIANO-REGGIANO*

Soak the skewers in water for at least 30 minutes to prevent splintering and burning.

Prepare a medium-hot charcoal fire, preheat a gas grill to medium-high, or position the rack in the top third of the oven and preheat to 450 degrees F.

Toss the shrimp with the olive oil in a medium bowl. Season the shrimp with the lemon-pepper. Thread 4 shrimp onto each of 4 skewers, threading through the head and tail so they will lay flat when cooking. Place the skewers on the grill rack and grill, turning frequently, until the shrimp are just opaque, about 8 minutes. If using the oven, place the skewered shrimp on a baking sheet and roast for 8 to 10 minutes.

Put the croutons in a large bowl with the 2 tablespoons dressing and toss. Add the mixed baby greens and romaine, and season with kosher salt and pepper to taste. Toss with enough dressing to coat, about $^1/_4$ cup. Add the Parmesan cheese and toss gently. Divide the salad between 2 plates and top each with 2 shrimp skewers.

Do-Ahead: The dressing can be made up to 1 week in advance and refrigerated.

Note: The Caesar dressing recipe (page 44) yields 1$^1/_2$ cups. This recipe requires only $^1/_2$ cup plus 2 tablespoons. So, if you're making the Caesar dressing just for this recipe, use the tasty extra to slather over shrimp or chicken, or as a dunk for veggies.

Mexican CHICKEN SALAD WITH TACO-RANCH DRESSING

Serves 2

   This salad evokes evenings spent south of the border and makes for a festive dinner, especially when paired with our Sauza Margaritas (page 222). For a great-tasting time-saver, we spice up a deli-roasted chicken with taco seasoning and onion powder.

TACO-RANCH DRESSING

$1/3$	CUP MAYONNAISE
$1/3$	CUP BUTTERMILK
$1 1/2$	TEASPOONS FRESH LIME JUICE
2	TEASPOONS TACO SEASONING
1	TEASPOON ONION POWDER
2	TABLESPOONS CHOPPED FRESH CILANTRO

CHICKEN

2	TEASPOONS TACO SEASONING
1	TEASPOON ONION POWDER
$1/2$	TEASPOON KOSHER SALT
2	SKINLESS, BONELESS CHICKEN BREAST HALVES (6 OUNCES EACH)
1	TABLESPOON CANOLA OIL

SALAD

1	CAN (15 OUNCES) BLACK BEANS, DRAINED AND RINSED
1	SMALL RIPE AVOCADO, PEELED, PITTED, AND CHOPPED INTO $3/4$-INCH PIECES
1	PLUM TOMATO, CUT INTO WEDGES
1	TEASPOON TACO SEASONING
4	CUPS CHOPPED ROMAINE LETTUCE
1	CUP CRUMBLED TORTILLA CHIPS, PREFERABLY RANCH-STYLE
$1/4$	CUP FRESH CILANTRO LEAVES
2	LIME WEDGES

Preheat the oven to 400 degrees F. Line a baking sheet with aluminum foil.

 TO MAKE THE TACO-RANCH DRESSING: Whisk together all the dressing ingredients in a medium bowl. Refrigerate until chilled, at least 30 minutes.

 TO PREPARE THE CHICKEN: Mix the taco seasoning, onion powder, and kosher salt in a small bowl. Season the chicken on both sides with the spice mixture and brush with the canola oil. Place the chicken on the prepared baking sheet and bake until opaque in the center, 15 to 20 minutes.

 TO MAKE THE SALAD: Combine the beans, avocado, tomato, and taco seasoning in a large bowl and toss gently. Add the lettuce, chips, and cilantro. Add $1/2$ cup of the dressing and toss, adding additional dressing if necessary. Divide between 2 plates. Slice the chicken and fan on top of the salads. Garnish each with a lime wedge.

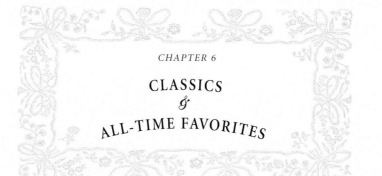

CHAPTER 6

CLASSICS
&
ALL-TIME FAVORITES

WHEN YOU GET MARRIED, THE NESTING INSTINCT KICKS IN. Setting up house is the first step in the fun, then comes creating and perpetuating that feeling of "there's no place like home." Food memories are some of the strongest associative memories we have. If you close your eyes and imagine your favorite childhood dish bubbling on the stovetop or warming in the oven, you can practically smell it cooking. There's a reason why foods like meat loaf, macaroni and cheese, lasagna, and chicken potpie are fondly referred to as comfort foods.

Our memories of frolicking in the backyard in the summertime are ignited the minute we get a whiff of a juicy steak sizzling on the grill. Our mom used to roast a chicken every Monday night, infusing the entire house with the aroma of rosemary, and her apron was perpetually stained from the lasagna she made most every weekend. Our grandmother's robust meat loaf was legendary, and our dad loved to impress us with his decadent beef Burgundy.

During our first few months of marriage, we were both homesick for the flavors of our childhood, so we fed our nostalgia by cooking our favorite comfort foods. As newlyweds, we incorporated our family recipes into our new lives as classics. These standbys have since evolved, becoming more modern versions of our can't-live-without-'em favorites.

In this chapter you'll find recipes for the best of these tried-and-true home-style meals. Many are adaptations of the family recipes we collected when we got married. We've attempted to give you old-fashioned flavors with updated twists. Every couple needs dishes like these in their lifelong culinary repertoire. This chapter is a delicious slice of Americana at its best!

BRIE AND CHAMPAGNE FONDUE

Makes: about 3 ³/₄ cups; *serves* **6 to 8**

Stick it, dip it, dunk it . . . just don't lose it! When we host fondue parties, we like to play a saucy game based on a popular custom. If one of the gals loses her bread cube in the fondue, she owes the fellow on her right a kiss. If the guy experiences the same mishap, he gets to kiss the hostess! Ooh-la-la! | Erik gave Sara a fondue pot for Christmas the first year they were married, and together they've made good use of it, preparing this decadent recipe and many more. Talk about a gift that is "first and forever"!

12	OUNCES IMPORTED SWISS CHEESE, SUCH AS EMMENTALER, GRATED
1¹/₄	POUNDS BRIE, RIND REMOVED, CUT INTO ¹/₂-INCH PIECES
2	TABLESPOONS CORNSTARCH
1	TEASPOON VEGETABLE OIL
1¹/₂	TEASPOONS MINCED GARLIC
1¹/₄	CUPS DRY (BRUT) CHAMPAGNE
1	TABLESPOON FRESH LEMON JUICE
¹/₈	TEASPOON FRESHLY GRATED NUTMEG, PLUS MORE AS NEEDED
¹/₂	TEASPOON KOSHER SALT, PLUS MORE AS NEEDED
	FRESHLY GROUND PEPPER
1	CRUSTY FRENCH BAGUETTE, CUT INTO CUBES

Combine the Swiss cheese, Brie, and cornstarch in a medium bowl. Set aside.

Heat the oil in a heavy-bottomed saucepan over medium heat. Add the garlic and cook, stirring, until aromatic and toasty, 2 to 3 minutes. Add the Champagne and lemon juice and bring to a simmer. Add 1 handful of the cheese at a time, whisking vigorously until the cheese is completely melted before adding more. (Do not allow the cheese mixture to get too hot or it will separate.) Whisk in the ¹/₈ teaspoon nutmeg, the ¹/₂ teaspoon kosher salt, and the pepper to taste. Taste and season with more nutmeg and kosher salt if nec-essary. Bring to a boil just before transferring to a fondue pot and keep warm over a low flame according to the manufacturer's directions. Serve immediately with the bread or other dipping ingredients of your choice.

Variation: Foods for Dunking: While bread cubes are a classic for dipping into cheese fondue, other foods are also delicious: cooked skinless, boneless chicken breasts, cut into bite-sized cubes; boiled new potatoes; blanched asparagus spears, broccoli florets or cauliflower florets; cooked tortellini; roasted mushrooms; and apple slices.

Individual FOUR-CHEESE PIZZAS

Serves 2

The Barbers make pizza once a week, religiously. There's big, BIG trouble on the horizon if Mary and Jack don't have pizza fixin's around, as their eldest son, Jackson, is becoming a real pizza connoisseur, even requesting variations on this stylish cheese pizza. Our four-cheese pie is sure to take your taste buds on a roller-coaster ride. As one of our culinary professors used to say, "Now *that's* Jimi Hendrix in your mouth!" | We store pizza dough in the freezer for quick, delicious weeknight meals. For the best pizza-parlor crisp crust, invest in a pizza stone, available at most cooking stores. During baking, the stone wicks moisture out of the dough and produces a wonderful crisp texture. If you don't have a stone, no problem. Simply bake the pizza on a ventilated pizza pan or on a baking sheet.

CORNMEAL FOR SPRINKLING (IF USING A BAKING SHEET)

$2/3$ CUP (2 OUNCES) SHREDDED FONTINA CHEESE

$2/3$ CUP (2 OUNCES) GRATED HIGH-QUALITY MOZZARELLA CHEESE

$1/4$ CUP (1 OUNCE) GRATED PARMESAN CHEESE, PREFERABLY PARMIGIANO-REGGIANO

$1/4$ CUP ($1^1/2$ OUNCES) CRUMBLED GORGONZOLA CHEESE

$1/2$ RECIPE PIZZA DOUGH AT ROOM TEMPERATURE (PAGE 41), OR 12 OUNCES PURCHASED FROZEN BREAD DOUGH AT ROOM TEMPERATURE (SEE NOTE)

$1/2$ TEASPOON CHOPPED FRESH ROSEMARY, OR $1/4$ TEASPOON DRIED ROSEMARY

EXTRA-VIRGIN OLIVE OIL FOR BRUSHING

Preheat the oven to 500 degrees F. Brush a ventilated pizza pan lightly with vegetable oil or spray with vegetable-oil cooking spray, or sprinkle a baking sheet with cornmeal.

Combine the fontina, mozzarella, Parmesan, and Gorgonzola cheeses in a medium bowl.

Divide the room-temperature dough in half and put on a lightly floured surface. Roll out or stretch the dough into two 8- to 10-inch disks. Place on the prepared pizza pan or baking sheet.

Top the pizzas with the cheese mixture, leaving a 1-inch border. Bake until the crust is golden, 12 to 15 minutes. Sprinkle with the rosemary and brush the edges with a little olive oil just before serving.

Note: Frozen bread dough can be found in the freezer section of most grocery stores. It makes a fine substitute for pizza dough if you don't have time to make your own from scratch. Thaw before using.

Variations: Just before baking the pizzas, top with:

1. Quartered fresh figs, then garnish with a handful of arugula just before serving.
2. Sautéed mushrooms (such as shiitakes, creminis, oysters, or portobellos), then drizzle with truffle oil just before serving.
3. Caramelized Onions (page 50). For added dimension, spread the dough with a thin layer of Roasted Garlic (page 34) before topping with the cheese.
4. Tomato slices, then garnish with chopped fresh basil just before serving.

Classic LASAGNA

Serves 8

Southern hospitality is all we've ever known. No baby was born, friend hospitalized, or out-of-town guest in for the weekend without our mother whipping up something yummy to congratulate, soothe, or welcome. We perpetuate the tradition with our lasagna—a dish that's perfect for giving because it can be made in advance, freezes well, and is universally loved. Once a labor-intensive creation that required hours bent over a colander, lasagna making is now new and improved. No-boil lasagna noodles have come to the cook's rescue, making the layering of this delectable dish a cinch.

8	OUNCES GROUND BEEF ROUND
8	OUNCES ITALIAN SAUSAGE LINKS, REMOVED FROM CASINGS AND CRUMBLED
1/2	TEASPOON KOSHER SALT
1/2	TEASPOON FRESHLY GROUND PEPPER
6	CUPS "GUSSIED-UP" MARINARA SAUCE (PAGE 36), OR 2 JARS (26 OUNCES EACH) MARINARA SAUCE
8	OUNCES RICOTTA CHEESE
8	OUNCES CREAM CHEESE AT ROOM TEMPERATURE
1	CUP (2 OUNCES) GRATED PARMESAN CHEESE, PREFERABLY PARMIGIANO-REGGIANO
1	PACKAGE (8 OUNCES; 12 SHEETS) "NO-BOIL" LASAGNA NOODLES
1	CUP LIGHTLY PACKED FRESH BASIL LEAVES, TORN INTO SMALL PIECES
2	CUPS (8 OUNCES) SHREDDED MOZZARELLA CHEESE

Preheat the oven to 375 degrees F. Lightly spray a 9-by-13-inch baking dish with vegetable-oil cooking spray.

Combine the ground beef and sausage in a large sauté pan over medium-high heat. Season with the kosher salt and 1/4 teaspoon of the pepper. Cook until the meat is lightly browned, 8 to 10 minutes. Using a slotted spoon, transfer the meat to a medium bowl. Add the marinara sauce to the meat and stir to combine. Set aside.

Mix the ricotta cheese, cream cheese, and Parmesan cheese in a medium bowl. Season with the remaining 1/4 teaspoon pepper. Set aside.

Cover the bottom of the prepared baking dish with 1 cup of the meat sauce. Arrange a single layer of uncooked lasagna noodles (3 sheets) on top of the sauce. Spread 1 1/2 cups of the meat sauce evenly on top. Add half of the cheese mixture by spoonfuls evenly over the meat sauce, then scatter half of the basil leaves on top. Top with a layer of lasagna noodles, 1 1/2 cups of the sauce, the remaining cheese mixture, and the remaining basil. Top with a layer of lasagna noodles, 1 1/2 cups of the meat sauce, and a final layer of lasagna noodles. Spread the remaining meat sauce over the top, and sprinkle with the mozzarella cheese.

Cover with aluminum foil and bake for 30 minutes. Uncover and bake until the cheese is bubbly and golden brown, 10 to 15 minutes more. Let stand for 15 minutes before serving.

ROAST CHICKEN AND VEGETABLES *for Two*

Serves 2

Nothing says "home, sweet home" like the inviting aroma of a chicken roasting in the oven. We roast a chicken once a week because it's incredibly easy to prepare, inexpensive, and great for leftovers. Whether you're home together or hosting friends for a casual dinner, this recipe works wonders. Few "full-meal deals" come easier or tastier. Because we roast a chicken so frequently, we often add an herb mixture, a rub, or a glaze to this classic recipe, to jazz things up a bit. The variations are limitless . . . experiment by rubbing the bird with jerk or Cajun seasoning, a cumin and coriander spice mixture, or coarse lavender salt (there are so many great spice rubs out in the marketplace to try). Brushing with a mixture of warm honey, rosemary, and cayenne is over the top, and basting with bacon grease and maple syrup is sweet home Carolina (tent with foil midway through roasting if using sweet glazes, to avoid burning). Regardless of which variation tickles your fancy, make this dish a part of your life.

3	CARROTS, CUT INTO THIRDS
6	SMALL RED NEW POTATOES, QUARTERED IF LARGE
1	MEDIUM YELLOW ONION, CUT INTO 6 WEDGES
3	TABLESPOONS UNSALTED BUTTER, MELTED, OR OLIVE OIL
	KOSHER SALT AND FRESHLY GROUND PEPPER
1	CHICKEN (3 TO 4 POUNDS)
1	LEMON, QUARTERED
2	FRESH ROSEMARY SPRIGS
4	CLOVES GARLIC, PEELED AND SMASHED

Preheat the oven to 425 degrees F.

Put the carrots, potatoes, and onion in a 9-by-13-inch glass baking dish. Toss the vegetables with 1 tablespoon of the butter. Season with kosher salt and pepper to taste. Spread the vegetables to the edges of the baking dish, making room for the chicken.

Remove the neck and giblets from the cavity of the chicken and discard. Rinse the bird under cold running water and pat dry. Put the chicken, breast-side up, in the center of the baking dish. Brush the chicken with the remaining 2 tablespoons butter. Season the cavity and skin generously with kosher salt and pepper to taste. Put the lemon quarters and rosemary sprigs inside the cavity. Put the garlic cloves under the chicken to prevent them from burning.

Roast for 45 minutes. Remove the dish from the oven. Using tongs, tilt the chicken, pouring the juices from the cavity onto the vegetables, and shake to coat. Baste the chicken with the pan juices. If the bird is browning too quickly, cover with aluminum foil. Continue roasting until the chicken is a deep golden brown and the juices run clear when the tip of a knife is inserted into the thigh joint, or until an instant-read thermometer inserted into the thigh, away from the bone, registers 170 to 175 degrees F, 25 to 30 minutes more.

Transfer the chicken to a platter, cover loosely with aluminum foil, and let stand for 10 to 15 minutes before carving. Using the back of a spoon, mash the garlic and squeeze some lemon into the pan juices. Toss the juices with the

CONTINUED

vegetables. Carve the chicken and serve the vegetables alongside. Drizzle any remaining juices over the chicken.

Note: Our favorite way to serve roasted chicken to our families is to carve all the meat from the bones after the meat has rested and chop it into bite-sized pieces. We then return the meat to the garlicky, lemony pan juices, re-season it with more salt and pepper, and toss with the vegetables. This way, every last bit of the chicken is well seasoned and moist throughout (breasts included).

CARVING A CHICKEN OR TURKEY

1. Anchor the breast of the bird with a carving fork and, using a boning or carving knife, cut through the skin between the thigh and the breast. Pull the leg and second joint outward. This exposes the joint at the bottom of the thigh, which is easily cut through.
2. Detach the leg and cut the thigh away from the drumstick. Turn the bird around and repeat with the other leg.
3. If serving the wings separately, pull the wing out from the breast and cut through the joint that connects the wing to the breast. Repeat with the other wing.
4. For chicken, you may opt to serve the breasts whole. To do this, cut between the meat and the bone, angling the knife toward the bone. Otherwise, cut thin slices of the breast meat on a diagonal to the breastbone, including a little skin with each slice.

PAN-FRIED PORK CHOPS WITH GLAZED APPLES

Serves 4

We just *love* "the other white meat"! This dish dates back to our childhood in North Carolina. Old-style classics like pork chops (cooked in bacon fat, of course) and applesauce were savored in our house. As down-home and nostalgic as pork chops make us feel, this recipe is 100 percent grown-up. Rich and hearty, salty and sweet, these chops are *jammed* with flavor (literally). Best of all, this dish takes little time to create. Don't let the "cure" scare you—this step couldn't be easier. Settle in with your spouse and a glass of wine, and cozy up together while your pork chops cure. If you don't have a stash of bacon grease on hand, we urge you to start the tradition (see Tip).

2   TABLESPOONS FIRMLY PACKED DARK BROWN SUGAR

1   TABLESPOON PLUS 1 TEASPOON KOSHER SALT

1   TABLESPOON CHOPPED FRESH ROSEMARY, OR
     1 TABLESPOON HERBES DE PROVENCE

4   THIN-CUT PORK CHOPS (ABOUT 1/2 INCH THICK EACH)
     FRESHLY GROUND PEPPER

1   TABLESPOON BACON GREASE, PLUS MORE IF NEEDED

2   SMALL TO MEDIUM RED APPLES, PEELED, CORED, AND
     CUT INTO 1/2-INCH PIECES

1¹/2 CUPS CHICKEN STOCK (PAGE 30) OR CANNED LOW-SODIUM CHICKEN BROTH

¹/3 CUP APRICOT JAM, PREFERABLY FRUIT SWEETENED

¹/4 CUP CALVADOS OR BRANDY

¹/4 TEASPOON GROUND CINNAMON

Combine the brown sugar, kosher salt, and rosemary in a small bowl and stir together. Coat the pork chops on both sides with the mixture, gently massaging the meat with your fingers to jump-start the curing process. Let stand for 15 minutes. Rinse the chops and pat dry with paper towels. Season the chops on both sides with pepper to taste.

Melt the 1 tablespoon bacon grease in a large heavy skillet over high heat, add the pork chops, and cook until crispy brown, about 2 minutes on each side.

Transfer the pork chops to a plate and cover with foil. Add the apples to the skillet and cook, stirring gently to brown slightly, about 30 seconds, adding a bit more bacon grease if the pan is dry. Add the stock, jam, Calvados, and cinnamon and stir well. Cook until the sauce thickens and is rich brown in color, about 10 minutes. (Don't cook down the sauce too much, but if you do, simply add a little more stock.)

Uncover the pork chops and top with the glazed apples.

Variation: In addition to apples, the pork chops are delicious with dried cranberries or cherries. Add them when you brown the apples in the skillet.

Tip: Whenever you fry bacon and have leftover grease, reserve it in a glass jar and refrigerate it. This gives you a flavorful and ready-to-use-anytime fat for sautéing.

Personalized CHICKEN POTPIES

Serves 4

It doesn't get any homier than potpies, and comfort food never goes out of fashion. Your mate will fall in love all over again with one glimpse of the sweet, monogrammed crust. Buy a rotisserie chicken, some frozen peas and carrots, and a jar of Alfredo sauce (a stray from the classic but time-saving and delicious). Then wrap yourself up in some flannel and feast on this treat. Despite its store-bought base, this pie's flavor will knock your socks off! Take it from us, you'll score serious points if you make an extra pie or two and pop them in the freezer for your mate to heat up on nights when you're away from home.

1	TABLESPOON OLIVE OIL
1	SMALL YELLOW ONION, CHOPPED
4	MEDIUM CLOVES GARLIC, CHOPPED
2	TEASPOONS CHOPPED FRESH THYME, OR 3/4 TEASPOON DRIED THYME
	KOSHER SALT AND FRESHLY GROUND PEPPER
1/2	CUP DRY WHITE WINE OR VERMOUTH
1	TABLESPOON ALL-PURPOSE FLOUR
2/3	CUP CHICKEN STOCK (PAGE 30) OR LOW-SODIUM CANNED CHICKEN BROTH
1	JAR (16 OUNCES) ALFREDO SAUCE, SUCH AS CLASSICO
3	CUPS SHREDDED PURCHASED ROAST CHICKEN
1	PACKAGE (10 OUNCES) FROZEN MIXED PEAS AND CARROTS, THAWED
1 1/2	RECIPES FLAKY PIECRUST (PAGE 39), OR 2 FROZEN PASTRY CIRCLES OR SHEETS FOR 9-INCH PIE
1	EGG, LIGHTLY BEATEN

Preheat the oven to 425 degrees F. Line a baking sheet with aluminum foil.

Heat the oil in a large saucepan over medium heat. Add the onion, garlic, and thyme and season lightly with kosher salt and pepper to taste. Cook, stirring frequently, until the onion is soft, 5 to 7 minutes. Add the wine and cook until it has evaporated but the onion is still moist, about 2 minutes more. Sprinkle the flour over the onion and cook for 1 minute. Add the stock and stir until well incorporated and slightly thickened.

Remove the pan from the heat. Stir in the Alfredo sauce, then the chicken and peas and carrots. Adjust the seasonings with more kosher salt and pepper if necessary. Divide the filling among four 1 1/2-cup ramekins. Set aside.

If using a homemade piecrust that has been refrigerated overnight, let it soften at room temperature for 30 to 45 minutes. If the piecrust has only been refrigerated for 45 minutes, it can be rolled out immediately. Divide in half and roll out each half as directed (see page 39). If using frozen pastry circles or sheets, place them on a work surface and let thaw slightly, about 10 minutes. Place a ramekin directly on the pastry. Using a knife, cut out a circle 1 inch wider than the bottom of the ramekin. Drape the pastry over the ramekin and seal by pressing gently on the sides of the

CONTINUED

ramekin. Repeat with the remaining ramekins. Cut pastry scraps into your sweetheart's initials, into hearts, or other decorative shapes and place on top of the pastry. Brush the pastry with the beaten egg. (You will have some leftover pastry. For a sweet treat, brush the scraps with butter, sprinkle with sugar and cinnamon, and bake at 350 degrees F until golden.)

Place the potpies on the prepared baking sheet and bake until the crust is golden, 35 to 45 minutes. Let stand for 15 minutes before serving.

Do-Ahead: The filling can be made and the pies assembled 1 day ahead. Cover and refrigerate, then bake as directed.

Note: We recommend baking 2 potpies and freezing the remaining 2. Do not brush the pastry with the beaten egg before freezing the pies. Cover the ramekins with foil and freeze. Bake the frozen pies, covered with foil, in a 425-degree F oven for about 30 minutes. Then remove the foil, brush with the beaten egg, and continue baking until the crust is golden, about 30 minutes.

BEEF BURGUNDY

Serves 4

As culinary icon Julia Child says, "Beef bourguignonne is certainly one of the most delicious dishes concocted by man." We wholeheartedly agree, so much so that we have made this classic the centerpiece of the annual Barber-Whiteford New Year's celebration. Boiled potatoes are the traditional accompaniment, but we love this hearty stew atop our Creamy-Dreamy Mashed Potatoes (page 163), egg noodles, or rice. We add a touch of color by garnishing with buttered peas or steamed French green beans. One of the best things about beef Burgundy is that it's better made a day or two in advance and freezes well. Pair it with a cool bottle of Pinot Noir (the principal Burgundy grape) to ring in the New Year with spirit.

4   BACON SLICES, ROUGHLY CHOPPED

1 1/2 POUNDS BONELESS BEEF STEW MEAT, SUCH AS BEEF
    CHUCK OR BOTTOM ROUND, CUT INTO 1-INCH CUBES

8   OUNCES CREMINI OR SHIITAKE MUSHROOMS, CLEANED
    AND QUARTERED (IF USING SHIITAKES, DISCARD STEMS)

1   MEDIUM YELLOW ONION, CHOPPED

1/8 TEASPOON FRESHLY GROUND PEPPER

3   TABLESPOONS ALL-PURPOSE FLOUR

2   CUPS GOOD-QUALITY RED WINE, SUCH AS BURGUNDY

3   CUPS BEEF BROTH (NOT DOUBLE STRENGTH)

3   TABLESPOONS TOMATO PASTE

    FRESH ROSEMARY SPRIG (4 INCHES LONG)

1   BAY LEAF

1   TABLESPOON FIRMLY PACKED DARK BROWN SUGAR

    ABOUT 20 PACKAGED PEELED BABY CARROTS

1   CUP FRESH PEARL ONIONS, PEELED, OR FROZEN
    PETITE WHOLE ONIONS, THAWED

    CHOPPED FRESH FLAT-LEAF PARSLEY FOR GARNISHING

Preheat the oven to 350 degrees F.

Fry the bacon in an ovenproof 6-quart heavy-bottomed pot or Dutch oven over medium heat until lightly browned and slightly crisp, about 5 minutes. Remove the pot from the heat. Using a slotted spoon, transfer the bacon to a paper towel–lined plate, leaving the fat in the pot.

Set the pot over high heat. Add the meat and cook until browned on all sides. Reduce the heat to medium-high and add the mushrooms, onion, and pepper. Cook, stirring constantly with a wooden spoon, until the onion is tender, about

5 minutes. Sprinkle with the flour and cook for 2 to 3 minutes more. Add the wine, broth, tomato paste, rosemary, bay leaf, brown sugar, and bacon. Stir, scraping up any browned bits from the bottom of the pot, and bring to a simmer.

Cover the pot and transfer to the oven. Bake for 1 1/2 hours. Remove the pot from the oven and add the carrots and pearl onions. Bake, uncovered, until the carrots and meat are tender, about 30 minutes more. Garnish with chopped parsley and serve.

"Oh-Baby!" BABY BACK RIBS

Serves 2 or 3

In the South, we had access to the most amazing barbecue and smoked ribs in all the land. After all, good ol' barbecue is the pride of North Carolina. In our years of cooking, we never dared fix ribs at home, fearing they'd fall short of the pit-smoked standard we grew up on. As California transplants, though, we missed barbecue fare. So we fiddled around with ribs until we created our own winning recipe. Our baby back ribs are fast, simple, and finger-lickin' good! No need for a pit or a grill. No need to parboil. And no fancy homemade barbecue sauce. These ribs are about a simple "rub and a bake" and there's nothin' intimidating about 'em (except eating them gracefully).

DRY RUB

$1/3$ CUP FIRMLY PACKED DARK BROWN SUGAR

3   TABLESPOONS PAPRIKA

2   TABLESPOONS ONION POWDER

1   TABLESPOON PLUS 1 TEASPOON KOSHER SALT

1   TABLESPOON FRESHLY GROUND PEPPER

2   SLABS (1 TO $1^1/_2$ POUNDS EACH) BABY BACK RIBS

1 TO $1^1/_2$ CUPS PREPARED BARBECUE SAUCE, PLUS MORE AS NEEDED

TO MAKE THE DRY RUB: Mix the brown sugar, paprika, onion powder, kosher salt, and pepper in a small bowl.

Press the dry rub onto the ribs, using 3 to 4 tablespoons for each slab. Any extra dry rub can be stored, tightly sealed, for several months. Put the ribs in a large sealable plastic bag. Let stand at room temperature for 1 hour or refrigerate for as long as overnight to allow the flavors of the spices to permeate the meat. If you refrigerated the ribs, let them stand at room temperature for 30 minutes to 1 hour before cooking.

Preheat the oven to 300 degrees F. Line a baking sheet with aluminum foil.

Remove the ribs from the plastic bag (don't scrape off the dry rub) and place on the prepared baking sheet. Slather the barbecue sauce (about $1/2$ cup per 1 pound of ribs) on both sides of each slab. Bake, meaty-side up, until the meat is no longer pink and an instant-read thermometer inserted into the center of the meat, away from the bone, registers 155 to 165 degrees F, about $1^1/_2$ hours. Brush with more barbecue sauce if necessary just before serving.

Cut between the bones to separate the ribs. Transfer to a platter and serve.

Note: If you're on a budget, substitute spareribs, which are meatier and less expensive than (though not as tender as) baby back ribs. Regardless, look for fresh ribs that have not been frozen.

SWEET-AND-SOUR BRISKET

Serves 6 to 8

Brisket is an integral part of the Texas barbecue tradition and is also popular in the Jewish kitchen, where it is customarily prepared for Rosh Hashanah. Our friends Carolyn Edwards and Emily Feinstein gave this recipe their stamp of approval (and so did their mother, Susan, who has been making brisket for over 20 years). The flavor of brisket gets better and better over time, assuming you can keep it around long enough. Our version is a little sassier (and saucier) than what you may be used to.

SWEET-AND-SOUR SAUCE

$1/2$ CUP RED WINE

1   CAN (14 OUNCES) LOW-SODIUM BEEF BROTH

$3/4$ CUP CHILI SAUCE, SUCH AS HEINZ (SEE NOTE)

$1/4$ CUP APPLE CIDER VINEGAR

$1/4$ CUP FIRMLY PACKED LIGHT BROWN SUGAR

$1/2$ TEASPOON DRIED THYME

1   BAY LEAF

1 BRISKET (ABOUT 5 POUNDS)

KOSHER SALT AND FRESHLY GROUND PEPPER

2 TABLESPOONS VEGETABLE OIL

4 MEDIUM YELLOW ONIONS, CUT INTO $1/2$-INCH-THICK SLICES

Preheat the oven to 350 degrees F.

TO MAKE THE SWEET-AND-SOUR-SAUCE: Combine the wine, broth, chili sauce, vinegar, brown sugar, thyme, and bay leaf in a medium bowl. Set aside.

Season the brisket on both sides with kosher salt and pepper to taste. Heat 1 tablespoon of the oil in a 6-quart pot or Dutch oven over medium-high heat. When the oil is hot add the brisket, fat-side down, and cook until golden brown, about 4 minutes. Turn the brisket over and cook until browned, 3 to 4 minutes more. Transfer to a plate. Add the remaining 1 tablespoon oil to the pot. Add the onions and cook, stirring occasionally, until they begin to caramelize, about 5 minutes. Place the brisket on top of the onions and cover with the sauce.

Cover the pot, place in the oven, and bake for $1^1/2$ hours. Transfer the brisket to a cutting board, scrape off the excess fat, and cut across the grain of the meat into $1/8$- to $1/4$-inch-thick slices. Return the slices to the pot, overlapping them. Spoon the sauce over the brisket, covering the meat well. Bake until the meat is fork-tender, $1^1/2$ to 2 hours more.

For the best flavor, let the brisket cool, then cover and refrigerate overnight. When ready to serve, preheat the oven to 350 degrees F. Put the brisket in a large pot and smother with the sweet-and-sour sauce to enhance the flavor and preserve moistness. Cover and bake for 20 to 30 minutes.

Note: Chili sauce is a mild condiment that resembles a slightly piquant ketchup.

Tip: This brisket freezes beautifully. Because the flavors get better over time, we refrigerate the brisket for a day or two before freezing. Thaw the brisket before reheating it.

TEXAS CHILI *with All the Fixin's*

Serves 8

In a desperate attempt to create the ultimate chili recipe, we invited a handful of friends over on a Sunday night for a chili cook-off and tasting. We tested chilis with chipotles, with molasses, with beer, with sausage, with hints of cinnamon, and even with chocolate. You can guess which version won, hands-down. Cowboys never got it this good! Don't forget the "fixin's"—they're this recipe's "giddy ap and go."

1	TABLESPOON BACON GREASE OR VEGETABLE OIL
2	MEDIUM YELLOW ONIONS, CHOPPED
3	TABLESPOONS CHOPPED GARLIC
3	TABLESPOONS CHILI POWDER
2	TABLESPOONS PAPRIKA
1	TABLESPOON CUMIN
2	TEASPOONS DRIED OREGANO
1	POUND GROUND BEEF CHUCK
1	POUND ITALIAN SAUSAGE LINKS, REMOVED FROM CASINGS AND CRUMBLED
2	TEASPOONS KOSHER SALT, PLUS MORE AS NEEDED
2	CANS (28 OUNCES EACH) CRUSHED TOMATOES WITH PURÉE
1	CAN (15 OUNCES) KIDNEY BEANS, RINSED AND DRAINED
1	CAN (15 OUNCES) BARBECUED BAKED BEANS, DRAINED
1	TABLESPOON MINCED CANNED CHIPOTLE CHILES IN ADOBO SAUCE, PLUS MORE AS NEEDED (SEE NOTE)

FIXIN'S

GRATED SHARP CHEDDAR CHEESE

CHOPPED GREEN ONION

SOUR CREAM

CRUMBLED CORN CHIPS

RED PEPPER FLAKES

CHOPPED JALAPEÑO CHILES

Heat the bacon grease in an 8-quart heavy-bottomed stockpot over medium heat. Add the onions and garlic and cook, stirring occasionally, until tender, 7 to 10 minutes. Add the chili powder, paprika, cumin, and oregano and stir until the spices are well combined. Add the ground chuck, sausage, and 1 teaspoon of the kosher salt. Increase the heat to medium-high and cook the meat, stirring frequently, until cooked through, 8 to 10 minutes.

Stir in the remaining ingredients. Reduce the heat to low, cover, and simmer, stirring occasionally, for 1 hour. Adjust the seasonings with more kosher salt or chipotle chiles if necessary. Serve with any or all of the suggested fixin's.

Note: You can find canned chipotle chiles in adobo sauce (smoked jalapeños in a thick red sauce) in supermarkets and Latino specialty markets.

Stovetop MACARONI AND CHEESE

Serves 2

    Call us if you know of one person who doesn't love macaroni and cheese! We have made good ol' mac and cheese 50 zillion ways—or so it seems. We've tried recipes with a classic béchamel sauce; a combination of designer cheeses; and with a traditional egg, milk, and cheese trio. Finally, though, we've nailed it. This adaptation of John Thorne's macaroni and cheese from his *Home Comfort Cook Book,* published in 1937, hits the spot. It is made with old-fashioned evaporated milk, an essential ingredient, believe it or not. Don't try to substitute regular milk as it tends to curdle. Cheddar cheese rules in this classic version, but cheeses like fontina and Monterey Jack also work well when you're hankerin' for something a little different.

BREAD CRUMBS

- $^1/_2$ TABLESPOON UNSALTED BUTTER
- $^1/_2$ CUP FRESH BREAD CRUMBS (SEE NOTE, FACING PAGE)
- PINCH OF KOSHER SALT

MACARONI AND CHEESE

- 1 EGG
- $3/_4$ CUP EVAPORATED MILK
- 1 TEASPOON DIJON MUSTARD
- $^1/_4$ TEASPOON KOSHER SALT, PLUS MORE AS NEEDED
- FRESHLY GROUND PEPPER
- DASH OF HOT RED PEPPER SAUCE
- 4 OUNCES (1 CUP) ELBOW MACARONI
- 1 TABLESPOON UNSALTED BUTTER
- $1^1/_2$ CUPS (2 OUNCES) SHREDDED SHARP CHEDDAR CHEESE

TO PREPARE THE BREAD CRUMBS: Melt the butter in a medium skillet over medium heat. When the foam begins to disappear, add the bread crumbs and cook for about 2 minutes, tossing gently for even browning. Add the kosher salt and set aside.

 TO MAKE THE MACARONI AND CHEESE: Lightly whisk the egg in a small bowl. Add the evaporated milk, mustard, the $^1/_2$ teaspoon kosher salt, freshly ground pepper to taste, and hot red pepper sauce.

 Fill a large saucepan three fourths full of water. Bring to a boil over high heat and add kosher salt. (We add $1^1/_2$ teaspoons kosher salt per quart of water.) Add the pasta and cook, stirring occasionally, until barely tender, 8 to 10 minutes. Drain and return the pasta to the pan. Set over low heat, add the butter, and stir until melted. Add the evaporated milk mixture and the cheese. Stir until the cheese melts and the mixture thickens, about 3 minutes. Adjust the seasonings with more kosher salt if necessary. Serve immediately, sprinkled with the bread crumbs. (If not eaten right away, macaroni and cheese will thicken. Just stir in some of the remaining evaporated milk to thin to the desired consistency.)

Note: As a time-saver, use purchased bread-crumbs; there is no need to sauté them in butter.

Better Than Grandma's MEAT LOAF

Serves 4

When Sara's father-in-law, Bill Whiteford, a food and drink aficionado, heard we were busy testing recipes for meat loaf, he insistently declared, "I'd rather eat meat loaf than filet mignon!" We couldn't agree more. We use sausage in our version of the classic because it gives the meat loaf unrivaled depth of flavor. When we're entertaining, we stuff this homespun mixture into red bell peppers for a stylish dish (see Variation). For a lighter version of meat loaf, substitute ground turkey for the beef, and chicken sausage for the breakfast sausage.

2	TEASPOONS VEGETABLE OIL
1	SMALL YELLOW ONION, CHOPPED
1/4	CUP MILK
1	CUP SOFT FRESH WHITE BREAD CRUMBS (SEE NOTE)
3/4	CUP KETCHUP
4	TEASPOONS WORCESTERSHIRE SAUCE
1	POUND GROUND BEEF ROUND
8	OUNCES GROUND BREAKFAST SAUSAGE
1	EGG, BEATEN
1 1/4	TEASPOONS MRS. DASH SEASONING MIX
1/2	TEASPOON GARLIC POWDER

Preheat the oven to 350 degrees F.

Heat the oil in a medium nonstick skillet over medium-high heat. Add the onion and cook, stirring occasionally, until tender, 5 to 7 minutes. Transfer to a large bowl.

Combine the milk and bread crumbs in a small bowl and set aside. Combine 1/4 cup of the ketchup and 2 teaspoons of the Worcestershire sauce in another small bowl and set aside.

Add the ground beef, sausage, the remaining ketchup and Worcestershire sauce, the egg, seasoning mix, garlic powder, and bread crumbs to the bowl with the onions. Mix until just incorporated.

Mound the meat loaf mixture in a 9-by-5-by-3-inch loaf pan. Bake for 45 minutes. Remove from the oven and pour off some of the fat. Spread the ketchup mixture over the top. Bake until an instant-read thermometer inserted into the center of the meat loaf registers 160 degrees F, about 30 minutes more. Let stand for 15 minutes before serving.

Note: To make fresh bread crumbs, place 2 slices of soft white sandwich bread, in the bowl of a food processor, fitted with the steel blade, and pulse until crumbled.

Variation: Stuffed Bell Peppers
Preheat the oven to 350 degrees F. Cut 4 medium red bell peppers in half lengthwise, keeping the stems intact. Remove the seeds and veins. Brush the insides of the pepper halves with olive oil and season with kosher salt. Arrange the pepper halves, cut-side up, on a foil-lined baking sheet and bake until softened, about 20 minutes. Remove from the oven and fill each pepper half with about 1/2 cup of the uncooked meat loaf mixture. Spread the ketchup mixture over the top and bake until an instant-read thermometer inserted into the center of the filling registers 160 degrees F, about 45 minutes.

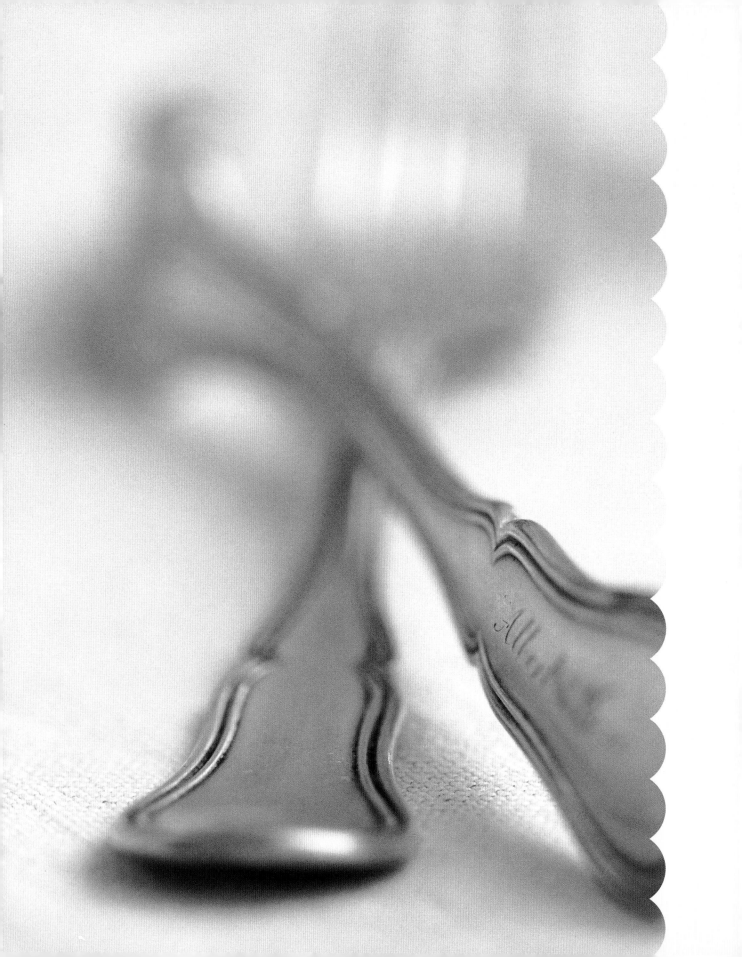

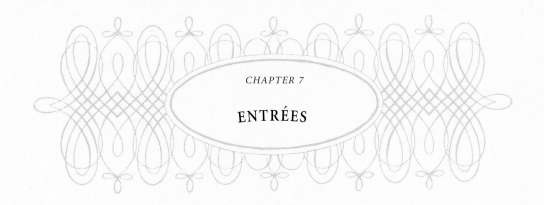

THIS CHAPTER IS ALL ABOUT THE MAIN EVENT—creating unforgettable entrées. We know that side dishes, salads, and desserts contribute to the overall dining experience, but more often than not, it's the main dish that really captures the spotlight at the dinner table. In this chapter we offer you a veritable cast of superstars. You'll find substantial, meaty fare for steak-and-potatoes types, chicken prepared three ways, fish dressed with seductive salsas and glazes, and super-satisfying pasta dishes.

When it comes to attention-grabbing entrées, we absolutely adore our Pork Tenderloin with Mango Salsa and Blackberry Syrup (page 141) for its elegant simplicity and our Pasta with Pesto, Shrimp, and Sweet 100s (page 126) as a weeknight winner. Our husbands lust after Lamb Chops with Mint-Mustard Sauce (page 142), and Grilled London Broil Fajitas (page 147) are fun to cook in tandem when casually entertaining friends.

No entrée chapter would be complete without a perfect casserole, easily prepared in advance, so we offer up our Chicken "Divine" (page 133)—we promise it's as wonderful as its name implies! And remember, turkey doesn't have to be just for Thanksgiving. We love to roast turkey on Sunday night and graze on it all week long. It's great for sandwiches, too.

Whether you want to pull out all the stops for guests or settle in for a sensational meal for two, you'll find an entrée here that fits your bill.

WILD MUSHROOM RISOTTO

Serves 2

For years, Sara worked at Splendido's, a Mediterranean restaurant in downtown San Francisco, where she practically "drowned" in risotto. She learned that the secret to a great risotto is to stir, stir, stir! Constant stirring (when you're tired, let your loved one take a turn) keeps the rice well distributed in the stock, ensuring even cooking and promoting the release of starch from the rice (not to mention, it gives your biceps a great workout). The result? Creamy perfection. For a touch of pure magic, take it one step further and drizzle truffle oil on top.

3¹/₂ CUPS CHICKEN STOCK (SEE PAGE 30) OR CANNED
      LOW-SODIUM CHICKEN BROTH

2¹/₂ TABLESPOONS OLIVE OIL

1   SMALL YELLOW ONION, CHOPPED

8   OUNCES SHIITAKE OR CREMINI MUSHROOMS, CLEANED
      AND SLICED (IF USING SHIITAKES, DISCARD STEMS)

1   TABLESPOON CHOPPED GARLIC

³/₄   CUP ARBORIO RICE (SEE NOTE)

¹/₂   CUP DRY WHITE WINE

¹/₄   CUP, PLUS 2 TABLESPOONS GRATED PARMESAN
      CHEESE, PREFERABLY PARMIGIANO-REGGIANO

¹/₂   TEASPOON CHOPPED FRESH THYME

1   TABLESPOON UNSALTED BUTTER

      KOSHER SALT AND FRESHLY GROUND PEPPER

      TRUFFLE OIL FOR DRIZZLING (OPTIONAL)

1   TABLESPOON CHOPPED FRESH CHIVES OR FLAT-LEAF PARSLEY

Bring the stock to a simmer in a small saucepan over medium-high heat. Reduce the heat to low, cover, and keep the stock hot.

Heat the olive oil in a large heavy-bottomed saucepan over medium-high heat. Add the onion and sauté, stirring frequently with a wooden spoon, for 2 minutes. Add the mushrooms and cook until tender and slightly brown, about 8 minutes. Add the garlic and cook for 2 minutes more. Add the rice and stir well, about 30 seconds. Add the wine and simmer, stirring constantly, until the liquid is absorbed, 2 to 3 minutes. Add ³/₄ cup of the hot stock, reduce the heat to medium, and cook, stirring frequently, until the stock is absorbed. Add the remaining hot stock ³/₄ cup at a time, stirring frequently and allowing each addition to be fully absorbed before adding more, until the rice is just tender and the risotto is creamy. The total cooking time is 20 to 25 minutes.

Stir in the ¹/₄ cup cheese, the thyme, and butter. If the rice appears dry, add up to ¹/₄ cup water to loosen the risotto slightly. Season with kosher salt and pepper to taste. (Beware: don't burn your tongue, as we have done numerous times!)

Divide the risotto between 2 large bowls and drizzle with truffle oil, if desired. Sprinkle with the 2 tablespoons cheese and the chives.

Note: Arborio, an Italian short-grain rice, is available in Italian markets and many supermarkets.

BOW TIE PASTA WITH ASPARAGUS, SUN-DRIED TOMATOES, AND BOURSIN

Serves 2

Garden fresh and "à la minute," this snappy pasta dish hits the spot. We make this whole-some pasta so often that, when we want to shake things up a bit, we substitute broccoli florets, spinach, or peas for the asparagus. Our secret to this simple fare is the Boursin. If you aren't familiar with this creamy French cheese flavored with garlic and herbs, it's all the more reason to try the dish. We promise a love affair. Stir the remaining Boursin into scrambled eggs, smear onto a toasted bagel, or spread onto raw vegetables—it adds a touch of magic.

1/3   *CUP PINE NUTS*

     KOSHER SALT

8   *OUNCES BOW TIE PASTA*

14   *MEDIUM ASPARAGUS SPEARS, PEELED (SEE NOTE, PAGE 152) AND CUT INTO 1 1/2-INCH PIECES*

1   *TABLESPOON OLIVE OIL*

4   *LARGE CLOVES GARLIC, MINCED*

1/3   *CUP DRAINED OIL-PACKED SUN-DRIED TOMATOES, CHOPPED (OPTIONAL)*

1/4   *CUP GRATED PARMESAN CHEESE, PREFERABLY PARMIGIANO-REGGIANO*

2   *OUNCES (1/3 CUP) GARLIC AND FINE HERBS BOURSIN*

1   *TABLESPOON CHOPPED FRESH DILL, OR 3/4 TEASPOON DRIED DILL WEED*

3/4   *TEASPOON LEMON PEPPER, PLUS MORE AS NEEDED*

     FRESH FLAT-LEAF PARSLEY LEAVES FOR GARNISHING (OPTIONAL)

Put the pine nuts in a dry small skillet over medium heat. Shake constantly until evenly toasted on all sides, about 4 minutes. Set aside.

Fill a large saucepan three fourths full of water. Bring to a boil over high heat and add kosher salt. (We add 1 1/2 teaspoons kosher salt per quart of water.) Add the pasta and cook, stir-ring occasionally, until barely tender, 8 to 10 min-utes. Add the asparagus to the pan and cook until tender-crisp, 1 to 2 minutes. Drain the pasta and asparagus, reserving 3/4 cup of the cooking water.

Set the pan over medium heat and heat the olive oil. Add the garlic and cook until fragrant and lightly brown, 1 to 2 minutes. Return the pasta and asparagus to the pan, then add the reserved cooking water. Add the tomatoes (if using), Parmesan cheese, Boursin, dill, and the 3/4 tea-spoon lemon pepper and toss to combine. Stir in the pine nuts. Season with kosher salt to taste and more lemon pepper if necessary.

Divide the pasta between 2 bowls and garnish with parsley, if desired. Serve immediately.

LINGUINE WITH SCALLOPS, SPINACH, AND BACON IN CHAMPAGNE-CREAM SAUCE

Serves 2 to 3

This recipe was inspired by the coquilles St. Jacques our mom made when we were growing up. The whole house was perfumed with the essence of vermouth-poached scallops. Those wafting aromas meant there was a very, very special occasion on the horizon. This dish, vaguely reminiscent of the classic concoction that Mom used to make, is also meant for an occasion—a special evening when you have a little extra time to spend in the kitchen. The subtle hints of shallots, aromatic thyme, and smoky bacon, combined with the sweetness of the Champagne and scallops, give this dish a sophisticated, decadent quality. Serve with a crusty loaf of French bread and a crisp, chilled Sauvignon Blanc. Now that's a splurge we all deserve!

3	BACON SLICES (PREFERABLY THICK-CUT), CHOPPED

CHAMPAGNE-CREAM SAUCE

5	LARGE SHALLOTS, THINLY SLICED (ABOUT 1½ CUPS)
	KOSHER SALT AND FRESHLY GROUND PEPPER
2	TEASPOONS ALL-PURPOSE FLOUR
1	CUP BRUT CHAMPAGNE
1¾	CUPS CHICKEN STOCK (PAGE 30) OR CANNED CHICKEN BROTH
½	CUP CRÈME FRAÎCHE
2	TEASPOONS DIJON MUSTARD
1	TABLESPOON CHOPPED FRESH THYME
1	TEASPOON SUGAR

	KOSHER SALT
8	OUNCES LINGUINE
½	OF A 10-OUNCE BAG PREWASHED SPINACH, ROUGHLY CHOPPED
8	OUNCES SEA SCALLOPS, PREFERABLY DAY BOAT
	FRESHLY GROUND PEPPER
⅓	CUP GRATED PARMESAN, PREFERABLY PARMIGIANO-REGGIANO

Fry the bacon in a large heavy skillet over medium heat, stirring frequently, until the fat is rendered and the bacon begins to brown, about 6 minutes. Using a slotted spoon, transfer the bacon to a paper towel–lined plate.

Add the shallots to the pan with the bacon grease, reduce the heat to medium-low, and season with kosher salt and pepper to taste. Cook, stirring frequently, until the shallots are soft and translucent, about 3 minutes. Sprinkle the flour over the shallots and cook 1 minute more, stirring frequently. Whisk in the Champagne, increase the heat to high, and cook for 1 minute. Whisk in the stock and cook, whisking frequently, until the sauce begins to thicken, about 3 minutes.

Remove the sauce from the heat and whisk in the crème fraîche, mustard, thyme, and sugar. Set aside.

Fill a large saucepan three fourths full of water. Bring to a boil over high heat and add kosher salt. (We add $1^{1}/_{2}$ teaspoons kosher salt per quart of water.)

Add the pasta and cook, stirring occasionally, until barely tender, according to the directions on the package. Add the spinach to the pan 1 minute before the pasta is ready. Drain the pasta and spinach, reserving $^{1}/_{4}$ cup of the cooking water. Return the pasta to the pan, add the reserved cooking water, and toss lightly.

Bring the cream sauce to a simmer over medium heat. Season the scallops lightly with kosher salt and pepper. Add them to the sauce, spoon the sauce over them, and cook for about 2 minutes. Turn and cook for 2 minutes more, then remove the pan from the heat. The scallops will continue to cook in the sauce.

Add about 1 cup of the sauce and the Parmesan cheese to the pasta and stir to incorporate. Toss thoroughly and season with kosher salt and pepper to taste. Divide the pasta between 2 bowls. Top with the remaining sauce and the scallops. Sprinkle with the bacon. Serve immediately.

Do-Ahead: The sauce can be made 1 day in advance and refrigerated. If you do this, we suggest searing the scallops in a medium skillet over high heat with 1 tablespoon of olive oil. The sauce can then be gently warmed in a saucepan. Scallops should be lightly seasoned with kosher salt and pepper before sautéing. Sauté until just opaque, 1 to 2 minutes on each side.

Note: Any dry/brut Champagne will work well in this recipe. We recommend buying a split (half-bottle) of Champagne, or buying a full bottle—and enjoying the remaining bubbly together. Take this opportunity to sip side-by-side as you cook!

PASTA WITH PESTO, SHRIMP, AND SWEET 100S

Serves 2

One of our fabulous recipe testers, Molly Naughton, made this dish for her boyfriend, a man who refuses to eat leftovers. After he devoured his dinner, Molly spotted him in the kitchen digging for Tupperware. He refrigerated what was left on her plate and ate the leftovers for breakfast the next morning. Need we say more?

KOSHER SALT

FRESHLY GROUND PEPPER

8 *OUNCES ANGEL HAIR PASTA*

1 *TABLESPOON OLIVE OIL*

8 *OUNCES LARGE SHRIMP, PEELED AND DEVEINED*

2 *TEASPOONS MINCED GARLIC*

1/2 *CUP PESTO, HOMEMADE (PAGE 48) OR PURCHASED*

1 *CUP HALVED SWEET 100S OR OTHER CHERRY TOMATOES*

GRATED PARMESAN, PREFERABLY PARMIGIANO-REGGIANO, FOR SERVING

LEMON WEDGES FOR GARNISHING

Fill a large saucepan three fourths full of water. Bring to a boil over high heat and add kosher salt. (We add 1½ teaspoons kosher salt per quart of water.) Add the pasta and cook, stirring occasionally, until barely tender, about 4 minutes. Drain the pasta, reserving 1 cup of the cooking water.

Heat the olive oil in the same pan over medium heat. Add the shrimp and cook for about 1 minute. Turn the shrimp over and add the garlic. Continue cooking until the shrimp is opaque in the center, about 1 minute more. Add the reserved cooking water and the pesto and stir until incorporated. Add the pasta and tomatoes and toss to combine. Season with kosher salt and pepper to taste.

Divide the pasta between 2 plates and top with cheese. Garnish each with a lemon wedge.

Tips for Perfect Pasta:

1. Fill a large pot three fourths full of cold water so that the noodles have room to squiggle and squirm.

2. Bring the water to a boil over high heat and salt generously. Add about 1½ teaspoons kosher salt per quart of water.

3. Don't overcook pasta. When tested, pasta should very slightly resist your bite. Stop boiling the pasta before it becomes soft. Even after draining, pasta continues to cook slightly. If you do cook your pasta a bit too long, rinse it with cold running water immediately to stop the cooking.

4. Drain pasta by pouring it into a colander.

5. Rinse pasta to prevent it from sticking *only* if you will not be serving it right away. If you are not assembling the final dish immediately, toss the rinsed pasta with butter or oil (olive oil, garlic oil, peanut oil—whatever is appropriate) to prevent it from sticking and to add flavor.

6. While the pasta is draining, heat the sauce in the pasta pot, then add the pasta and toss to coat with the sauce.

SALMON WITH HONEY-MUSTARD GLAZE

Serves 2

We have carried on our mom's tradition of topping broiled fish with Ritz crackers, which lend a crispy, buttery taste and toasty texture. Sophisticated yet casual, this salmon is surprisingly easy to make. We are just as likely to serve this dish to our families on Monday night as we are to serve it to guests at a dinner party. When purchasing the fish, we suggest requesting the thinner tail-end portion of the fillet so you'll get more mustard flavor with every bite of salmon.

2	SKINLESS SALMON FILLETS (8 OUNCES EACH)
3	TABLESPOONS STONE-GROUND MUSTARD
2	TABLESPOONS CRÈME FRAÎCHE OR SOUR CREAM
2	TEASPOONS HONEY
$1/2$	TEASPOON DRIED DILL WEED
8	CRACKERS, SUCH AS RITZ, CRUMBLED

Preheat the oven to 400 degrees F. Line a baking sheet with aluminum foil.

Place the salmon on the prepared baking sheet. Combine the mustard, crème fraîche, honey, and dill weed in a small bowl. Spread the mixture on top of the fillets. Sprinkle with the cracker crumbs just before placing in the oven. Bake until the salmon is barely cooked through, 12 to 15 minutes. Serve immediately.

Note: We keep crème fraîche on hand but understand from our friends in other parts of the country that it can be hard to find. Substitute sour cream, or make your own crème fraîche by combining $1/2$ cup sour cream with $1/2$ cup heavy cream (not ultrapasteurized) and let stand, covered, in a warm place until thick, 8 to 24 hours.

CORN CHIP–CRUSTED HALIBUT WITH CREAMY SALSA AND CILANTRO

Serves 2

Picture this: We were vacationing in Hawaii and after a long day of sailing, we were sunburned, tired, and ravenous. It was late, the kids were cranky, and there was no time to go to the store. So we turned to the sparsely stocked pantry and fridge in our rental home for inspiration. What we found was a bag of Doritos, a jar of salsa, some spices, and some sour cream. Oh, heavens! Thankfully, we'd purchased a gorgeous piece of halibut that morning. With some quick improvising, we created this dish to the wild applause of our hungry family and friends. | When we're pressed for time, we often rely on this quick, now slightly updated entrée and still chuckle over its origin. For wonderful accompaniments, try our Sweet Corn with Jalapeño Essence (page 155) and Butter Lettuce with Mango, Goat Cheese, and Mighty Mint Vinaigrette (page 83).

2	HALIBUT FILLETS (8 OUNCES EACH)
	KOSHER SALT
1/2	TEASPOON GROUND CUMIN
2	TABLESPOONS UNSALTED BUTTER, MELTED
1	TABLESPOON FRESH LIME JUICE
2	HANDFULS CORN CHIPS
3/4	CUP MEDIUM SALSA (SEE NOTE)
3	TABLESPOONS SOUR CREAM
2	TABLESPOONS FRESH CILANTRO LEAVES

Preheat the oven to 400 degrees F. Line a baking sheet with aluminum foil.

Place the halibut on the prepared baking sheet. Season both sides of the fillets with kosher salt to taste and the cumin. Combine the butter and lime juice in a small bowl and drizzle over the fillets.

Put the corn chips in a sealable plastic bag and crush into small pieces using the palm of your hand (you should have about 1/4 cup). Top each fillet with a thick layer of the crumbs. Cover loosely with aluminum foil to prevent excess browning. Bake until the fish is opaque in the center, about 20 minutes, removing the foil after about 10 minutes.

Whisk together the salsa and sour cream in a small saucepan over low heat. Heat until just warmed through, 2 to 3 minutes.

Place the halibut fillets on individual plates, top with the creamy salsa, and garnish with the cilantro leaves.

Note: Believe it or not, we actually prefer this dish made with a premium-quality bottled salsa rather than with one of the fresh salsas sold in the refrigerated case at the supermarket. Bottled salsas tend to be thicker and have a depth of flavor that works especially well in this dish.

GRILLED TUNA WITH SOY-GINGER GLAZE AND PICKLED CUCUMBERS

Serves 2

We have a HUGE crush on tuna served with the pungent, aromatic flavors of Asia. The stark contrast of the warm tuna and soy-ginger glaze piled high with cool, crispy cucumbers makes this dish unforgettable. Please, oh please, be careful not to overcook the tuna. We think tuna is at its best served rare in the center. Complete the meal with a side of Coconut Rice (page 170), and a flurry of snow peas drizzled with sesame oil. | Don't forget to raise a warm thimble full of sake in celebration of this Asian-inspired meal.

MARINADE

3/4	CUP DRY SHERRY
2	TABLESPOONS SOY SAUCE
1	TABLESPOON PLUS 1 TEASPOON HONEY
2	MEDIUM CLOVES GARLIC, MINCED
2	TEASPOONS FRESH LIME JUICE
1	TEASPOON ASIAN CHILI SAUCE
1	TEASPOON PEELED AND FINELY CHOPPED FRESH GINGER
2	AHI TUNA STEAKS (6 TO 8 OUNCES EACH)

PICKLED CUCUMBERS

1	CUP PAPER-THIN SLICES CUCUMBER (SEEDS REMOVED)
1/4	VERY SMALL RED ONION, SLICED PAPER-THIN
1/4	CUP SEASONED RICE VINEGAR (SEE NOTE)

VEGETABLE OIL FOR BRUSHING
2 TEASPOONS DARK SESAME OIL
CILANTRO SPRIGS FOR GARNISHING

Combine the sherry, soy sauce, honey, garlic, lime juice, chili sauce, and ginger in a small saucepan. Put the tuna steaks in a baking dish and pour 1/4 cup of the marinade over the steaks. Let stand at room temperature for at least 30 minutes, or refrigerated up to 2 hours.

Put the cucumber and red onion in a small bowl. Add the vinegar and toss to coat evenly. Cover with plastic wrap and refrigerate for at least 15 minutes or up to 2 days.

Prepare a medium-hot charcoal fire or preheat a gas grill to medium-high. Or set a grillpan over high heat until it is hot and beginning to smoke.

Remove the tuna steaks from the marinade and pat dry. Brush the steaks on both sides with vegetable oil. Grill, turning once, for 3 to 5 minutes on each side, or to your liking. Be careful, as the tuna will get dry if overcooked.

Meanwhile, put the remaining marinade in a small saucepan over medium-high heat and cook until reduced to a syrupy consistency (about 1/4 cup), about 10 minutes. Remove from the heat and stir in the sesame oil. Serve the tuna steaks with the soy-ginger glaze and top with a heaping portion of the pickled cucumbers. Garnish with cilantro sprigs.

Note: If you cannot find seasoned rice vinegar, add 1 1/2 tablespoons sugar and 1 teaspoon kosher salt to 1/4 cup unseasoned rice vinegar.

CHICKEN WITH PROSCIUTTO, FONTINA, AND MUSHROOM SAUCE

Serves 2

Mary's husband, Jack, adores this rustic chicken dish. We think you will, too. It makes great weeknight fare when prepared with white button mushrooms—and is out of this world for entertaining when made with earthy, exotic mushrooms and drizzled with truffle oil. If you're unfamiliar with exotic mushrooms, this is the time to experiment. Shiitakes add their signature nuttiness to the sauce, but you can't go wrong with creminis, either. If prosciutto and fontina cheeses are hard to find, use Westphalian ham and Swiss cheese, or honey-cured ham and Gouda.

2	SKINLESS, BONELESS CHICKEN BREAST HALVES
	KOSHER SALT AND FRESHLY GROUND PEPPER
2	TEASPOONS MINCED FRESH SAGE, OR 1 TEASPOON DRIED SAGE
2	PAPER-THIN PROSCIUTTO SLICES
1/2	CUP (1 OUNCE) GRATED FONTINA CHEESE
1	TABLESPOON OLIVE OIL
4	OUNCES SLICED SHIITAKE, CREMINI, OR WHITE BUTTON MUSHROOMS, CLEANED AND SLICED (IF USING SHIITAKES, DISCARD STEMS) (ABOUT 2 1/2 CUPS)
1/2	SMALL YELLOW ONION, CHOPPED
2	TEASPOONS ALL-PURPOSE FLOUR
1/2	CUP DRY WHITE WINE
1	CUP CHICKEN STOCK (PAGE 30) OR LOW-SODIUM CANNED CHICKEN BROTH
3	TABLESPOONS HEAVY CREAM
	TRUFFLE OIL FOR DRIZZLING (OPTIONAL)

Preheat the oven to 425 degrees F. Line a baking sheet with aluminum foil and spray lightly with vegetable-oil cooking spray.

Place a chicken breast half between 2 sheets of plastic wrap. Using a mallet or the back of a wooden spoon, pound it forcefully. You want to increase the surface area of the chicken by about 50% and to tenderize the meat. Repeat with the remaining chicken breast.

Place the chicken breasts on the prepared baking sheet and open them like a book. Season lightly with kosher salt and pepper to taste. Sprinkle half of the sage on each breast. Top each with 1 slice of the prosciutto and half of the cheese, and leave the breasts open to cook. Bake until the chicken is opaque in the center, about 15 minutes.

Meanwhile, heat the olive oil in a large skillet over medium-high heat. Add the mushrooms and onion and season lightly with kosher salt and pepper to taste. Sauté until the mushrooms are golden brown, 6 to 8 minutes. Sprinkle the flour over the vegetables and stir to coat. Cook for 1 minute. Add the wine and cook until evaporated, 1 to 2 minutes. Add the stock and cream, increase the heat to high, and cook until the sauce thickens, 3 to 5 minutes.

Transfer each chicken breast to a plate and top with the mushroom sauce. Drizzle with truffle oil, if desired, and serve.

CHICKEN "DIVINE"

Serves 4

This is our spin on the classic Chicken Divan and as we Southerners say, it is "diviiiine!" Don't be daunted by the rather long ingredient list; the dish comes together lickety-split. We often make an extra one and freeze it for a rainy day. When we deliver a comforting casserole to a new mom or an ailing friend, this is one of our trusty favorites.

4	*CUPS FRESH BROCCOLI FLORETS, OR 2 PACKAGES (10 OUNCES EACH) FROZEN BROCCOLI FLORETS, THAWED*
2	*TEASPOONS OLIVE OIL*
1	*MEDIUM YELLOW ONION, CHOPPED*
2	*TEASPOONS CHOPPED FRESH THYME, OR 1/4 TEASPOON DRIED THYME*
1/4	*TEASPOON KOSHER SALT*
1/8	*TEASPOON FRESHLY GROUND PEPPER*
1/2	*CUP DRY WHITE WINE, SUCH AS CHARDONNAY*
1	*JAR (16 OUNCES) ALFREDO SAUCE, SUCH AS CLASSICO*
2	*CUPS (4 OUNCES) GRATED SMOKED GOUDA OR EDAM CHEESE*
1/2	*CUP MILK*
1/8	*TEASPOON FRESHLY GRATED NUTMEG*
4	*CUPS COOKED PENNE, MACARONI, OR ORECCHIETTE (SEE NOTE)*
2	*CUPS SHREDDED ROAST CHICKEN, HOME COOKED (PAGE 105) OR PURCHASED*
1/4	*CUP DRY ITALIAN-STYLE BREAD CRUMBS*
	PAPRIKA FOR SPRINKLING

Preheat the oven to 375 degrees F.

If using fresh broccoli, cook the florets in a steamer until tender-crisp, 3 to 4 minutes. Rinse with cold water to stop the cooking and drain thoroughly. If using thawed frozen broccoli, squeeze out the excess liquid. Set aside.

Heat the olive oil in a medium saucepan over medium heat. Add the onion, thyme, kosher salt, and pepper. Cook, stirring occasionally, until the onion is tender, about 5 minutes. Add the wine, increase the heat to high, and cook until the liquid has evaporated, 2 to 3 minutes. Remove from the heat. Stir in the Alfredo sauce, 1/2 cup of the cheese, the milk, and nutmeg. Then stir in the cooked pasta, broccoli, and chicken and mix thoroughly.

Transfer to an 8-inch square baking dish. Top with the remaining 1 1/2 cups cheese and the bread crumbs. Sprinkle with paprika, cover with aluminum foil, and bake for 30 minutes. Uncover and bake until golden brown, 10 to 15 minutes more.

Do-Ahead: This casserole can be made 1 day in advance and refrigerated. It can also be assembled and then frozen. If the casserole was frozen, thaw in the refrigerator and bake as directed.

Note: About 3 cups dried penne pasta yields 4 cups cooked.

GRILLED CHICKEN WITH ROASTED RED PEPPER SALSA

Serves 2

Dress up an ordinary chicken breast with an aromatic spice blend of cumin and cinnamon, paired with golden raisins, olives, and fresh cilantro. This is Mediterranean fare at its headiest and most seductive—great for a candlelit dinner for 2. That said, this beautiful dish is also a good candidate for the buffet table. For equally great results, try the salsa on grilled halibut or swordfish.

3/4 CUP COARSELY CHOPPED ROASTED RED BELL PEPPERS (SEE NOTE)

1/4 CUP CHOPPED PITTED GREEN OLIVES

1/4 CUP GOLDEN RAISINS

3 TABLESPOONS CHOPPED RED ONION

3 TABLESPOONS CHOPPED FRESH CILANTRO

1/2 TEASPOON ORANGE ZEST

JUICE OF 1 ORANGE

KOSHER SALT

2 BONELESS CHICKEN BREAST HALVES

2 TABLESPOONS OLIVE OIL

1 TEASPOON GROUND CUMIN

1/2 TEASPOON GROUND CINNAMON

1/8 TEASPOON CAYENNE PEPPER

Combine the bell peppers, olives, golden raisins, red onion, cilantro, orange zest, and orange juice in a small bowl. Season with kosher salt to taste.

Prepare a medium-hot charcoal fire, or preheat a gas grill to medium-high.

Place a chicken breast half between 2 sheets of plastic wrap. Using a mallet or the back of a wooden spoon, pound to about 1/2-inch thickness. Repeat with the remaining chicken breast. Set aside.

Heat the olive oil in small heavy skillet over medium heat. Add the cumin, cinnamon, and cayenne and stir until fragrant, about 1 minute. Add half of the spice mixture to the bell pepper mixture. Brush the remaining spice mixture on the chicken and season with kosher salt to taste.

Grill the chicken until just cooked through, about 4 minutes on each side. Be careful not to overcook as the chicken breasts are thin. (Alternatively, grill the chicken in a hot well-seasoned ridged grill pan over medium-high heat.) Transfer each chicken breast to a plate. Spoon the salsa over the chicken and serve.

Note: To roast bell peppers, preheat the oven to 350 degrees F. Line a baking sheet with aluminum foil. Cut 1/4-inch slices off the top and bottom of 2 medium peppers. Remove the stem from the top pieces. Pull the core out of the center of each pepper. Make 1 slit down one side of each pepper and lay flat, skin-side down. Using a sharp knife, remove the ribs and seeds. Arrange the pepper pieces, skin-side up, on the prepared baking sheet. Press gently to flatten the peppers. Drizzle with about 1 tablespoon olive oil and brush evenly onto the peppers. Roast until the peppers are soft and caramelized, 30 to 40 minutes. Transfer the peppers to a bowl, cover with plastic wrap, and let stand for 20 to 30 minutes, then peel and chop.

Holiday TURKEY

Serves 8 to 10

Trust us! We wouldn't ask you to brine a turkey if we didn't think it was the true secret to success . . . guaranteeing an unbelievably moist bird that is flavorful to the bone. Follow these straightforward directions and this recipe will be your "first-and-forever" holiday turkey. When we are faced with the intimidating task of preparing the traditional celebratory feast, we cook our bird (without the stuffing) in advance and let it rest. We then carve it and decoratively arrange it on a platter an hour or so before our guests arrive (a cooked turkey can sit at room temperature, safely, for up to 2 hours before serving). That way, we don't have to hassle with carving while we are entertaining our guests. Though the turkey is room temperature, we make certain that the gravy is piping hot. For a stress-free holiday, see our detailed timeline on page 242.

1	FRESH TURKEY (ABOUT 14 POUNDS)
1	CUP KOSHER SALT OR $^1/_2$ CUP TABLE SALT, PLUS MORE AS NEEDED
$^1/_2$	CUP SUGAR
1	GALLON PLUS $3^1/_4$ CUPS WATER, PLUS MORE AS NEEDED
2	PLASTIC TURKEY-SIZED OVEN BAGS, MADE BY REYNOLDS
	FRESHLY GROUND PEPPER
3	MEDIUM YELLOW ONIONS, EACH CUT INTO 8 WEDGES
2	CARROTS, CUT INTO 2-INCH CHUNKS
1	CELERY STALK, LEAVES REMOVED, CUT INTO 2-INCH PIECES
12	FRESH THYME SPRIGS
2	HEADS OF GARLIC, HALVED HORIZONTALLY
1	BAY LEAF
$1^1/_2$	CUPS WHITE WINE
4	TABLESPOONS UNSALTED BUTTER, MELTED
3	TABLESPOONS CORNSTARCH
3	CUPS CHICKEN STOCK (PAGE 30) OR CANNED CHICKEN BROTH

Remove the neck and giblets from the body and neck cavities of the turkey. Store the neck and giblets separately in the refrigerator for making gravy. Remove and discard excess fat from the turkey and rinse the bird under cold running water.

Combine the 1 cup kosher salt, the sugar, and the 1 gallon water in a large bowl, stirring to dissolve the salt and sugar. Put 1 plastic oven bag inside the other to create a double thickness. Put the bag in a large roasting pan. Fold back the top one third of the bag to form a collar. Put the turkey inside the bag, unfold the top of the bag, and

pour the brine over the bird. Squeeze out the excess air and seal the bag tightly with a twist tie. Refrigerate for at least 6 hours and preferably 12 hours. If you are short on time, double the amount of salt and sugar and refrigerate for 4 to 6 hours.

Remove the turkey from the brine and rinse the bird thoroughly under cold running water to remove the salt. Pat dry inside and out with paper towels. Let the turkey stand at room temperature for about 2 hours. (If time doesn't permit, no worries. Just add an additional 30 minutes to the roasting time.)

CONTINUED

Position the rack in the lowest position of the oven and preheat to 400 degrees F.

If the turkey has a plastic or metal hook in the tail area, insert the ends of the drumsticks into the hook. If not, tie the drumsticks together with string.

To secure the wings, twist the wing tip underneath the shoulder. You may need to break the wing joint to do this. If the wings won't stay, tie them to the sides of the turkey with string.

Season the body and neck cavities with kosher salt and pepper to taste. Fill with about one fourth of the onions, carrots, and celery along with the thyme. Scatter the remaining onions, carrots, and celery along with the garlic, bay leaf, neck, and giblets in the bottom of the pan. Pour in the wine and 3 cups of the water.

Brush the turkey breast with half of the melted butter. Season with kosher salt and pepper to taste. Set a V-shaped rack in a large heavy-bottomed roasting pan. Place the turkey, breast-side down, on the rack. Brush the back side of the bird with the remaining butter and season with kosher salt and pepper to taste. Roast for 1 hour. Remove the pan from the oven (close the oven door). Using wads of paper towels to protect your hands, turn the bird breast-side up. Baste with the pan juices and return to the oven.

After 30 minutes, baste the turkey again. If the liquid in the pan has evaporated, add more water as needed. Roast for 30 minutes more, or until an instant-read thermometer inserted into the thickest part of the thigh, away from the bone, registers 170 to 175 degrees F. The meatiest part of the breast should register 165 degrees F.

Transfer the turkey to a cutting board or serving platter and cover loosely with aluminum foil. Let rest until ready to carve, at least 30 minutes.

Meanwhile, combine the cornstarch and the remaining $1/4$ cup water in a small bowl, stirring to dissolve the cornstarch. Set aside. Place the roasting pan across 2 burners over medium-high heat. Add the stock and stir to scrape up any browned bits from the bottom of the pan. Using a wooden spoon, mash the garlic into the juices and stir. Using a slotted spoon, transfer the vegetables from the pan into a strainer set over a small saucepan. Pour the juices from the roasting pan over the vegetables and press firmly on them with the back of a spoon. Set the saucepan over medium-high heat, bring to a simmer, and stir in the cornstarch mixture. Cook until thickened, about 1 minute. Season with kosher salt and pepper to taste. Carve the turkey and serve with the gravy.

TURKEY TIPS

1. Allow at least 1 pound of meat per person ($1^1/2$ pounds if you want ample leftovers).

2. Purchase a fresh turkey if available. It has superior flavor to a frozen one.

3. Smaller birds are much easier to handle than larger ones. Limit your turkey to 14 pounds.

4. For the crispiest skin, brine your turkey 24 hours prior to cooking. Remove the bird from the brine after 12 hours, and let it air-dry in the refrigerator for up to 8 hours before roasting.

5. Don't be shy when turning the bird in the roasting pan. Layer paper towels between the turkey and your pot holders, grab the turkey above the legs, and flip it over.

6. For carving tips, see page 106.

PRIME RIB WITH RED WINE GRAVY

Serves 6 to 8

Prime rib, the granddaddy of intimidating dishes, is as easy to overcook as it is to undercook. We have demystified the dish, giving you the confidence to make a rosy-pink-all-the-way-through prime rib every time. In a quest for a foolproof recipe, we tested a full range of temperatures—from 200 degrees to 500 degrees F. Follow the directions to a T, and you'll be guaranteed a *perfectly* cooked prime rib.

1   3-RIB STANDING RIB ROAST (ABOUT 7 POUNDS), CHINE BONE REMOVED
    AND TIED BACK ON
    KOSHER SALT AND FRESHLY GROUND PEPPER
3   YELLOW ONIONS, CUT INTO 2-INCH PIECES
3   CARROTS, CUT INTO 2-INCH PIECES
1   HEAD OF GARLIC, HALVED HORIZONTALLY
8   FRESH THYME SPRIGS
1   BAY LEAF
2   CUPS RED WINE
1 1/4 CUPS WATER
1/4   CUP CORNSTARCH
3   CUPS BEEF BROTH

Let the roast stand at room temperature for about 2 1/2 hours.

Preheat the oven to 200 degrees F.

Place a large, heavy-bottomed roasting pan across 2 burners and heat over medium-high heat. Season the roast generously with kosher salt and pepper to taste. When the pan is hot but not smoking, place the roast, fat-side down, in the pan. Cook on all sides until crispy golden brown, about 10 minutes.

Transfer the roast to a platter. Scatter the onions, carrots, garlic, thyme, and bay leaf in the pan. Pour the wine and 1 cup of the water over the vegetables. Set a V-shaped or wire rack in the pan and place the roast on the rack, fat-side up. Roast until an instant-read thermometer inserted into the center of the meat, away from the bone, registers 130 degrees F for medium-rare, 3 to 3 1/2 hours. Transfer the roast to a cutting board and let rest for at least 20 minutes or up to 1 hour.

Meanwhile to make the gravy, combine the cornstarch and the remaining 1/4 cup water in a small bowl, stirring to dissolve the cornstarch. Set aside. Place the roasting pan across 2 burners over medium-high heat. Add the broth and stir to scrape up any browned bits from the bottom of the pan. Using a slotted spoon, transfer the vegetables from the pan into a strainer set over a small saucepan. Pour the juices from the roasting pan over the vegetables and press firmly on them with the back of a spoon. Set the saucepan over medium-high heat, bring to a simmer, and stir in the cornstarch mixture. Cook until thickened, about 1 minute. Season with kosher salt and pepper to taste.

To carve the roast, place it on the cutting board with rib bones pointing up. Cut the strings holding the rib bones to the roast and remove the bones. Set the roast, cut-side down, and carve into thick slices. Serve with the gravy.

PORK TENDERLOIN WITH MANGO SALSA AND BLACKBERRY SYRUP

Serves 3 or 4

Our friends often ask us for advice on food and entertaining. This recipe is one of our fondest recommendations; it impresses *every* time. As beautiful on the plate as it is on your taste buds, this pork has another plus—it can be prepared in less than an hour. For a perfect dinner, serve with our Roasted Asparagus (page 152) and Coconut Rice (page 170). In summer we often substitute white peaches or nectarines for the mangoes.

MANGO SALSA

1 $1/2$ *CUPS DICED MANGO (ABOUT 1 LARGE MANGO)*

2   *TABLESPOONS FINELY CHOPPED RED ONION*

1   *TABLESPOON CHOPPED FRESH MINT*

$1/2$ *TEASPOON SEEDED, DERIBBED, AND CHOPPED JALAPEÑO CHILE, PLUS MORE AS NEEDED*

$1/2$ *TEASPOON GRATED LIME ZEST*

2   *TEASPOONS FRESH LIME JUICE, PLUS MORE AS NEEDED*

$1/4$ *TEASPOON KOSHER SALT, PLUS MORE AS NEEDED*

BLACKBERRY SYRUP

$3/4$ *CUP RASPBERRY VINEGAR*

3   *TABLESPOONS SEEDLESS BLACKBERRY PRESERVES*

$1/8$ *TEASPOON KOSHER SALT*

2   *PORK TENDERLOINS (ABOUT 12 OUNCES EACH)*

1 $1/4$ *TEASPOONS KOSHER SALT*

$1/2$ *TEASPOON FRESHLY GROUND PEPPER*

2   *TABLESPOONS VEGETABLE OIL*

      MINT SPRIGS FOR GARNISHING

Preheat the oven to 450 degrees F. Line a baking sheet with aluminum foil.

TO MAKE THE MANGO SALSA: Combine the mango, red onion, mint, the $1/2$ teaspoon jalapeño, the lime zest, the 2 teaspoons lime juice, and the $1/4$ teaspoon kosher salt in a medium bowl. Season with more jalapeño, lime juice, and kosher salt if necessary. Let stand, covered, at room temperature.

TO MAKE THE BLACKBERRY SYRUP: Whisk together the vinegar, preserves, and kosher salt in a small saucepan and simmer over medium- high heat until reduced to about $1/4$ cup, about 10 minutes. Keep an eye on the reduction during the final stages of cooking to avoid over-reducing or burning.

Season the pork with the kosher salt and pepper. Heat the oil in a large heavy-bottomed skillet over high heat. Add the pork and sauté, turning as needed, until golden, 2 to 3 minutes per side. Transfer to the prepared baking sheet. Roast until pork is just cooked through but is still pink in the center, 8 to 12 minutes. An instant-read thermometer inserted into the center of the meat should register 150 degrees F.

Transfer the pork to a cutting board and let rest for at least 5 minutes, then slice on the diagonal. Fan the slices on a serving plate, top with the mango salsa, and drizzle with the blackberry syrup. Garnish with mint sprigs.

LAMB CHOPS WITH MINT-MUSTARD SAUCE

Serves 2

You've heard of the Clean Plate Club, right? Well, this dish inspires diners to go one step further. The first time Mary served these lamb chops at a small dinner party, her husband, Jack, apologized in advance for his behavior and then picked up his plate and licked it clean. How's that for an endorsement! | We actually prefer the less expensive rib lamb chops to the pricier loin chops, because they have more flavor. We can't seem to get enough of this sauce—a jazzy new take on the traditional mint jelly accompaniment. For a Mediterranean-inspired feast, serve the chops with Couscous with Melted Leeks and Thyme (page 171), or try them alongside Sweet Peas with Red Onion and Mint (page 158).

3	TABLESPOONS MINT JELLY
1	TABLESPOON WHITE WINE VINEGAR
1	TABLESPOON STONE-GROUND MUSTARD
1/4	CUP CHICKEN STOCK (PAGE 30) OR CANNED CHICKEN BROTH
1	TABLESPOON VEGETABLE OIL
6	LAMB CHOPS (4 OUNCES EACH), PREFERABLY RIB CUT
	KOSHER SALT AND FRESHLY GROUND PEPPER

Whisk together the mint jelly, vinegar, mustard, and stock in a small bowl. Set aside.

Heat the oil in a large heavy-bottomed skillet over high heat. Season both sides of the lamb chops with kosher salt and pepper to taste. Add the chops and cook for about 3 minutes on each side for medium-rare. Transfer the chops to a platter, cover loosely with aluminum foil, and let rest.

Remove the pan from the heat, discard the fat, and add the mint jelly mixture. Set over medium-high heat and cook, stirring occasionally, until the liquid is reduced to 1/4 cup or is slightly thickened, 2 to 4 minutes. Drizzle the warm sauce over the lamb chops and serve.

GRILLED BUTTERFLIED LEG OF LAMB
WITH LEMON AND ROSEMARY

Serves 6 to 8

This recipe pays homage to our friend, Diane Morgan, who inspired us to pack each side of the meat with herbs. We have adapted her recipe and added grilled lemons—after all, lamb loves lemon. One of the best things about a leg of lamb is its leftover potential. We create sensational sandwiches by layering leftover thinly sliced meat on rosemary foccacia, topped with Caramelized Onions (page 50), fresh basil, and goat cheese.

MARINADE

3/4   *CUP OLIVE OIL*

6   *LARGE CLOVES GARLIC, PEELED*

     JUICE OF 1 LEMON

1 1/2 *TEASPOONS KOSHER SALT*

1   *TEASPOON FRESHLY GROUND PEPPER*

1   *LEMON, CUT INTO ABOUT 8 THIN SLICES*

1   *BUTTERFLIED LEG OF LAMB (3 1/2 TO 4 1/2 POUNDS)*

     OLIVE OIL FOR BRUSHING

     KOSHER SALT AND FRESHLY GROUND PEPPER

     SCANT 1/4 CUP DRIED ROSEMARY, CRUMBLED

     SCANT 1/4 CUP OREGANO

TO MAKE THE MARINADE: Combine the oil, garlic, lemon juice, kosher salt, and pepper in a blender and blend until smooth.

Put the lemon slices on a plate and brush lightly with some of the marinade. Set aside.

Remove any string from the lamb if necessary. Put the lamb on a flat surface and, using a rolling pin, mallet, or the back of a saucepan, pound about 40 times, concentrating on the thickest area of the meat. This ensures more even cooking. Put the lamb, fat-side down, in a large baking dish and pour the remaining marinade evenly over the lamb, massaging the meat on both sides with your fingers. This helps to jump-start the marinating process. The more you massage the meat, the better, especially if your time is limited. Let the lamb and lemons stand at room temperature for 1 hour or refrigerate for up to 24 hours.

Prepare a medium-hot charcoal fire or preheat a gas grill to medium-high.

Remove the lamb from the marinade. Brush with the oil and season both sides with kosher salt and pepper to taste. Coat one side with the rosemary and the other with oregano, pressing the herbs into the meat. Put the lamb (fat-side down) on the grill. Cook, with the grill covered, for about 15 minutes. Turn the lamb over, cover the grill, and cook for an additional 5 minutes. Place the lemons on the grill, and cook for 2 to 3 minutes per side, until soft and lightly charred. An instant-read thermometer inserted into the center of the meat should register 120 to 130 degrees F. Do not overcook the lamb, as it will continue to cook while resting. Remove the lamb and lemons from the grill.

Transfer the lamb and lemons to a high-sided baking sheet (or grooved cutting board), cover loosely with aluminum foil, and let rest for 15 to 20 minutes. Transfer the lamb to a cutting board and slice the lamb against the grain into thin slices. Serve with 2 to 3 lemon slices per person.

GRILLED LONDON BROIL FAJITAS

Serves 4

Years ago, Mary and Jack served London broil fajitas for a dinner party . . . thank goodness they had invited close friends. Delicious as the fajitas were, Mary, Jack and their guests learned the hard way that eating fajitas made with thick slices of meat makes for an awkward experience. Noticing their guests were struggling with unmanageable strips of London broil, Jack quickly got out the forks and knives. You'll have no need for silverware with this recipe if you remember to slice the meat into short, ultrathin pieces. These fajitas are great for entertaining . . . rock, wrap 'em, and roll!

SALSA

2 1/2   CUPS CHOPPED TOMATOES (ABOUT 5 PLUM TOMATOES)

1/2   TEASPOON KOSHER SALT, PLUS MORE AS NEEDED

3   TABLESPOONS PICANTE SAUCE

3   TABLESPOONS MINCED YELLOW ONION

1/2   JALAPEÑO CHILE, MINCED, PLUS MORE AS NEEDED

2   TABLESPOONS CHOPPED FRESH CILANTRO

1   TABLESPOON FRESH LIME JUICE

1 1/2   TEASPOONS MINCED GARLIC, PLUS MORE AS NEEDED

FAJITAS

1 1/2   POUNDS LONDON BROIL

2   TEASPOONS CHILI POWDER

1   TEASPOON GARLIC POWDER

1   TEASPOON ONION POWDER

2   TEASPOONS KOSHER SALT

1   TEASPOON GROUND CUMIN

1 1/2   TEASPOONS FIRMLY PACKED DARK BROWN SUGAR

2   TABLESPOONS VEGETABLE OIL

2   RED BELL PEPPERS, SEEDED, DERIBBED, AND THINLY SLICED

1/2   LARGE YELLOW ONION, THINLY SLICED

1/8   TEASPOON FRESHLY GROUND PEPPER

8   FLOUR TORTILLAS (10 TO 12 INCHES DIAMETER),
WARMED (SEE NOTE)

1   RECIPE GUACAMOLE (PAGE 58)

OPTIONAL CONDIMENTS:

FRESH CILANTRO LEAVES

SOUR CREAM

GRATED MONTEREY JACK CHEESE

SLICED JALAPEÑO CHILES

SPICY CHIPOTLE BLACK BEANS (PAGE 162)

CONTINUED

TO MAKE THE SALSA: Put the tomatoes in a strainer. Add the $1/2$ teaspoon kosher salt and toss. Let drain for 10 to 15 minutes. Combine the picante sauce, onion, the $1/2$ jalapeño, the cilantro, lime juice, tomatoes, and the $11/2$ teaspoons garlic in a medium bowl. Add more salt, jalapeño, and garlic if necessary. The salsa may be made 6 to 8 hours in advance and refrigerated.

TO MAKE THE FAJITAS: Place the London broil between 2 pieces of plastic wrap. Using a rolling pin or a mallet, pound to a uniform $1/2$-inch thickness.

Combine the chili powder, garlic powder, onion powder, 1 teaspoon of the kosher salt, the cumin, and brown sugar in a small bowl. Rub the mixture evenly into the meat, coating both sides. Let stand at room temperature for at least 30 minutes or up to 2 hours.

Prepare a hot charcoal fire or preheat a gas grill to high. Or, set a grill pan over high until it is hot and beginning to smoke. Generously oil the grill rack.

Grill the London broil for 3 to 4 minutes on each side for medium-rare or to desired doneness. (Alternatively, grill the meat on a stovetop grill pan for 8 to 12 minutes.) Transfer the steak to a cutting board and let stand for 5 minutes. Cut into 2-inch-wide pieces and slice each as thinly as possible. Sprinkle with $1/2$ teaspoon of the kosher salt. Arrange the slices on a platter.

Heat the oil in a large skillet over medium-high heat until hot but not smoking. Add the bell peppers, onion, the remaining $1/2$ teaspoon kosher salt, and the pepper. Sauté, stirring occasionally, until the bell peppers are softened, about 15 minutes. Transfer to the platter with the London broil. Drizzle any juices from the cutting board over the meat and the pepper mixture. Serve with the tortillas, salsa, guacamole, and condiments, if desired.

Note: To warm the tortillas, preheat an oven to 200 degrees F. Wrap the tortillas in a dampened paper towel, cover the bundle with aluminum foil, and heat for 10 to 15 minutes. To serve, remove the paper towel from the foil packet and place the foil-wrapped tortillas in a basket. Cover the foil with a colorful napkin or tea towel for a pretty presentation.

FILETS MIGNONS WITH GREEN PEPPERCORNS AND BRANDY-CREAM SAUCE

Serves 2

The best steak *au poivre* we ever had was in a little town near Joigny, France, on our way to cooking school at La Varenne. What set this sophisticated dish apart from others we'd eaten was the green peppercorn sauce. Traditionally, steak *au poivre* is made with a crushed black peppercorn crust, which we find overpowering. We like green peppercorns (along with a sprinkling of white and black pepper), because they are less pungent than the black variety, yet add an explosive depth of flavor. Green peppercorns are soft, under-ripe pepper berries, preserved in brine, and are easily found in your grocery store. We've created a recipe reminiscent of the steak we tasted on that spring night in France. It is peppery, and creamy, with complementary notes of brandy and mustard.

2	8-OUNCE FILETS MIGNON (ABOUT 1^{1}/$_{2}$ INCHES THICK)
	KOSHER SALT
	FRESHLY GROUND BLACK PEPPER
	FRESHLY GROUND WHITE PEPPER
1	TABLESPOON OLIVE OIL
1	TABLESPOON UNSALTED BUTTER
3	MEDIUM SHALLOTS, FINELY CHOPPED (ABOUT ^{1}/$_{2}$ CUP)
1	LARGE GARLIC CLOVE, MINCED
1	TEASPOON ALL-PURPOSE FLOUR
3/4	CUP BEEF BROTH
1/4	CUP HEAVY CREAM
3	TABLESPOONS BRANDY
2	TABLESPOONS DRAINED GREEN PEPPERCORNS (IN BRINE), COARSELY CHOPPED
1	TABLESPOON DIJON MUSTARD

Season both side of the steaks with kosher salt and black and white peppers to taste. Heat the oil in a medium heavy skillet, over high heat. Add the steaks, reduce heat to medium, and cook to desired doneness, about 5 minutes per side for medium-rare. Transfer steaks to a plate, and cover loosely with foil.

Using a paper towel, wipe out the skillet and set over medium heat. Melt the butter in the skillet and add the shallots and garlic. Cook, stirring frequently, until soft and translucent, 3 to 5 minutes. Sprinkle the flour over the shallots and garlic and cook for about 1 minute. Whisk in the broth, cream, and brandy, then the green peppercorns and mustard. Increase heat to medium-high and cook until the sauce is thick enough to coat the back of a spoon, about 5 minutes. Spoon over steaks, and serve immediately.

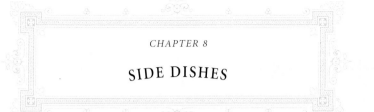

CHAPTER 8

SIDE DISHES

IT USED TO BE THAT EVERY MEAL CAME WITH AT LEAST TWO OR THREE "SIDES." We love the generous spirit of the all-American blue plate special, so we've done our best to fill this chapter with side dishes that go with just about everything and even stand strongly on their own. When you head into the kitchen to prepare dinner together, decide who will prepare the main-course, and which spouse gets to choose and prepare the perfectly matched side-dish.

When selecting sides, think about complementary colors, flavors, opposing textures, and what is in season. Roasted or grilled red meats and bright green vegetables make great mates, for example, while a moist salmon fillet is ideal nestled up to a pile of crispy roasted potatoes. Starches make great partners to most main-course dishes— just remember not to serve two starchy sides.

Sara's husband, Erik, says mashed potatoes don't come creamier than our creamy-dreamy version (he'd bathe in them, if he could). Mary's husband, Jack, has developed a serious pepper habit, the result of our subtly spiced Sweet Corn with Jalapeño Essence (page 155). We share our Southern roots with you in our home-style Roasted Tomato Pie (page 160), and we've given you plenty of ways to gussy up those vitamin-packed greens. Broccoli with Sun-Dried Tomatoes and Parmesan (page 156) is a sexy side, not to mention Spinach with Raisins and Pine Nuts (page 153), which we can't seem to get enough of.

We've created great side dishes for entertaining, too. Holiday buffets get a splash of color and flavor with Maple-Glazed Spiced Carrots (page 157) or Wild Rice with Dried Cranberries, Green Onions, and Pecans (page 169). And Sweet Peas with Red Onion and Mint (page 158) turns ordinary peas into a bright-tasting special-occasion side. For a sophisticated edge, stir melted leeks and fresh thyme into our enticing version of couscous, or fry up our positively addictive potato pancakes topped with sour cream and chives.

ROASTED ASPARAGUS

Serves 2

Whether you like 'em long and lean or short and fat, these sweet, caramelized spears will win you over. Roasting vegetables is super easy and the results, fantastic! We are fans of roasting because it concentrates the vegetables' flavors and intensifies their natural sugars. When asparagus is not in season, try roasting carrots, parsnips, Brussels sprouts, sweet potatoes, or mushrooms until they are tender when pierced with a knife.

16 ASPARAGUS SPEARS, TRIMMED, PEELED IF
    NECESSARY (SEE NOTE)

1 1/2 TEASPOONS EXTRA-VIRGIN OLIVE OIL

    KOSHER SALT AND FRESHLY GROUND PEPPER

    LEMON WEDGE OR DASH OF BALSAMIC
    VINEGAR (OPTIONAL)

Preheat the oven to 450 degrees F.

Put the asparagus in a large baking pan. Drizzle with the olive oil and season with kosher salt and pepper to taste. Toss to coat. Roast until the asparagus is tender-crisp, 8 to 15 minutes, shaking the pan halfway through the cooking time. (Total cooking time depends on the thickness of the spears.) Season with a squeeze of lemon or a dash of vinegar, if desired.

Note: How to trim asparagus:

THIN ASPARAGUS: Hold the base of an asparagus spear with one hand and grab the spear a few inches higher with the other hand. Applying pressure, snap the spear where the tender and tough parts meet. (The tough part will break off more or less voluntarily.) Using the cut spear as your guide, trim the remaining ones accordingly.

THICK ASPARAGUS: Cut thick asparagus spears with a knife, rather than breaking them, as they have a tendency to break virtually anywhere along the stalk, leading to unnecessary waste. Cut the stalks where you see a color change. Then take a small bite of the cut spear to see if it remains tough or stringy. If so, cut a little higher up on the stalk. Using the cut spear as your guide, trim the remaining ones accordingly.

DO I HAVE TO PEEL ASPARAGUS?

If the stalks are thick, peeling is a must, as the base of the asparagus can be tough and unpalatable. To peel, use a sharp vegetable peeler and peel the stalks away from the tip, about two thirds of the way down. It is not necessary to peel pencil-thin asparagus spears.

SPINACH WITH RAISINS AND PINE NUTS

Serves 2 or 3

Just as you and your spouse were meant to be together, this combination of bright, velvety spinach leaves, plump raisins, and creamy pine nuts make for a beautiful marriage. We eat this sumptuous dish for lunch and dinner, served hot or at room temperature, made with kale or chard instead of spinach, and garlic in place of onion. We even add orzo and goat cheese to create an out-of-this-world pasta salad. When we prepare a large batch for entertaining, we find it's easier to plunge the spinach (in batches) into boiling salted water for about 1 minute, rather than sautéing in a pan.

2   HEAPING TABLESPOONS RAISINS

1   PACKAGE (10 OUNCES) PREWASHED SPINACH

1/8 TEASPOON KOSHER SALT, PLUS MORE AS NEEDED

1   TABLESPOON UNSALTED BUTTER OR OLIVE OIL

1/2 SMALL YELLOW ONION, THINLY SLICED
    FRESHLY GROUND PEPPER

2   HEAPING TABLESPOONS PINE NUTS, TOASTED (SEE NOTE)
    PINCH OF FRESHLY GRATED NUTMEG, PLUS MORE AS NEEDED

Put the raisins in a small bowl, add hot water to cover, and let stand for 15 minutes. Drain and set aside.

Put 1/4 cup water in a large sauté pan and bring to a boil over medium heat. Add the spinach and the 1/8 teaspoon kosher salt. (If you don't have a large sauté pan with straight sides, sauté the spinach in 2 batches.) Cook over medium-high heat, turning the spinach as needed, until wilted and tender, 2 to 3 minutes. Transfer the spinach to a colander to drain. When the spinach is cool enough to handle, squeeze it thoroughly to remove any excess water.

Wipe out the pan and melt the butter or heat the olive oil over medium heat. When the butter or oil begins to sizzle, add the onion and season with a pinch of kosher salt and pepper to taste. Cook, stirring occasionally, until tender, about 8 minutes. Add the spinach, raisins, pine nuts, and nutmeg. Sauté briefly to warm through. Adjust the seasonings by adding more kosher salt, pepper, and nutmeg if necessary. Serve warm or at room temperature.

Note: To toast pine nuts, place them in a dry small pan over medium-low heat. Shake the pan constantly until the nuts are browned, about 5 minutes.

SWEET CORN WITH JALAPEÑO *Essence*

Serves 2 or 3

Fiery hot, this is not! Instead, this corn dish captures the wonderful, subtle essence of jalapeño without imparting its panicky-hot flavor. The jalapeño's assertiveness actually enhances the corn's sweetness. Remove the seeds and veins from the chile, where its fire is concentrated. And do your best to keep your hands to yourself for a while after deseeding chiles. The capsicum oil contained within the jalapeño is hot stuff! The bottom one third of the jalapeño is generally free of seeds, making it easy to cut seedless rounds.

1   *TABLESPOON UNSALTED BUTTER*

6   *THIN SLICES JALAPEÑO CHILE, SEEDED AND DEVEINED, PLUS MORE AS NEEDED*

2   *CUPS CORN KERNELS (CUT FROM 2 EARS OF CORN)*

2 TO 4 TABLESPOONS WATER, PLUS MORE AS NEEDED

1/2   *TEASPOON KOSHER SALT*

FRESHLY GROUND PEPPER

Combine the butter and jalapeño in a large sauté pan over medium-high heat. Cook until the butter is bubbling, 1 to 2 minutes. Add the corn, 2 tablespoons of the water, and the kosher salt and cook until the corn is tender, 4 to 7 minutes (see Note). Add the remaining 2 tablespoons water or more to the pan if necessary to prevent the corn from turning brown. (This is usually necessary for older corn as it does not emit any juices during cooking. Fresh summer corn releases enough liquid in the pan.) Season with pepper to taste and additional jalapeño slices, if desired!

Note: If your corn is very fresh (at the height of the summer season), cook it for the shortest amount of time possible, just until hot. However, if the corn is older, cook it longer, about 7 minutes.

BROCCOLI WITH SUN-DRIED TOMATOES AND PARMESAN

Serves 2 or 3

This is no "Broccoli-shmoccoli!" Ordinary steamed broccoli gets a boost from tart sun-dried tomatoes and a smattering of toasted pine nuts. If you're one of those people who just can't get excited about broccoli, this dish may prompt you to reevaluate your relationship with these brightly flavored florets. The kicker is the addition of freshly grated Parmigiano-Reggiano cheese. Keep a chunk of it on hand in the refrigerator and grate it yourself as you need it. It elevates this dish to new heights.

4   CUPS BROCCOLI FLORETS (ABOUT 1 BUNCH)

1   TABLESPOON UNSALTED BUTTER

2   TABLESPOONS PINE NUTS

1/4   CUP DRAINED OIL-PACKED SUN-DRIED TOMATOES, CHOPPED

FRESHLY GROUND PEPPER

2   TABLESPOONS GRATED PARMESAN CHEESE, PREFERABLY PARMIGIANO-REGGIANO

KOSHER SALT

Cook the broccoli florets in a steamer until tender, about 5 minutes. Plunge into heavily salted ice water. (We add 1 1/2 teaspoons kosher salt per quart of water.) Drain well and set aside.

Combine the butter and pine nuts in a medium skillet over medium heat. Cook, stirring constantly, until the nuts and butter begin to brown, 1 to 2 minutes. Add the broccoli, sun-dried tomatoes, and pepper to taste and stir until warm, 1 to 2 minutes. Add the cheese and remove from the heat. Toss and season with kosher salt to taste. Serve immediately.

MAPLE-GLAZED SPICED CARROTS

Serves 2

If your memories of eating cooked carrots as a child conjure up images of bland, over-cooked nubs, these orange beauties will most definitely change your outlook. This versatile side dish is long on mellow sweetness and full of gentle spice. We love to add it to our holiday buffet offerings and serve it regularly as a dressed-up side dish for weeknight suppers. It's wonderful alongside our Sweet-and-Sour Brisket (page 113) or paired with our Prime Rib with Red Wine Gravy (page 139).

3   MEDIUM CARROTS (ABOUT 8 OUNCES TOTAL),
     PEELED AND CUT DIAGONALLY INTO $^1/_4$-INCH-THICK
     SLICES (SEE NOTE)

$^1/_4$ CUP WATER

2   TABLESPOONS UNSALTED BUTTER

2   TEASPOONS MAPLE SYRUP

$^3/_4$ TEASPOON FRESH LEMON JUICE, PLUS MORE AS NEEDED

$^1/_4$ TEASPOON CURRY POWDER

$^1/_4$ TEASPOON KOSHER SALT, PLUS MORE AS NEEDED
     PINCH OF GROUND CINNAMON
     PINCH OF CAYENNE PEPPER

Combine the carrots, water, butter, maple syrup, the $^3/_4$ teaspoon lemon juice, the curry powder, the $^1/_4$ teaspoon kosher salt, the cinnamon, and cayenne pepper in a small nonstick saucepan over high heat. Bring to a boil, reduce the heat to medium-high, and cook, stirring frequently, for 5 minutes. Reduce the heat to low and cook until the liquid has reduced to a glaze and the carrots

are tender, about 8 minutes. Just before serving, adjust the seasonings by adding more lemon juice and kosher salt if necessary.

Note: To save time, you may use 8 ounces (a scant 2 cups) packaged peeled baby carrots. After reducing the heat to low, cook for about 10 minutes.

SWEET PEAS WITH RED ONION AND MINT

Serves 2 or 3

The combination of mint and peas is as natural and harmonious as two peas snuggled together in a pod. Add red onion for a mellow backdrop, and the result is a delicate spring-fresh gift from the garden. We make this recipe year-round. It's great in the springtime, when baby peas come fresh from the market, and is also delicious prepared with frozen peas in the winter. Serve with a seared halibut fillet topped with our quick and easy blender Hollandaise Sauce (page 175), or offer these little gems with Lamb Chops with Mint-Mustard Sauce (page 142).

2   *CUPS FRESH PEAS, OR 1 BOX (10 OUNCES) FROZEN BABY PEAS*

2   *TEASPOONS UNSALTED BUTTER*

1/4   *SMALL RED ONION, CHOPPED*

1/4   *TEASPOON KOSHER SALT*

1   *TABLESPOON CHOPPED FRESH MINT, OR 1 TEASPOON DRIED MINT*

2   *TEASPOONS EXTRA-VIRGIN OLIVE OIL FRESHLY GROUND PEPPER*

If using frozen peas, put them in a strainer or colander. Run cold water over them to remove any ice crystals. Let thaw for about 10 minutes.

Heat the butter in a small saucepan over medium heat. Add the red onion and 1/8 teaspoon of the kosher salt and cook, stirring occasionally, until tender, about 5 minutes. Add the peas and cook until warm, 3 to 5 minutes. Stir in the mint, olive oil, the remaining 1/8 teaspoon kosher salt, and pepper to taste.

ROASTED TOMATO PIE

Serves 6 to 8

Every Southern family we know has their own cherished recipe for tomato pie. Some are strewn with Vidalia onions, some with spring onions. Some cooks include Cheddar cheese and others, Swiss. Some recipes call for basil and others, thyme. We grew up eating Mom's version of tomato pie each summer but always complained that hers was oozing with an abundance of liquid. We've remedied Mom's "pie problem" by roasting the tomatoes, which concentrates their flavor and reduces the amount of juices.

2	POUNDS RIPE SUMMER TOMATOES OR PLUM TOMATOES, CUT IN $^{1}/_{2}$-INCH-THICK SLICES
2	TABLESPOONS OLIVE OIL
$^{1}/_{2}$	TEASPOON KOSHER SALT
	FRESHLY GROUND PEPPER
1	RECIPE FLAKY PIECRUST (PAGE 39), OR ONE 9-INCH FROZEN PIE SHELL (NOT DEEP DISH)
$1^{1}/_{4}$	CUPS (3 OUNCES) GRATED PARRANO OR SHARP WHITE CHEDDAR CHEESE (SEE NOTE)
10	MEDIUM FRESH BASIL LEAVES, THINLY SLICED, PLUS MORE FOR GARNISHING (SEE TIP)
$^{1}/_{4}$	TEASPOON DRIED OREGANO
$^{1}/_{2}$	CUP (2 OUNCES) GRATED PARMESAN CHEESE, PREFERABLY PARMIGIANO-REGGIANO
$^{1}/_{2}$	CUP MAYONNAISE

Preheat the oven to 350 degrees F. Line a baking sheet with aluminum foil and brush with olive oil.

Place the tomatoes on the baking sheet, brush with the olive oil, and season with the kosher salt and pepper to taste. Roast until the tomatoes are slightly dehydrated but not completely dry, 1 to 1$^{1}/_{2}$ hours. (Plum tomatoes take about 1 hour. Peak-of-season summer tomatoes take about 1$^{1}/_{2}$ hours.)

If using a homemade piecrust, bake it blind as directed. If using a frozen pie shell, prebake it according to the package directions. While the crust is still warm, sprinkle with $^{1}/_{2}$ cup of the Parrano cheese.

Adjust the oven to 400 degrees F. Layer half of the tomatoes on top of the cheese and sprinkle with half of the basil. Layer the remaining tomatoes on top and sprinkle with the remaining basil.

Combine the oregano, Parmesan cheese, mayonnaise, and pepper to taste in a small bowl. Spoon the mixture on top of the tomatoes. Top with the remaining $^{3}/_{4}$ cup Parrano cheese. Place the pie on the prepared baking sheet and bake until the cheese is lightly browned, 20 to 30 minutes.

Serve slightly warm or at room temperature. Garnish with sliced basil before serving.

Note: Parrano cheese is a Gouda cheese made from goat's milk. It is tangy and has a smooth, firm body and a substantial nutty taste. If you can't find Parrano, substitute sharp white Cheddar cheese.

Tip: To slice basil, stack 10 leaves one on top of the other and roll them up like a jelly roll, then cut into thin ribbons. This is called a chiffonade.

SAUSAGE AND ROASTED GARLIC STUFFING

Serves 8

Stuffing loyalties run deep in our family. Sara likes nuts and dried fruit soaked in port. Mary prefers cornbread and sausage. Dad insists on cutting his own bread cubes, while Mom turns to packaged seasoned bread cubes for convenience. Needless to say, it's a challenge to please everybody with a single stuffing, but this is a recipe we can all agree on—it's an all-around favorite. We love the simple and familiar combination of good ol' breakfast sausage and sweet sautéed onions and celery with heady roasted garlic and sage. Do yourself a favor and make this versatile tried-and-true stuffing more than just once a year.

1	PACKAGE (14 OUNCES) SEASONED BREAD CUBES, SUCH AS PEPPERIDGE FARM
4	TABLESPOONS UNSALTED BUTTER
1	LARGE YELLOW ONION, CHOPPED
2	LARGE CELERY STALKS, CHOPPED
1/4	TEASPOON KOSHER SALT
1/8	TEASPOON FRESHLY GROUND PEPPER
12	OUNCES GROUND BREAKFAST SAUSAGE
13/4	CUPS WATER
1/4	CUP ROASTED GARLIC, HOMEMADE (PAGE 34) OR PURCHASED
1/4	CUP CHOPPED FRESH FLAT-LEAF PARSLEY
1	TABLESPOON CHOPPED FRESH SAGE, OR 1 TEASPOON DRIED SAGE
1	TABLESPOON CHOPPED FRESH THYME, OR 1 TEASPOON DRIED THYME

Preheat the oven to 350 degrees F. Spray a 9-by-13-inch glass baking dish with vegetable-oil cooking spray.

Put the bread cubes in a large bowl.

Melt 1 tablespoon of the butter in a large skillet over medium-high heat. Add the onion, celery, kosher salt, and pepper and cook, stirring occasionally, until the onion is soft and lightly browned, 8 to 10 minutes. Pour over the bread cubes. Set the skillet over medium heat and put the sausage in the pan. Cook, breaking the sausage into small pieces with a wooden spoon, until browned, about 5 minutes. Using a slotted spoon, transfer the sausage to the bowl. Pour off excess fat from the skillet.

Return the skillet to medium heat. Add the water, roasted garlic, the remaining 3 tablespoons butter, the parsley, sage, and thyme and stir to scrape up the browned bits. Bring to a simmer, then pour into the bowl and stir well to combine. Transfer to the prepared baking dish, cover with aluminum foil, and bake for 25 to 30 minutes. Uncover and bake until the top crisps slightly, 5 to 10 minutes more.

Do-Ahead: The stuffing can be assembled up to 1 day in advance. Cover with aluminum foil and refrigerate. Bring to room temperature, then bake as directed.

Spicy CHIPOTLE BLACK BEANS

Serves 2

If you've never experienced chipotle chiles, get yourself to the store, and fast! Even folks who normally steer clear of hot peppers have been known to launch a lusty affair with these little devils. Chipotle chiles are smoked jalapeños. They can be fiery, but their unique smokiness is what hits you first and adds an unexpected dimension to beans, chili, and stewed meat dishes. These beans hold their own against our Grilled London Broil Fajitas (page 147) or Corn Chip–Crusted Halibut with Creamy Salsa and Cilantro (page 129). Serve a bowl of these brazen beans with a grilled chicken breast or an extra-thick pork chop smothered with Mango Salsa (page 141)—positively delish!

2   TEASPOONS VEGETABLE OIL

1   SMALL RED BELL PEPPER, SEEDED, DERIBBED,
     AND FINELY CHOPPED

1   TEASPOON FINELY CHOPPED GARLIC

1/4   TEASPOON KOSHER SALT, PLUS MORE AS NEEDED

1/4   TEASPOON GROUND CUMIN

1/8   TEASPOON GROUND CINNAMON

1   CAN (15 TO 16 OUNCES) BLACK BEANS, DRAINED AND RINSED

1/4   CUP WATER

2   TABLESPOONS MILD PICANTE SAUCE

1/4   TEASPOON MINCED CANNED CHIPOTLE CHILES IN
      ADOBO SAUCE, PLUS MORE AS NEEDED (SEE NOTE, PAGE 114)

Heat the vegetable oil in a medium heavy-bottomed skillet over medium heat. Add the bell pepper, garlic, the 1/4 teaspoon kosher salt, the cumin, and cinnamon. Cook, stirring occasionally, until soft and fragrant, about 5 minutes. Reduce the heat to low. Add the black beans, water, picante sauce, and the 1/4 teaspoon chipotle chiles. Cook until warmed through and the flavors begin to meld, about 10 minutes. Add more kosher salt and chipotle chiles, if necessary.

Creamy-Dreamy MASHED POTATOES

Serves 4

Mom taught us early on that a hint of onion juice transforms ordinary mashed potatoes into an unforgettably delicious offering. But our latest mashed-potato revelation came by way of our trusted recipe tester Molly Naughton. Molly sold us on the easy-to-handle, inexpensive potato ricer, and we will never, ever make mashed potatoes again without one. Pick up a ricer and follow our simple tips for the creamiest, dreamiest mashers ever. The addition of white Cheddar cheese adds to the richness and dimension of these spuds.

KOSHER SALT

2 *POUNDS YUKON GOLD POTATOES, PEELED AND CUT INTO 2-INCH PIECES*

3/4 *CUP HEAVY CREAM*

2 *TABLESPOONS UNSALTED BUTTER*

1/4 *CUP MILK, PLUS MORE AS NEEDED*

1 *CUP (2 OUNCES) GRATED WHITE CHEDDAR CHEESE*

2 *TEASPOONS GRATED ONION, PLUS MORE AS NEEDED (SEE NOTE)*

FRESHLY GROUND PEPPER

Put the potatoes in a large saucepan and cover with cold salted water. (We use 2 teaspoons kosher salt per quart of water.) Bring just to a boil over high heat. Reduce the heat to low, and simmer until the potatoes are tender when pierced with a fork, about 20 minutes. Drain the potatoes.

Meanwhile, heat the cream, butter, and the 1/4 cup milk in a small saucepan over medium heat or in the microwave. While the potatoes are still hot, press them through a potato ricer. Alternatively, mash with a potato masher or a large fork. Return the potatoes to the large saucepan and fold in the warm cream mixture, then the cheese and the 2 teaspoons onion. Season with kosher salt and pepper and more onion to taste, thinning with additional milk to the desired consistency.

Note: Using the finest grate on a handheld grater, grate the onion into a bowl. You can also put small pieces of onion through a garlic press. Sometimes the result will be onion juice and other times, it will have the consistency of onion purée. Either is suitable for this dish. The purée is a little stronger, so add with caution.

OUR SECRETS FOR THE CREAMIEST, DREAMIEST MASH:

1. Yukon Golds make THE best mashed potatoes.
2. Don't cut the potatoes too small or too big (2 inches is just perfect), or they will absorb too much water and become grainy.
3. Pieces should be uniform in size for even cooking.
4. Always salt the cooking water.
5. Never boil potatoes; simmer them gently.
6. Do not overcook the potatoes or their texture will be grainy, not smooth.
7. Always warm cream, butter, and milk before adding them to the mashed potatoes.

POTATO PANCAKES WITH SOUR CREAM AND CHIVES

Serves 4 to 6

Whether you call them latkes or potato pancakes, these perfectly crisp-on-the-outside, soft-on-the-inside potato cakes are unbeatable. (We like these a lot-ke!) We generally eat half the pancakes and freeze the rest, as they crisp up beautifully when reheated (see Do-Ahead below). They make a divine first course, layered with smoked salmon, crème fraîche, and dill sprigs. For a more traditional presentation, try them with a little applesauce and a dollop of sour cream.

2   MEDIUM RUSSET POTATOES (ABOUT 1^1/$_2$ POUNDS TOTAL), PEELED

1   SMALL YELLOW ONION

3   EGGS, LIGHTLY BEATEN

3   TABLESPOONS MATZO MEAL OR 1^1/$_2$ TABLESPOONS ALL-PURPOSE FLOUR (SEE NOTE)

1^1/$_2$ TEASPOONS KOSHER SALT

^{1}/$_4$ TEASPOON FRESHLY GROUND PEPPER

VEGETABLE OIL OR REFINED PEANUT OIL FOR FRYING

2   TABLESPOONS SOUR CREAM

1   TEASPOON CHOPPED FRESH CHIVES

Using a food processor fitted with the metal shredding blade, grate the potatoes. (Lay the potatoes horizontally in the feed tube to maximize the length of the potato strands.) Halve the onion and grate it directly onto the potatoes. Wrap the potatoes and onion in a clean dish towel and squeeze tightly, extracting as much moisture as possible. Transfer to a bowl. Add the eggs, matzo meal, kosher salt, and pepper and mix well.

Pour oil to a depth of about ^{1}/$_8$ inch into a large cast-iron or heavy nonstick skillet over medium-high heat. When the oil is hot (a piece of potato will sizzle when added), drop ^{1}/$_4$-cup spoonfuls of the potato mixture into the skillet; do not overcrowd the skillet. Using a fork, spread into thin 3-inch pancakes. Fry until crispy and golden brown, about 5 minutes per side. If the edges darken quickly, reduce the heat. To prevent excess absorption of oil, flip the pancakes only once. Transfer the pancakes to a paper towel–lined plate. Add more oil between batches as needed.

Just before serving, top each pancake with a dollop of sour cream and a sprinkling of chives.

Do-Ahead: To freeze potato pancakes, fry as directed and let cool to room temperature, then place in sealable plastic bags (lay flat in freezer) or transfer to an airtight container. To reheat, let the pancakes thaw at room temperature. Place a wire rack on a baking sheet. Place pancakes on the rack and bake at 375 degrees F until warm and crisp, about 15 minutes.

Note: Although flour can be substituted, we prefer matzo meal because it provides additional binding power. Matzo is sold in most supermarkets.

Matzo is a thin unleavened bread traditionally eaten during Jewish Passover holiday seders. Matzo meal is used in a variety of foods. It is also used to thicken soups and to bread foods before frying.

Killer ROASTED POTATOES

Serves 2

Nothin' better than taters with a crispy exterior and tender interior. These roasted potatoes are the only ones we've ever had that are extremely crispy and downright crunchy. You can actually hear your neighbor at the table "crunch" with every bite. Not right until they are ultra-crispy, these killer potatoes are a winner every time and are simple to prepare. Use russet potatoes—no other variety produces the same results.

1	TABLESPOON UNSALTED BUTTER
1	TABLESPOON VEGETABLE OIL
1	LARGE RUSSET POTATO (ABOUT 1 POUND), PEELED AND CUT INTO 1-INCH PIECES
1/4	TEASPOON KOSHER SALT
1/8	TEASPOON FRESHLY GROUND PEPPER

Preheat the oven to 450 degrees F.

Combine the butter and oil in an 8-inch square baking dish and place in the oven. When the butter has melted, remove the dish from the oven, add the potato, and toss in the butter-oil mixture until well coated. Add the kosher salt and pepper and toss to mix. Arrange the potato pieces in a single layer so they do not overlap. Roast, turning the potato pieces at least twice, until they are crispy and golden brown, about 1 hour and 15 minutes. Serve immediately. When potatoes cool, they lose their crispness.

Note: Crisp, crisp, crisp is our motto when it come to perfect roasted potatoes. The key is to avoid overcrowding the pan, which is why we call for such a large baking dish. If the potatoes are layered on top of each other, they will steam and get soggy instead of crisping.

Variation: Toss the potatoes with 1 tablespoon chopped fresh rosemary before roasting.

SWEET POTATOES WITH PRALINE TOPPING

Serves 8

Sara's husband, Erik, thought he hated sweet potatoes. On their first Thanksgiving together, he fell in love with this dish at first bite. To make this voluptuously creamy casserole, we combine pale tan-skinned sweet potatoes with darker red-skinned ones, also known as garnet yams. The pale-skinned potatoes are drier and have a lower sugar content than yams. A blend of the two strikes the perfect chord for us. Erik is now crushed that Thanksgiving only comes around once a year!

1 1/2	POUNDS MEDIUM TAN-SKINNED SWEET POTATOES (SEE NOTE)
1 1/2	POUNDS MEDIUM RED-SKINNED SWEET POTATOES (YAMS)
1	CAN (5 OUNCES) EVAPORATED MILK
4	TABLESPOONS UNSALTED BUTTER, CUT INTO PIECES
2	EGGS, LIGHTLY BEATEN
2	TABLESPOONS FIRMLY PACKED LIGHT BROWN SUGAR
1	TABLESPOON VANILLA EXTRACT
	CONTENTS OF 1 VANILLA BEAN (OPTIONAL) (SEE NOTE, PAGE 201)
1	TABLESPOON BRANDY
1/2	TEASPOON KOSHER SALT

TOPPING

1	CUP FIRMLY PACKED DARK BROWN SUGAR
1/3	CUP ALL-PURPOSE FLOUR
4	TABLESPOONS UNSALTED BUTTER, MELTED
1/3	CUP (1 OUNCE) CHOPPED PECANS
1/4	TEASPOON KOSHER SALT

Preheat the oven to 425 degrees F. Line a baking sheet with aluminum foil.

Rinse the sweet potatoes and prick in several places with a fork. Place on the prepared baking sheet and bake until very soft when pierced with a knife, 1 1/4 to 1 1/2 hours. Remove the sweet potatoes from the oven and reduce the oven to 325 degrees F.

When the sweet potatoes are cool enough to handle, peel them and put the pulp in the bowl of a food processor. Add the evaporated milk, butter, eggs, brown sugar, vanilla, contents of vanilla bean, if desired, brandy, and kosher salt. Process until smooth and creamy. Transfer the potato mixture to an 8-inch square glass baking dish.

TO MAKE THE TOPPING: Combine the brown sugar, flour, butter, pecans, and kosher salt in a medium bowl. Spoon the topping evenly over the potatoes. Bake until the topping is golden brown, 25 to 35 minutes.

Do-Ahead: The sweet potato purée can be made 1 day in advance and refrigerated. The topping can be prepared 3 to 5 days in advance and stored in a sealable plastic bag in the refrigerator. Spoon the topping over the potatoes just before baking.

Note: If you are unable to find tan-skinned sweet potatoes, reduce the brown sugar in the purée to 1 tablespoon and use a little less evaporated milk.

WILD RICE WITH DRIED CRANBERRIES, GREEN ONIONS, AND PECANS

Serves 4

This snazzy, earthy pilaf plots the tartness of dried cranberries against the nuttiness of pecans and the dense, rustic flavor of wild rice. It is rich, healthful fare, perfect for autumnal entertaining. For a lighter pilaf, combine wild rice with brown rice, or experiment with other grains, such as quinoa or bulgur. Grains are delicious tossed with dried fruits, toasted nuts, and a drizzle of high-quality oil. If there are leftovers, add them to a handful of dressed baby greens for a sumptuous salad.

1/3   CUP (1 OUNCE) PECANS

1   CUP WILD RICE

1   TABLESPOON HIGH-QUALITY EXTRA-VIRGIN OLIVE OIL OR
*   NUT OIL, SUCH AS PECAN, HAZELNUT, OR WALNUT*

1/3   HEAPING CUP DRIED CRANBERRIES

2   TABLESPOONS SLICED GREEN ONION, BOTH WHITE
*   AND GREEN PARTS*

*   KOSHER SALT AND FRESHLY GROUND PEPPER*

Preheat the oven to 350 degrees F.

Put the pecans on a baking sheet and roast until aromatic and lightly browned, about 10 minutes. (After 6 to 8 minutes, shake the pan and rotate, if necessary, to ensure even baking.) Let cool, then roughly chop the pecans or break into pieces by hand.

Cook the wild rice according to the package directions. (Most recipes do not call for salted water, but we recommend adding $1/2$ teaspoon kosher salt per 2 cups of water.) When the rice is tender, drain and transfer to a medium bowl. Add the olive oil, dried cranberries, pecans, and green onion. Season with kosher salt and pepper to taste.

COCONUT RICE

Serves 2

This is one of the creamiest, most luxurious side dishes we've tasted. Coconut milk adds a distinctive, slightly tropical flavor and complements the nuttiness of the rice. For this recipe, we always use basmati, a mellow, long-grain rice whose name translates as "queen of fragrance." Look for basmati in the Asian section of your supermarket or in an ethnic grocery store. We often top the rice with chopped jalapeños, fresh cilantro, or toasted shredded coconut. This dish is superb served alongside Pork Tenderloin with Mango Salsa and Blackberry Syrup (see page 141) or Grilled Tuna with Soy-Ginger Glaze and Pickled Cucumbers (see page 131).

$3/4$ CUP PLUS 2 TABLESPOONS WELL-STIRRED UNSWEETENED COCONUT MILK

$3/4$ CUP WATER

$1/2$ TEASPOON KOSHER SALT

$3/4$ CUP BASMATI RICE

$1/2$ TEASPOON FINELY CHOPPED LIME ZEST

2 TEASPOONS THINLY SLICED GREEN ONION, BOTH WHITE AND GREEN PARTS

Combine the $3/4$ cup coconut milk, the water, and kosher salt in a medium saucepan over high heat and bring to a boil. Stir in the rice. Reduce the heat to low, cover, and simmer until most of the liquid is absorbed, about 15 minutes. Remove the pan from the heat and let stand, covered, for 5 minutes. Stir in the 2 tablespoons coconut milk, the lime zest, and green onion.

COUSCOUS WITH MELTED LEEKS AND THYME

Serves 2

Bet ya' our melted leeks will melt your heart. The humble bulb's sweet, subtle onion flavor shines in this simple recipe, transforming couscous into something special. This dish is among our favorites for its ease of preparation and its versatility.

2   MEDIUM LEEKS, WHITE PART PLUS 1 INCH OF GREEN PART, CUT INTO $^1/_4$-INCH-WIDE PIECES (ABOUT 2 CUPS)

3/4   CUP COUSCOUS

1   CUP HOMEMADE CHICKEN STOCK (SEE PAGE 30), VEGETABLE STOCK (PAGE 31), OR CANNED VEGETABLE BROTH

1   TABLESPOON UNSALTED BUTTER

KOSHER SALT AND FRESHLY GROUND PEPPER

$^1/_2$ TEASPOON CHOPPED FRESH THYME, OR $^1/_8$ TEASPOON DRIED THYME

EXTRA-VIRGIN OLIVE OIL FOR DRIZZLING

Put the leeks in a bowl of water and swish them around with your hands to free them of excess sand or dirt.

Put the couscous in a medium bowl. Bring the stock to a boil in a small saucepan over high heat. Add the boiling stock to the couscous and stir until thoroughly moistened. Cover tightly with plastic wrap and let stand until the stock is absorbed, about 5 minutes.

Meanwhile, melt the butter in a large nonstick skillet over medium heat. Using a strainer or a slotted spoon, lift the leeks out of the water and transfer to the skillet. (A little extra water in the pan helps to keep the leeks from browning.) Season with kosher salt and pepper to taste and cook, stirring occasionally, until tender but not brown, 6 to 8 minutes.

Fluff the couscous with a fork. Stir in the leeks and thyme. Drizzle with olive oil and season with kosher salt and pepper to taste.

CHAPTER 9

BREAKFAST
&
BRUNCH

WITH THIS CHAPTER WE CHALLENGE YOU to think outside the traditional eggs-and-bacon box. Starting your day together by sharing a meal is a marital ritual we urge you to establish. We especially love easing into the weekends with our husbands, and there's no better eye-opener than a batch of our Mom's "Flyaway" Pancakes with Melted Berries (page 183), served with fresh-squeezed orange juice.

Why not make brunch an occasion to entertain? It's a great way to end the hectic work week on an upbeat note and entertain on a more relaxed scale. Keep it casual and invite some friends over in their pajamas. Whip up some Mary's Bloody Marys (page 229) and a Frittata with Sun-Dried Tomatoes, Cream Cheese, and Basil (page 177), and brunch becomes satisfaction guaranteed. Or, on a more formal note, impress with Eggs Benedict (page 175) or French Toast with Hot Buttered Rum–Maple Syrup (page 180).

No one is alone in his or her fear of entertaining "the in-laws" for the first time. For us, it didn't matter that we'd both been cooking our entire lives, we still felt overwhelmed at the prospect. It wasn't until we jumped in with both feet that we realized that while it's scary to cook for others, it's also quite easy to impress with fantastic food.

Years ago, Sara's in-laws took to our Unbelievable Banana Bread (page 188) with great affection, and as breakfast progressed, their hearts grew fonder for the meal (and for Sara!). On Mary and Jack's first anniversary, Mary made the Sausage and Cheddar Cheese Strata (page 178) for a celebratory brunch, and her in-laws are still raving about it years later.

EGGS BENEDICT

Serves 2

Wonderful for Valentine's Day, Easter, Mother's Day, or any time you want to treat your sweetheart to breakfast in bed, eggs Benedict is a good old-fashioned splurge we all deserve every now and then. When it comes to the egg-rich hollandaise sauce, there's no need for a double boiler. Our foolproof blender hollandaise ensures you won't end up with "scrambled eggs"—and tastes every bit as luxuriant as the traditional labor-intensive version. Better yet, we've broken down this recipe into 10 easy steps. Your eggs Benedict will be perfect every time.

4	*CANADIAN BACON SLICES*
2	*TEASPOONS KOSHER SALT*
2	*TABLESPOONS DISTILLED WHITE VINEGAR*

HOLLANDAISE SAUCE:

2	*EGG YOLKS AT ROOM TEMPERATURE*
2	*TEASPOONS HEAVY CREAM AT ROOM TEMPERATURE*
$^1/_4$	*TEASPOON KOSHER SALT, PLUS MORE AS NEEDED*
	DASH OF CAYENNE PEPPER
$^1/_2$	*CUP (1 STICK) PLUS 2 TABLESPOONS UNSALTED BUTTER, MELTED AND HEATED UNTIL BUBBLING BUT NOT BROWN (SEE NOTE)*
2	*TEASPOONS FRESH LEMON JUICE AT ROOM TEMPERATURE*
1	*TEASPOON WHITE WINE VINEGAR*
	SUGAR
2	*ENGLISH MUFFINS*
4	*EGGS*
	FRESHLY GROUND PEPPER
	CHOPPED FRESH TARRAGON OR DILL FOR GARNISHING (OPTIONAL)

Preheat the oven to 200 degrees F.

1) Put the Canadian bacon in a large nonstick skillet. Set over a burner but do not turn on the burner. Put 2 ovenproof plates in the oven to warm.

2) Fill a medium nonstick skillet nearly to the rim with water. Add the kosher salt and vinegar and bring to a simmer over high heat. Alternatively, fill an egg poacher with water and season with salt.

3) *TO MAKE THE HOLLANDAISE SAUCE:* Put the egg yolks, cream, the $^1/_4$ teaspoon kosher salt, and cayenne in a blender. Blend on high speed until smooth and frothy, 2 to 3 seconds. With the blender still on high speed, add the hot butter in a thin, steady stream, then add the lemon juice and white wine vinegar. Season with kosher salt to taste and a generous pinch of sugar. Transfer the sauce to a microwave-safe cup or bowl. Alternatively, put the sauce in the top pan of a double boiler or in a bowl set over a saucepan of simmering water.

CONTINUED

4) Cut the English muffins in half and lightly toast them.

5) Carefully break an egg into a cup and slide it into the simmering water, or into the cups of an egg poacher. Repeat with the remaining eggs. (Arrange the eggs in a clockwise pattern in the skillet so you will know which one you put in first. Remove the eggs in the same order.) Remove the skillet from the heat and cook until the yolks are medium-firm, 3 to 4 minutes.

6) Meanwhile, heat the Canadian bacon over high heat until slightly crisp, about 1 minute.

7) Place 2 English muffin halves on each of 2 warmed plates.

8) Top each muffin half with a slice of Canadian bacon.

9) Using a slotted spoon, carefully lift out each egg and drain over the skillet. Blot the eggs lightly with a paper towel. Gently place 1 egg on top of each Canadian bacon slice.

10) If not keeping the hollandaise sauce warm in a double boiler, warm it in the microwave for about 10 seconds and pour generously on top of the eggs and around the English muffins. Season with pepper to taste and garnish with tarragon, if desired. Serve immediately.

Note: We heat the butter in a glass measuring cup in the microwave until it begins to boil. In order for the egg yolks to thicken the sauce, the butter must be very hot and the egg yolks, cream, and lemon juice must be at room temperature when you begin blending.

Do-Ahead: Believe it or not, hollandaise sauce can be made 1 day in advance and refrigerated. To reheat the sauce, warm it in the microwave in 10-second increments until warm but not hot. (If the sauce gets too hot, it will separate.) Alternatively, put the sauce in the top pan of a double boiler or in a bowl set over a saucepan of simmering water.

When entertaining, the eggs can be cooked several hours in advance. After poaching the eggs, transfer them to a bowl of ice water. Store them in the ice water in the refrigerator until ready to serve. Reheat the eggs by lowering them into a pan of simmering water for about 45 seconds. Drain and serve as directed.

Variation: Substitute smoked salmon for the Canadian bacon and top with blanched asparagus tips, then with the eggs.

FRITTATA WITH SUN-DRIED TOMATOES, CREAM CHEESE, AND BASIL

Serves 2

It's the classic Saturday-morning dilemma . . . hit the snooze button and sleep in late, or get up early and make a killer breakfast? Problem solved. You can whip up this creamy frittata in about 10 minutes. Start the coffee before you begin, pop some bread in the toaster while the frittata is under the broiler and, within minutes, you'll have a perfectly delicious breakfast for you and the one you love. Sara's husband, Erik, often says, "I'll love you a lotta if you'll make that frittata."

1/2	TABLESPOON BUTTER
1/2	SMALL YELLOW ONION (ABOUT 1/2 CUP)
	PINCH OF KOSHER SALT, PLUS 1/4 TEASPOON
	FRESHLY GROUND PEPPER
4	EGGS
2	TABLESPOONS GRATED PARMESAN CHEESE, PREFERABLY PARMIGIANO-REGGIANO
1/3	CUP SUN-DRIED TOMATOES PACKED IN OIL, DRAINED AND ROUGHLY CHOPPED
2	TABLESPOONS THINLY SLICED FRESH BASIL
1	OUNCE CREAM CHEESE, CRUMBLED
	TABASCO SAUCE FOR SERVING

Set the rack about 8 inches from the top of the oven and preheat the broiler.

Melt the butter in an 8-inch ovenproof non-stick skillet over medium-high heat. Add the onion and season with the pinch of kosher salt and pepper to taste. Cook, stirring occasionally, until the onion is soft, about 5 minutes.

Whisk together the eggs, Parmesan cheese, 1/4 teaspoon kosher salt, and pepper to taste in a medium bowl. Add the sun-dried tomatoes and basil, reserving a bit of each for garnishing. Pour the egg mixture into the skillet and stir gently to combine with the onion. Reduce the heat to medium-low. Scatter the cream cheese on top. Cook until the eggs are set on the bottom, about 5 minutes. While the eggs are cooking, lift an edge of the frittata with a spatula and let the uncooked eggs flow underneath. Repeat in a few places.

When the eggs are almost cooked, put the skillet under the broiler. Broil until the frittata is lightly browned and the eggs are set in the center, about 1 minute. Garnish with the reserved sun-dried tomatoes and basil. Season with Tabasco sauce to taste.

SAUSAGE AND CHEDDAR CHEESE STRATA

Serves 8 to 10

One of our favorite weekend get-togethers that we ever hosted was a "Breakfast for Dinner" party, where everyone brought his or her favorite breakfast casserole. We all shared and tasted numerous versions—some were prepared with Jiffy cornbread mix, others featured grits and white bread. Some came topped with Swiss cheese, others with Cheddar, and even a few were made with Kraft singles! Our friend Lucy Bowen Taylor brought the winning recipe, which got rave reviews for its creamy, soufflélike texture. Our adaptation of Lucy's strata has become a staple in our households. Make this for Saturday brunch and freeze the leftovers in squares for weekday breakfasts.

1 1/2	POUNDS GROUND BREAKFAST SAUSAGE (12 OUNCES HOT, 12 OUNCES REGULAR)
4	EGGS, BEATEN
2 1/2	CUPS HALF-AND-HALF
1	TEASPOON DRIED SAGE
3/4	TEASPOON KOSHER SALT
1/4	TEASPOON FRESHLY GROUND PEPPER
6	POTATO BREAD OR OTHER SOFT WHITE BREAD SLICES, CRUSTS REMOVED
2	CUPS (6 OUNCES) GRATED EXTRA-SHARP CHEDDAR CHEESE
2	TABLESPOONS CHOPPED FRESH CHIVES, FLAT-LEAF PARSLEY, OR GREEN ONION, BOTH WHITE AND GREEN PARTS

Preheat the oven to 350 degrees F. Butter a 9-by-13-by-2-inch baking dish.

Heat a large skillet over medium-high heat. Put the sausage in the skillet and cook, stirring occasionally, until it is thoroughly browned, 5 to 7 minutes. Using a slotted spoon, transfer the sausage to a paper towel–lined plate to drain.

Whisk together the eggs, half-and-half, sage, kosher salt, and pepper in a medium bowl. Layer the bread in the prepared baking dish and top with the sausage. Pour the egg mixture over the sausage and top with the cheese. Bake until the strata is set in the middle, about 30 minutes. Do not overcook. Let cool for 15 to 20 minutes. Garnish with the chives just before serving.

FRENCH TOAST WITH HOT BUTTERED RUM–MAPLE SYRUP

Serves 2

We consider ourselves French toast purists, wanting nothing but warm maple syrup poured over the soufflélike toast. Our husbands occupy an opposing camp. They adore this dish with sliced bananas warmed in the syrup. If you side with the guys, you may want to try the bananas or even raisins or blueberries. We've added a splash of rum to this recipe for an extra burst of flavor. If serving a brunch crowd, cook the French toast in batches, cover with aluminum foil, and keep warm in a 200-degree F oven.

$^1/_2$	CUP HALF-AND-HALF
2	EGGS
1	TABLESPOON GRANULATED SUGAR
2	TEASPOONS VANILLA EXTRACT
$^1/_4$	TEASPOON, PLUS A PINCH OF KOSHER SALT
$^1/_8$	TEASPOON GROUND CINNAMON
2	TABLESPOONS UNSALTED BUTTER
4	CHALLAH BREAD SLICES (1 INCH THICK)
$^1/_3$	CUP MAPLE SYRUP
1	TABLESPOON LIGHT RUM
	POWDERED SUGAR FOR DUSTING

Whisk together the half-and-half, eggs, granulated sugar, vanilla, the $^1/_4$ teaspoon kosher salt, and the cinnamon in a wide, shallow bowl. Heat a large nonstick skillet over medium heat and melt 1 tablespoon of the butter. Dip the bread in the egg mixture, coating both sides. Arrange the bread in the skillet and cook until golden brown, 1 to 2 minutes on each side. Transfer 2 pieces of toast to each of 2 warmed plates.

Remove the skillet from the heat and combine the maple syrup, the remaining 1 tablespoon butter, the rum, and a pinch of kosher salt in the pan. Swirl until the butter melts. Pour over the French toast, dust with powdered sugar, and serve immediately.

PEANUT BUTTER TOAST WITH ICY-COLD BANANA MILK

Serves 2

We discovered banana milk after Mary's son Jackson was born. In a desperate attempt to get him to drink milk, Mary dropped a freckled banana in the blender with some whole milk, strained it into a bottle, and Jackson guzzled every last drop. This wholesome milk has been a favorite breakfast beverage ever since—and not just for Jackson! Pair it with toast slathered with warm peanut butter and drizzled with honey for a "stick-to-your-ribs" breakfast.

2	*CHALLAH OR OTHER SOFT WHITE BREAD SLICES (1 INCH THICK)*
2	*CUPS MILK*
2	*SMALL RIPE BANANAS*
1/4	*CUP MAPLE SYRUP*
2	*TEASPOONS VANILLA EXTRACT*
3	*TABLESPOONS CREAMY PEANUT BUTTER*
	HONEY FOR DRIZZLING
	POWDERED SUGAR FOR DUSTING
	PINCH OF NUTMEG (OPTIONAL)

Toast the bread.

Combine the milk, bananas, maple syrup, vanilla, and a handful of ice cubes in a blender. Blend until smooth and frothy, about 1 minute.

Put the peanut butter in a small bowl or ramekin and heat in the microwave until warm, about 10 seconds. Spread the peanut butter on the toast and drizzle with honey. Dust with powdered sugar.

Pour the banana milk into the glasses. Sprinkle with nutmeg, if desired.

Mom's "Flyaway" PANCAKES WITH MELTED BERRIES

Serves 2 to 4

We luuv Mom's light and airy pancakes. This recipe conjures up memories of long, lazy breakfasts in the country. Dad would send us out to the chicken coop for some fresh eggs, en route to the raspberry patch, to gather the ingredients for this recipe. Our recollections of those feisty chickens, the raspberries' briery bushes, and Mom's cloudlike pancakes will never "fly away." We continue her pancake-making tradition and assure you, these are worth the effort. The batter can be transformed into delicious waffles or made into extra special pancakes by pouring it into decorative metal cookie cutters. Nothing like surprising your loved one with a stack of hearts! If you're short on time, use your favorite prepackaged mix, and top the pancakes with our syrupy melted berries. (Be sure to check the dates on your baking soda and baking powder. If they have expired, these pancakes will not "fly away".)

MELTED BERRIES:

1	CUP FRESH OR FROZEN BLUEBERRIES
1	CUP FRESH OR FROZEN RASPBERRIES
1/4	CUP SUGAR, PLUS MORE AS NEEDED
1	TABLESPOON UNSALTED BUTTER
	PINCH OF KOSHER SALT
	FRESH LEMON JUICE AS NEEDED

PANCAKES

1 1/4	CUPS ALL-PURPOSE FLOUR
2	TEASPOONS GRANULATED SUGAR
1 1/2	TEASPOONS BAKING POWDER
1 1/2	TEASPOONS KOSHER SALT
2	EGGS
1	CUP BUTTERMILK
1/2	CUP SOUR CREAM
1	TEASPOON BAKING SODA
	UNSALTED BUTTER, MELTED
	POWDERED SUGAR FOR DUSTING (OPTIONAL)

TO MAKE THE MELTED BERRIES: Combine the blueberries, raspberries, the 1/4 cup sugar, the butter, and kosher salt in a small saucepan over low heat. Cook until the berries soften and render their juices, 2 to 3 minutes if fresh, 3 to 4 minutes if frozen. Add more sugar and a squeeze of lemon juice if necessary. Remove from the heat.

TO MAKE THE PANCAKES: Stir together the flour, granulated sugar, baking powder, and kosher salt in a small bowl. Whisk the eggs in a medium bowl, then add the buttermilk, sour cream, and baking soda. Add the flour mixture and whisk until well incorporated. Stir in the 1 tablespoon of melted butter.

Spray a large nonstick skillet with vegetable-oil cooking spray and set over medium heat, or cook a dollop of butter over medium heat until the butter begins to bubble but not brown. Spoon

CONTINUED

¹/₄ cup batter into the skillet for each pancake, and cook until small bubbles begin to form on top, 2 to 3 minutes. You may need to reduce the heat slightly at this point. Using a spatula, flip the pancakes and cook until golden brown and puffy, 2 to 3 minutes. Remove from the pan and stack the pancakes, drizzling melted butter between each pancake. Dust with powdered sugar, if desired, and serve with the melted berries.

Note: If you have leftover batter, cover and refrigerate it for up to 1 day. The pancakes will be tasty, but they will not rise as high.

Quick-and-Easy DROP BISCUITS

Makes 6 biscuits

The first time we made these biscuits, we stood over the stove and ate the entire batch. No butter, no jam, nothing! Try them—or our Cheddar cheese–dill version (see Variation)—and you just might find yourself doing the same. These biscuits are quick and easy, requiring no rolling pin or fancy cutters.

1   CUP PLUS 2 TABLESPOONS ALL-PURPOSE FLOUR
     (SEE NOTE)

1 1/2 TEASPOONS BAKING POWDER

1 1/2 TEASPOONS SUGAR

3/4 TEASPOON KOSHER SALT

1   CUP CHILLED HEAVY CREAM, PLUS MORE
     AS NEEDED

Position the rack in the center of the oven and preheat to 400 degrees F.

Stir together the flour (to measure flour accurately, spoon it into your measuring cup and level with a knife), baking powder, sugar, and kosher salt in a large bowl. Add the 1 cup cream and stir just until a dough forms. The dough should be slightly sticky. If it seems dry, add a little more cream. Drop 1/4 cup of the batter onto a baking sheet for each biscuit, spacing them about 1 inch apart. Bake until the biscuits are pale golden on the top and golden brown on the bottom, 18 to 20 minutes. Let cool for 5 minutes before serving.

Variation: Cheddar cheese–dill biscuits: Add 3/4 cup (1 1/2 ounces) Cheddar cheese, 1/2 teaspoon dried dill weed, and an additional 2 tablespoons all-purpose flour (1 1/4 cups total) to the batter.

Do-Ahead: These biscuits freeze beautifully. Drop the biscuit dough onto a baking sheet as directed but do not bake. Instead, place the baking sheet in the freezer, then transfer the frozen biscuits to a sealable plastic bag. When ready to bake, preheat the oven to 400 degrees F. To prevent the bottoms of the biscuits from browning, put the frozen biscuits on a baking sheet stacked atop another sheet, place in the top third of the oven, and bake for 25 to 30 minutes.

Note: For exceptionally light, tender biscuits, we like to use a low-protein flour like most of those produced in the South. Our favorite is White Lily. You can purchase this flour at www.whitelily.com or by calling (800) 264-5459.

YOGURT-GRANOLA PARFAITS

Serves 2

Bed-and-breakfast fare comes home when you greet the new day with this energy-packed parfait. Indulge your loved one or your guests by serving the parfait on a flower-laden tray with a tumbler of freshly squeezed O.J.

1	*RIPE BANANA*
1	*CUP VANILLA YOGURT*
1/4	*TEASPOON VANILLA EXTRACT*
1 1/2	*CUPS GRANOLA*
8	*STRAWBERRIES, HULLED AND SLICED,* *PLUS 2 WHOLE STRAWBERRIES*

Coarsely mash the banana in a small bowl with a fork. Add the yogurt and vanilla and stir to combine. Put 1/2 cup granola in each of 2 parfait or red wineglasses. Top each with a heaping 1/4 cup yogurt mixture and 2 sliced strawberries. Repeat the layering process by adding 1/4 cup granola followed by a heaping 1/4 cup yogurt mixture and 2 sliced strawberries. Garnish each parfait with 1 whole strawberry.

Unbelievable BANANA BREAD

Makes 2 loaves

When it comes to sweet treats, we always prepare extra—some for us and the rest to share with our neighbors or friends. This recipe makes 2 loaves. Should you decide the bread is just too good to part with, slice the second loaf, wrap the slices individually in plastic wrap, and freeze. Pull a thick slice straight from the freezer, pop it in the toaster, and slather with butter for breakfast. Absolute heaven.

1 1/2 CUPS (5 OUNCES) WALNUTS

2 1/4 CUPS ALL-PURPOSE FLOUR

1 TEASPOON KOSHER SALT

1/2 TEASPOON GROUND CINNAMON

3/4 CUP VEGETABLE OIL

2 1/4 CUPS SUGAR

3 EGGS, LIGHTLY BEATEN

1 1/2 TEASPOONS VANILLA EXTRACT

1 1/2 TEASPOONS BAKING SODA

1/2 CUP BUTTERMILK

2 CUPS VERY RIPE MASHED BANANAS (ABOUT 5 SMALL BANANAS)

Position the rack in the center of the oven and preheat to 350 degrees F.

Put the walnuts on a baking sheet and roast until aromatic and lightly browned, 12 to 15 minutes. After 6 to 8 minutes, shake the pan and rotate if necessary to ensure even browning. When broken in half, the interior of the walnuts should be golden. Let cool, then roughly chop the walnuts or break into pieces by hand. Keep the oven set at 350 degrees F.

Spray two 9-by-3-inch loaf pans with vegetable-oil cooking spray.

Stir together the flour, kosher salt, and cinnamon in a medium bowl. Set aside.

Combine the oil and sugar in the bowl of a stand mixer fitted with the paddle attachment. Alternatively, use a hand mixer. Beat on low

speed, until combined. Add the eggs and vanilla and beat until incorporated, about 1 minute.

Stir the baking soda into the buttermilk in a small bowl. Add one third of the dry ingredients to the mixer, followed by half of the buttermilk, and mix on low speed until barely combined, 10 to 15 seconds. Repeat. Scrape down the sides and mix in the remaining dry ingredients. Add the mashed bananas and walnuts and mix until just incorporated. Do not overmix.

Pour the batter into the prepared pans. Bake until the bread is golden brown and a toothpick inserted into the center comes out clean, about 1 hour. Transfer the pans to wire racks and let cool for 5 minutes, then remove the loaves from the pans and let cool on the racks for at least 10 minutes before serving.

Rise-and-Shine SMOOTHIE

Serves 2

After writing two books on smoothies and testing literally thousands of them, we can say from experience that this is the No. 1 breakfast smoothie. Chock-full of vitamin C, potassium, and calcium, it's sure to get the morning off to a great start for you and your loved one. Feel free to substitute any juice, fruit, or yogurt in the proportions listed below. So "rise and shine, and give yourself some glory, glory."

$^1/_2$ CUP FRESH ORANGE JUICE

1 CUP QUARTERED FROZEN STRAWBERRIES (8 TO 10 STRAWBERRIES) (SEE NOTE)

1 FROZEN RIPE BANANA, SLICED (SEE NOTE)

1 CUP VANILLA YOGURT

Combine the orange juice, strawberries, banana, and yogurt in a blender. Blend on medium speed until smooth. Pour into glasses and serve.

Note: For convenience, freeze several ripe bananas at a time. Peel them, put in a sealable plastic bag, and freeze for up to 2 weeks. When strawberries are in season, rinse, dry, hull, and quarter the berries, then freeze in a sealable plastic bag for up to 2 weeks. When fresh berries are not in season, purchased frozen strawberries are the best bet.

WE'RE SUCKERS FOR SWEET ENDINGS, so in this chapter, we offer you a dessert for every occasion. And, because there's nothing quite like plying the object of your desire with sugar-riddled kisses, we've come up with plenty of treats created expressly for you and your honey to enjoy.

Bake your way into your partner's heart with Strawberry Shortcakes d'Amour (page 197) or Peanut Butter Pie Sealed with Kisses (page 202). Send cupid's arrow soaring with "Hidden-Treasure" Bread Pudding (page 219), filled with molten chocolate, or tease those taste buds with Puckery Lemon Parfaits with Summer Berries (page 217). Nibbled as an afternoon delight or savored as the finale to a romantic dinner, our Nectarine Tarts for Two (page 207) are too good to be true! You won't believe how easy they are to make.

Our classic, comforting treats are inspired by our childhood sweet-tooth fantasies, among them our Harvest Apple Crisp (page 208), prepared every Sunday night during fall and winter, and our Daddy's Oatmeal Cookies (page 211), affectionately referred to as "oaties." We honestly think that Sara's husband finally proposed after 10 years of dating because she fed him a new version of cheesecake, now known as our Very Vanilla Cheesecake (page 200). And, believe it or not, we've even been offered a month-long stay at our friend's fabulous Sonoma country home in exchange for just one cheesecake left in the fridge when we leave.

When entertaining, we often turn to our Spiced Carrot Cake with Fluffy Cream Cheese Icing (page 193), which always earns applause. Or, we make a grand entrance with dinner's finale. Our Shhh, Don't Tell—Chocolate Fudge Birthday Cake (page 195) gets a standing ovation every time, birthday or not.

SPICED CARROT CAKE WITH *Fluffy* CREAM CHEESE ICING

Serves 8 to 10

Sara and Erik love this cake sooo much that they chose it for their wedding cake! The secret to this supermoist cake is the carrot purée. Believe it or not, a couple of jars of baby food (yes, baby food!) will save you the trouble of puréeing carrots. For a simple, stylish presentation, sprinkle the cake and the accompanying platter with vibrant orange and yellow rose petals.

CARROT CAKE

3	CUPS ALL-PURPOSE FLOUR
2 3/4	CUPS GRANULATED SUGAR
1	TABLESPOON BAKING SODA
2	TEASPOONS GROUND CINNAMON
2	TEASPOONS KOSHER SALT
4	EGGS, LIGHTLY BEATEN
1 1/2	CUPS CORN OIL
2	TEASPOONS VANILLA EXTRACT
1 1/2	CUPS GRATED CARROT, ABOUT 1 LARGE CARROT
2	JARS (4 OUNCES EACH) CARROT PURÉE (BABY FOOD)
1	CUP SHREDDED SWEETENED COCONUT

CREAM CHEESE ICING

3 1/2	CUPS POWDERED SUGAR
12	OUNCES CREAM CHEESE AT ROOM TEMPERATURE
1/2	CUP (1 STICK) UNSALTED BUTTER AT ROOM TEMPERATURE
2	TEASPOONS VANILLA EXTRACT
1/4	TEASPOON KOSHER SALT

EDIBLE FLOWER PETALS FOR DECORATING (OPTIONAL)

Position the rack in the center of the oven and preheat to 350 degrees F. Spray two 9-inch cake pans with vegetable-oil cooking spray.

TO MAKE THE CAKE: Sift together the flour, granulated sugar, baking soda, cinnamon, and kosher salt into the bowl of a stand mixer fitted with the paddle attachment. In a separate bowl, whisk together the eggs, oil, and vanilla and add to the dry ingredients. Beat on low speed for about 1 minute. Add the grated carrot, carrot purée, and coconut and mix until just incorporated.

Pour the batter into the prepared pans and bake until a knife inserted into the center of the cakes comes out clean, 40 to 50 minutes. Do not overcook. Transfer the pans to a wire rack and let cool completely.

TO MAKE THE ICING: Sift the powdered sugar into a medium bowl and set aside. In the bowl of a stand mixer fitted with the paddle attachment, beat together at medium speed the cream cheese, butter, vanilla, and kosher salt, scraping down the sides of the bowl at least once, until the mixture is

CONTINUED

smooth, with no lumps, 1 to 2 minutes. Slowly add the powdered sugar and beat until light, fluffy, and well blended, scraping down the sides of the bowl halfway through.

To assemble, place 1 cake, flat-side up, on a platter. Spread part of the icing over the top of the cake. Top with the second cake, flat-side up, and spread the remaining icing over the top and sides of the cake. Just before serving, decorate with edible flower petals, if desired.

Do-Ahead: The cake can be baked up to 2 days in advance. Wrap the unfrosted cake tightly with plastic wrap and store at room temperature. Make the icing up to 1 week in advance, cover, and refrigerate; bring to room temperature before frosting the cake. The cake can be frosted 1 day before serving and refrigerated in a covered container. Bring the cake to room temperature before serving.

Shhh, Don't Tell—CHOCOLATE
FUDGE BIRTHDAY CAKE!

Serves 8 to 10

During most of our years in the culinary world, we scoffed at the idea of a boxed cake. We've always made our cakes from scratch. Until now. When creating recipes for this book, we decided to test a boxed cake, comparing it with our own favorite homemade cake. We held a tasting at our friend Carolyn Edwards's birthday party for 12: Believe it or not, this boxed-cake recipe earned unanimous approval over the homemade, time-consuming recipe we've been making for years! We were shocked but excited. The cake's winning feature? Unbelievable moistness. It's fine to use a boxed cake, but please no shortcuts on the icing. Fortunately, this unctuous icing is a cinch to prepare. Red garnishes are magnificent against this cake. Think fresh raspberries, cherries, or red rose petals.

CAKE

1	BOX DEVIL'S FOOD CAKE MIX, SUCH AS DUNCAN HINES
1	CUP WATER
3	EGGS
$^1/_3$	CUP CORN OIL
$^1/_3$	CUP SOUR CREAM
2	TEASPOONS VANILLA EXTRACT
$^1/_2$	TEASPOON KOSHER SALT
1	CUP SEMISWEET CHOCOLATE CHIPS

ICING

1	12-OUNCE BAG (2 CUPS) SEMISWEET CHOCOLATE CHIPS
2	CUPS SUGAR
$^2/_3$	CUP MILK
1	CUP (2 STICKS) UNSALTED BUTTER, CUT INTO PIECES
$^1/_4$	TEASPOON KOSHER SALT
1	TEASPOON VANILLA EXTRACT

Position the rack in the center of the oven and preheat to 350 degrees F. Butter 3 nonstick 8-inch cake pans with 1½-inch sides.

TO MAKE THE CAKE: Combine the cake mix, water, eggs, oil, sour cream, vanilla, and kosher salt in the bowl of a stand mixer fitted with the paddle attachment. Alternatively, use an electric hand mixer. Beat on low speed until the mixture is well blended. Increase the speed to medium if using a stand mixer (high for a hand mixer) and beat for 2 minutes. Stir in the chocolate chips.

Pour the batter into the prepared pans and bake until a knife inserted into the center of the cakes comes out clean, about 25 minutes. Transfer the pans to wire racks and let cool for 10 to 15 minutes. Remove the cakes from the pans and let cool completely on the racks.

TO MAKE THE ICING: Put the chocolate chips in the metal bowl of a stand mixer fitted with the whisk attachment. Alternatively, use an electric hand mixer. Combine the sugar, milk, butter, and kosher salt in a medium saucepan over high heat

CONTINUED

and bring to a boil, stirring occasionally. Let boil vigorously for exactly 1 minute. Pour the hot sugar mixture over the chocolate. Add the vanilla. Beat on medium speed until the mixture begins to thicken to a spreadable consistency, 10 to 15 minutes.

To assemble, place 1 cake, flat-side up, on a platter. Spread one third of the icing (about 3/4 cup) over the top of the cake. Top with the second cake, flat-side up, and spread one third of the icing (about $^3/_4$ cup) over the top. Top with the third cake, flat-side up, and spread a thin layer of the remaining icing over the top and sides of the cake.

Note: If your kitchen is warm, refrigerate the cake for about 15 minutes after frosting the second layer. This will prevent the cake from sliding.

STRAWBERRY SHORTCAKES *d'Amour*

Serves 2

We simply adore Strawberry Shortcakes d'Amour. Luscious red berries enveloped in their sweet juices, topped with snow-white clouds of whipped cream, all of it sandwiched between a heart-shaped biscuit and dusted with powdered sugar. Seduced? Prepare this recipe only when strawberries are perfectly ripe and rosy red, and the mood at home is right. The recipe is tailored to serve 2, but the biscuit recipe yields 6 shortcakes. We suggest freezing the additional unbaked shortcakes, precut into hearts. Save them for another red-hot occasion, or pull them out of the freezer and bake them fresh for your loved one's breakfast, topped with preserves—a sure-fire bet for preserving the sweetness in any marriage!

SHORTCAKES

3   CUPS CAKE FLOUR, PLUS MORE AS NEEDED

1/4   CUP PLUS 1 TABLESPOON, PLUS 2 TEASPOONS GRANULATED SUGAR

2 1/2 TEASPOONS BAKING POWDER

1   TEASPOON KOSHER SALT

6   TABLESPOONS COLD UNSALTED BUTTER, CUT INTO PIECES

1 1/2 CUPS HEAVY CREAM

1   EGG LIGHTLY BEATEN WITH 1 TABLESPOON WATER

STRAWBERRIES

2   CUPS HULLED AND QUARTERED STRAWBERRIES

1   TABLESPOON RASPBERRY PRESERVES

2   TEASPOONS GRANULATED SUGAR

1/4   TEASPOON FRESH LEMON JUICE

WHIPPED CREAM

1/3   CUP COLD HEAVY CREAM

1   TABLESPOON SOUR CREAM

1 1/2 TEASPOONS GRANULATED SUGAR

1/4   TEASPOON VANILLA EXTRACT

POWDERED SUGAR FOR DUSTING

6 MINT SPRIGS

Position the rack in the center of the oven and preheat to 400 degrees F. Spray a baking sheet with vegetable-oil cooking spray.

TO MAKE THE SHORTCAKES: Sift together the flour, the 1/4 cup plus 1 tablespoon granulated sugar, the baking powder, and kosher salt in a medium bowl. Transfer to the bowl of a food processor fitted with the steel blade. Add the butter and pulse 3 or 4 times at 2-second intervals until the dough resembles coarse meal. Add the cream and process until the dough begins to come together, a few seconds more. It will still be crumbly at this point. Do not overwork or the shortcakes will be tough.

CONTINUED

Transfer the dough to a well-floured work surface. If the dough is sticky, sprinkle it with more flour. Using a lightly floured rolling pin, roll out the dough into a rectangle about 12 inches long. Fold the left end to the middle and the right end up over the left end to form 3 layers. Roll out the dough to $^3/_4$-inch thickness. Using a 3-inch-wide heart-shaped cutter, cut into 3 individual cakes. Gather the scraps, roll out the remaining dough, and cut out 3 more hearts.

Place the shortcakes at least 2 inches apart on the prepared baking sheet. Brush the tops lightly with the beaten egg mixture and sprinkle with the 2 teaspoons granulated sugar. Bake until the shortcakes are light golden brown, 15 to 20 minutes.

MEANWHILE, PREPARE THE STRAWBERRIES: Stir together the strawberries, raspberry preserves, granulated sugar, and lemon juice in a medium bowl. Put 1 cup of the mixture in a small bowl and mash with a fork or potato masher. Add to the strawberry mixture and set aside.

TO MAKE THE WHIPPED CREAM: **Combine the** heavy cream, sour cream, granulated sugar, and vanilla in the bowl of a stand mixer fitted with the whisk attachment. Beat on high speed until soft peaks form, about 1 minute. The cream should slowly fall over forward when lifted with a whisk. Alternatively, use an electric hand mixer.

To serve, using a serrated knife, cut 2 short-cakes in half horizontally and place the bottom halves on each of 2 plates. Top with the strawberries, dividing evenly. Add a dollop of whipped cream and top with the remaining shortcake halves. Dust with powdered sugar and garnish with the mint sprigs.

Do-Ahead: These shortcakes freeze beautifully. Freeze the uncooked shortcakes on a baking sheet as directed but do not bake. Instead, place the baking sheet in the freezer, then transfer the frozen cakes to a sealable plastic bag. When ready to bake, preheat the oven to 400 degrees F and bake for 25 to 30 minutes. To prevent the bottom of the cakes from browning, put the frozen short-cakes on a baking sheet stacked atop another sheet, place in the top third of the oven, and bake for 15 to 20 minutes.

When we entertain, we whip the cream before our guests arrive, refrigerate it, and whisk to the desired consistency just before serving. We also like to warm the shortcakes just before serving.

Very VANILLA CHEESECAKE

Serves 10 to 12

We're vanilla addicts and have always loved cheesecake. We created this VERY vanilla cheesecake to indulge both passions. The ethereal top layer, made from sour cream, sugar, and vanilla, is what sets this cheesecake apart from all the others. It lightens the rich cream cheese base, adding an unforgettable velvety finish. Our friend John McCulloch tells us that he literally dreams about this dessert! Now you can deliver the fantasy, too. If you don't have vanilla beans on hand, increase the amount of vanilla extract by $1/2$ teaspoon for both the filling and the topping.

CRUST

1 $1/4$ CUPS GRAHAM CRACKER CRUMBS (FROM TEN 5-BY-$2^1/2$-INCH GRAHAM CRACKERS)

$1/3$ CUP SUGAR

4 TABLESPOONS UNSALTED BUTTER, MELTED AND COOLED SLIGHTLY

PINCH OF KOSHER SALT

FILLING

4 EGGS AT ROOM TEMPERATURE, LIGHTLY BEATEN

1 $1/2$ TEASPOONS VANILLA EXTRACT

CONTENTS OF $1/2$ VANILLA BEAN (SEE NOTE)

$1/2$ TEASPOON KOSHER SALT

3 PACKAGES (8 OUNCES EACH) CREAM CHEESE AT ROOM TEMPERATURE

1 CUP SUGAR

TOPPING:

3 CUPS SOUR CREAM

$1/2$ CUP SUGAR

1 TEASPOON VANILLA EXTRACT

CONTENTS OF $1/2$ VANILLA BEAN (OPTIONAL) (SEE NOTE)

$1/4$ TEASPOON KOSHER SALT

Position the rack in the center of the oven and preheat the oven to 350 degrees F. Lightly spray a 9-inch springform pan with vegetable-oil cooking spray.

TO MAKE THE CRUST: Mix the graham cracker crumbs, sugar, butter, and kosher salt in a small bowl. Using your fingers, press the mixture evenly into the bottom and one third of the way up the sides of the prepared pan. Bake for 10 minutes. Transfer the pan to a wire rack and let cool, about 15 minutes. Reduce the oven to 325 degrees F.

TO MAKE THE FILLING: Combine the eggs, vanilla extract, contents of $1/2$ vanilla bean, and kosher salt in a small bowl. Set aside.

In the bowl of a stand mixer fitted with the paddle attachment, beat the cream cheese on low speed until creamy, about 1 minute. Alternatively, beat with an electric hand mixer on low speed. With the mixer running, slowly add the sugar, then stop the mixer and scrape down the sides of the bowl. Continue beating until light and creamy, about 30 seconds. With the mixer running, slowly add the egg mixture in three additions, scraping down the sides of the bowl after each addition. Do not overbeat; if too much air is incorporated, the cheesecake will crack. Pour the filling into the cooled crust. Put the pan on a baking sheet and bake until the cheesecake is just barely set in the center (it will still jiggle when moved), 45 to 55 minutes.

MEANWHILE, MAKE THE TOPPING: In the bowl of a stand mixer fitted with the paddle attachment, lightly beat the sour cream, sugar, vanilla extract, contents of 1/2 vanilla bean, and kosher salt about

1 minute on low speed until incorporated. Remove cheesecake from the oven (keep the oven set at 300 degrees F). Spread the topping over the cheesecake and bake for 5 minutes. Transfer the pan to a wire rack and let cool, then refrigerate for at least 6 hours or preferably overnight before serving.

Note: To remove the contents of a vanilla bean, using a sharp knife, split the bean lengthwise and scrape out the small seeds. If the bean is hard and difficult to cut, soak it in boiling water until soft, 5 to 10 minutes. When the bean is cool enough to handle, proceed as directed.

Do-Ahead: This is an ideal do-ahead dessert, as it tastes best when made a day or two in advance. Keep refrigerated until ready to serve.

PEANUT BUTTER PIE *Sealed with Kisses*

Serves 6

Signed, sealed, and delivered with an abundance of kisses, this affection-inspired creation is loaded with lovin' spoonfuls of silky, satiny, nutty delight. Make this pie for your "better half," and discover that the way to your lover's heart is indeed through his or her stomach!

CRUST

30	*VANILLA OR CHOCOLATE WAFERS*
$1/3$	*CUP LIGHTLY SALTED DRY-ROASTED PEANUTS*
2	*TABLESPOONS UNSALTED BUTTER, MELTED*

FILLING

$3/4$	*CUP SMOOTH PEANUT BUTTER AT ROOM TEMPERATURE*
$1 1/2$	*CUPS HEAVY CREAM*
$3/4$	*CUP POWDERED SUGAR*
1	*TEASPOON VANILLA EXTRACT*
18	*CHOCOLATE KISSES, SUCH AS HERSHEY'S*
	CHOCOLATE SAUCE (PAGE 214) OR PURCHASED CHOCOLATE SYRUP FOR DRIZZLING

Position the rack in the center of the oven and preheat to 325 degrees F.

TO MAKE THE CRUST: Combine the wafers and peanuts in the bowl of a food processor fitted with the steel blade, and process until finely ground. Add the butter and pulse a few times until incorporated. Using your fingers, press the mixture evenly into the bottom and all the way up the sides of a 9-inch pie dish, pressing it firmly. Bake until fragrant, about 15 minutes. Transfer the pie dish to a wire rack and let cool completely.

MEANWHILE, MAKE THE FILLING: Put the peanut butter in a medium bowl. Set aside. Combine the cream, powdered sugar, and vanilla in the bowl of a stand mixer fitted with the whisk attachment. Beat on medium-high speed until soft peaks form, about $1 1/2$ minutes. The cream should slowly fall over forward when lifted with a whisk. Alternatively, use an electric hand mixer.

Using a rubber spatula, gently stir about half of the whipped cream mixture into the peanut butter. Then transfer this mixture into the remaining whipped cream mixture and beat on medium-high speed until just incorporated. Do not overmix.

Pour the filling into the cooled crust and spread evenly. Arrange the chocolate kisses in a circular fashion on the outside edge of the filling, $1/2$ inch in from the crust. Refrigerate until firm, at least 3 hours or as long as overnight. Slice and serve with an artful drizzle of chocolate sauce.

Silken CHOCOLATE TART

Serves 8

Life isn't worth living without this silky chocolate tart! We like to serve this devilish delight slightly warm with perfectly whipped cream. Our alcohol-spiked "whips du jour" add an element of surprise to any occasion. It's fun to experiment with flavored whips—cream lightly blended with after-dinner liqueurs, such as Grand Marnier, Frangelico, crème de menthe, framboise, and Kahlua.

CHOCOLATE TART

1   *RECIPE FLAKY PIECRUST (PAGE 39), OR 1 FROZEN PASTRY CIRCLE OR SHEET FOR A 9-INCH TART PAN*

1   *CUP HEAVY CREAM*

8   *OUNCES HIGH-QUALITY SEMISWEET CHOCOLATE, ROUGHLY CHOPPED, OR 1$^1/_3$ CUPS SEMISWEET CHOCOLATE CHIPS*

1   *TEASPOON VANILLA EXTRACT*

$^1/_4$ *TEASPOON KOSHER SALT*

2   *EGGS AT ROOM TEMPERATURE, LIGHTLY BEATEN*

WHIPPED CREAM

1   *CUP HEAVY CREAM*

2   *TEASPOONS SUGAR*

1   *TABLESPOON LIQUEUR OF CHOICE, PLUS MORE AS NEEDED*

COCOA POWDER FOR DUSTING

TO MAKE THE CHOCOLATE TART: Position the rack in the center of the oven. If using a homemade piecrust, bake it blind as directed. If using a frozen pastry circle or sheet, let thaw slightly and mold into a 9-inch tart pan. Prebake according to the package directions. Transfer to a wire rack and let cool.

Adjust the oven to 350 degrees F.

Bring the cream to a simmer in a small saucepan over medium heat. Remove from the heat and whisk in the chocolate until smooth. Add the vanilla and kosher salt and whisk until incorporated. Let cool to lukewarm, then whisk in the eggs. Pour into the tart shell and bake until the filling trembles in the middle when lightly shaken, 20 to 25 minutes. Transfer the pan to a wire rack and let cool for at least 30 minutes before serving.

JUST BEFORE SERVING, MAKE THE WHIPPED CREAM: Combine the cream, sugar, and the 1 table-spoon liqueur in the bowl of a stand mixer fitted with the whisk attachment. Beat on high speed until soft peaks form, about 1 minute. The cream should slowly fall over forward when lifted with a whisk. Alternatively, use an electric hand mixer. Add more liqueur if desired.

Tip: If you are in a pinch, you can make this tart using a store-bought 9-inch pie shell (not deep dish). Prebake according to the package directions. Be sure to let the finished tart cool for at least 1 hour before serving.

PUMPKIN PIE WITH BOURBON-SPIKED WHIPPED CREAM

Serves 6 to 8

We just can't understand why pumpkin pie is made only once a year, at Thanksgiving. Merely smelling the spices as the pie is baking makes us thankful to be alive. Spice up Thanksgiving or any occasion with this spirited variation on pumpkin pie. Canned pumpkin sits on store shelves year-round, so don't wait until November to make this decadent dessert. This pie's lively filling will get everyone talking, but it's the bourbon-spiked topping that will make your guests feel dizzy with delight. | For a stylish holiday presentation, we like to use leaf cookie cutters to create a festive seasonal garnish. Cut a few leaf shapes from the extra pie dough, gently brush with beaten egg, and bake separately until lightly browned. Place a few leaves on each slice before serving.

PUMPKIN PIE

1	RECIPE FLAKY PIECRUST (PAGE 39), OR ONE 9-INCH DEEP-DISH FROZEN PIE SHELL
3/4	CUP SUGAR
1	TEASPOON KOSHER SALT
1	TEASPOON GROUND CINNAMON
1/2	TEASPOON GROUND GINGER
1/8	TEASPOON GROUND CLOVES
	PINCH OF FRESHLY GRATED NUTMEG
2	EGGS
1	CAN PUMPKIN (15 OUNCES)
1 1/2	CUPS HEAVY CREAM
2	TEASPOONS VANILLA EXTRACT
1	TABLESPOON BOURBON
1	TABLESPOON MILK

WHIPPED CREAM

1	CUP HEAVY CREAM
3	TABLESPOONS SUGAR
1	TABLESPOON BOURBON, PLUS MORE AS NEEDED

TO MAKE THE PUMPKIN PIE: If using a homemade piecrust, bake it blind as directed for about 17 minutes. (For this recipe, it is not necessary to bake the crust for an additional 8 minutes before adding the filling.) If using a frozen pie shell, prebake it according to the package directions.

Adjust the oven to 425 degrees F. Position the rack in the lower third of the oven and put a baking sheet on the rack.

Stir together the sugar, kosher salt, cinnamon, ginger, cloves, and nutmeg in a small bowl. Set aside.

Whisk the eggs in a large bowl. Add the pumpkin, cream, vanilla, bourbon, and the sugar-and-spice mixture and mix well.

Brush the outer edge of the piecrust with the milk. Remove the baking sheet from the oven. Put the pie shell on the baking sheet and fill the shell to the rim with the pumpkin mixture. (Depending on the pie shell and the dish, you may have as much as $1/3$ cup of the pumpkin mixture left over.)

Bake for 15 minutes. Reduce the oven to 350 degrees F and bake until the pie is set in the center, 40 to 50 minutes more. (The filling will still jiggle when moved.) Transfer the pie to a wire rack and let cool completely.

JUST BEFORE SERVING, MAKE THE WHIPPED CREAM: Combine the cream, sugar, and the 1 tablespoon bourbon in the bowl of a stand mixer fitted with the whisk attachment. Beat on high speed until soft peaks form, about 1 minute. The cream should slowly fall over forward when lifted with a whisk. Alternatively, use an electric hand mixer. Add more bourbon, if desired.

Serve each slice with a dollop of whipped cream.

NECTARINE TARTS *for Two*

Serves 2

Make these sweet tarts for your sweetheart in no time flat, as the preparation only requires 10 quick minutes! Ripe nectarines are a wondrous thing—so tender, juicy, and aromatic, particularly if you can find white nectarines in the summertime. When nectarines are not at their peak, experiment with other seasonal fruits, creating your own combo based on what's available at your produce stand. For example, in the winter, try apples with oatmeal cookies and apple jelly. Although the tarts are best served fresh out of the oven, they can be made several hours in advance and warmed just before serving. A warm nectarine tart, topped with vanilla bean ice cream and drizzled with a warm (store-bought) caramel sauce is pure and simple perfection.

1   SHEET FROZEN PUFF PASTRY (10 INCHES SQUARE),
    SUCH AS PEPPERIDGE FARM

1   EGG, LIGHTLY BEATEN WITH 1 TABLESPOON WATER

2   TABLESPOONS GINGERSNAP CRUMBS (ABOUT 2 COOKIES)

1   RIPE YET FIRM NECTARINE, HALVED, PITTED, AND CUT INTO
    ABOUT 16 VERY THIN SLICES, EACH ABOUT $^{1}/_{8}$ INCH WIDE

2   TEASPOONS GRANULATED SUGAR

2   PINCHES OF GROUND CINNAMON

1   TABLESPOON APRICOT JAM (WITHOUT CHUNKS)

1   TEASPOON UNSALTED BUTTER
    POWDERED SUGAR FOR DUSTING

Position the rack in the center of the oven and preheat to 400 degrees F. Line a baking sheet with aluminum foil and lightly spray with vegetable-oil cooking spray.

Remove the sheet of puff pastry from the freezer. Using a heavy knife, cut the pastry in half crosswise and return the remaining half to the freezer for later use. Lay the pastry flat, let thaw, and cut it in half again crosswise, creating two 5-inch squares. Place the squares on the prepared baking sheet.

Fold the sides of each pastry square about $^{1}/_{2}$ inch towards the center. Use your index finger to make indentions and lightly squeeze the dough around your finger, creating a fluted effect around the edges. (This forms a "little boat" for the nectarines.) Brush the edges of the tarts with the beaten egg mixture.

Sprinkle the cookie crumbs evenly in the center of each pastry. Fan 8 slices of nectarines, slightly overlapping in the center of each pastry. Sprinkle each tart with 1 teaspoon of the granulated sugar and a pinch of cinnamon. Warm the apricot jam in a microwave until warm and syrupy, about 10 seconds. Drizzle evenly over the nectarines. Dot each tart with $^{1}/_{2}$ teaspoon of the butter. Bake until the crust is golden brown, 25 to 35 minutes. Let cool slightly and dust with powdered sugar just before serving.

Harvest APPLE CRISP

Serves 6 to 8

This dessert may seem old-fashioned, but it never goes out of style. We have made this crisp countless times, and it's always a smashing success. It's one of those desserts we prepare when we're in a pinch, without our recipe box handy. We just remember 5 apples, some sugar and spice for the filling, and "1, 1, 1"— 1 stick butter, 1 cup brown sugar, and 1 cup flour for the topping. Then we finish it off with a spoonful of oats. Using this quick, foolproof formula, you can turn out a delicious dessert anytime, anywhere.

FILLING

5   GRANNY SMITH APPLES, PEELED, CORED, AND CUT
        INTO 1-INCH PIECES

$^1/_2$ CUP GRANULATED SUGAR

2   TEASPOONS FRESH LEMON JUICE

        CONTENTS OF 1 VANILLA BEAN (SEE NOTE, PAGE 201), OR
        1 TEASPOON VANILLA EXTRACT

$1^1/_2$ TEASPOONS GROUND CINNAMON

$^1/_2$ TEASPOON GROUND NUTMEG, PREFERABLY FRESHLY GRATED

$^1/_4$ TEASPOON KOSHER SALT

STREUSEL TOPPING

$^1/_2$ CUP (1 STICK) UNSALTED BUTTER

1   CUP FIRMLY PACKED LIGHT BROWN SUGAR

$^1/_4$ TEASPOON KOSHER SALT

1   CUP ALL-PURPOSE FLOUR

$^1/_3$ CUP ROLLED OATS OR QUICK-COOKING OATS

Position the rack in the center of the oven and preheat to 350 degrees F.

TO MAKE THE FILLING: Combine the apples, granulated sugar, lemon juice, contents of 1 vanilla bean, cinnamon, nutmeg, and kosher salt in an 8-inch square glass baking dish and mix well. Set aside.

TO MAKE THE STREUSEL TOPPING: Melt the butter in a medium saucepan over medium heat. Remove from the heat, and stir in the brown sugar and kosher salt. Add the flour and oatmeal and stir until just incorporated. Do not overwork. Crumble the mixture evenly over the apple filling. (If your kitchen is warm and humid, the mixture

may resemble cookie dough. That is OK. Simply crumble the pieces over the apples.) Put the baking dish on a baking sheet and bake until the topping is golden brown and the filling is bubbling, 50 to 60 minutes.

Do-Ahead: Prepare the apple filling and the streusel topping 6 to 8 hours in advance, but do not crumble the topping over the apple filling until you are ready to bake. Refrigerate the filling and topping separately. When ready to bake, crumble the topping over the filling and proceed as directed.

SHORTBREAD SWEETHEARTS

Makes about 20 cookies

Sometimes the simplest gesture is the one that touches the most. Make our heart-shaped shortbread cookies and see for yourself. These buttery beauties will express your affection simply and sweetly. They also inspire "oohs and aahs" when added to a bridal-shower sweets table. Your guests will eat to their hearts' content!

- 3/4 CUP (1 1/2 STICKS) UNSALTED BUTTER AT ROOM TEMPERATURE
- 2/3 CUP POWDERED SUGAR, PLUS MORE FOR DUSTING (OPTIONAL)
- 1 TEASPOON VANILLA EXTRACT
- 1/2 TEASPOON KOSHER SALT
- 1 1/2 CUPS ALL-PURPOSE FLOUR
- ABOUT 2 TABLESPOONS GRANULATED SUGAR

In the bowl of a stand mixer fitted with the paddle attachment, beat the butter on medium-low speed until light and fluffy, about 1 minute. Alternatively, use an electric hand mixer. Add the 2/3 cup powdered sugar and beat until incorporated. Add the vanilla and kosher salt and beat well, scraping down the sides of the bowl. Add the flour, a spoonful at a time, and beat until just incorporated.

Gather the dough into a ball and place on a large piece of plastic wrap. Flatten the dough into a disk and wrap well. Refrigerate until chilled, at least 1 hour or as long as overnight.

Position the rack in the center of the oven and preheat to 325 degrees F.

Let the dough soften slightly at room temperature for about 15 minutes. Place the dough between 2 layers of plastic wrap. Roll out the dough to 1/4-inch thickness. Using a 2-inch heart-shaped cookie cutter, cut out cookies and place about

2 inches apart on a baking sheet. Gather the scraps into a ball and repeat the rolling and cutting process. Sprinkle the cookies with granulated sugar. Bake until the cookies are slightly golden brown around the edges, about 20 minutes. Let the cookies cool on the baking sheets for 2 to 3 minutes, then transfer the cookies to a wire rack and let cool completely. Dust with powdered sugar, if desired.

Note: For an irresistible presentation, we arrange these cookies on a platter with chocolate-dipped strawberries. To make the strawberries, dip large, stemmed berries into warm, melted chocolate. For an extra-special touch, melt about 2 ounces white chocolate and put it in a sealable plastic bag. Cut the tip off one corner and drizzle an artful pattern onto the dipped berries.

Daddy's OATMEAL COOKIES

We may be married with families of our own, but we still have little girls' crushes on our dad. For as long as we can remember, Dad has had an uncontrollable sweet tooth, and he absolutely adores these irresistible cookies, which he affectionately refers to as "oaties." Every time we bake them, we break into nostalgic grins over Dad's unrequited romance with oatmeal cookies.

2	CUPS ALL-PURPOSE FLOUR
1	TEASPOON BAKING SODA
1	TEASPOON KOSHER SALT
1	TEASPOON GROUND CINNAMON
2	EGGS AT ROOM TEMPERATURE
2	TEASPOONS VANILLA EXTRACT
1	CUP (2 STICKS) UNSALTED BUTTER AT ROOM TEMPERATURE
2	CUPS FIRMLY PACKED LIGHT BROWN SUGAR
2	CUPS ROLLED OATS OR QUICK-COOKING OATS
1	CUP RAISINS

Position the rack in the center of the oven and preheat to 350 degrees F. Spray 2 or more baking sheets with vegetable-oil cooking spray or line with parchment paper.

Stir together the flour, baking soda, kosher salt, and cinnamon in a small bowl. Set aside.

Stir together the eggs and vanilla in a small bowl. In the bowl of a stand mixer fitted with the paddle attachment, beat the butter and brown sugar on medium speed until creamy and blended. Alternatively, use an electric hand mixer. Add the egg mixture to the butter mixture in two additions and beat until incorporated. Scrape down the sides of the bowl after each addition. Reduce the speed to low, slowly add the dry ingredients, and beat until just incorporated. Scrape down the sides of the bowl if necessary. Stir in the oatmeal and raisins.

Drop rounded tablespoons of dough about 2 inches apart onto the prepared baking sheets. Bake until the edges of the cookies are golden and the centers are barely cooked, about 10 minutes. Let the cookies cool on the baking sheets for 2 to 3 minutes, then transfer the cookies to wire racks and let cool completely.

Tips: Invest in 4 good-quality baking sheets. Look for professional-quality bakeware constructed of heavy-duty materials. The pans will conduct heat fast and evenly, so cookies will brown nicely and not burn on the bottom.

For fastest results, fill 2 baking sheets with cookie dough and bake. Meanwhile, fill 2 other baking sheets with dough. This allows you to make 48 cookies in less than an hour.

Do-Ahead: Bake half the cookie dough, then wrap the rest in plastic wrap and refrigerate or freeze for later baking. The dough keeps for 1 week in the refrigerator and 1 month frozen.

Our Favorite CHOCOLATE CHIP COOKIES
(Mary vs. Sara)

Makes about 24 cookies

In our quest to create the ideal chocolate chip cookie, we tried dozens of recipes and polled everyone we knew. We both agree that the best chocolate chip cookie is one with an ooey-gooey center, loads of chocolate chips, and freshly toasted nuts. What we don't agree on is the butter-versus-margarine debate . . . Mary and Jack are adamant about using margarine (shameless, but true) for a softer, chewier result, while Sara and Erik "stick" with butter for its undeniable, buttery taste and the crispy outer crust it creates. Whether you side with Mary or Sara, the true secret to these cookies is their baking time. If overcooked, the cookies are unremarkable, but when slightly undercooked, they are the epitome of moist, chewy perfection. | Wouldn't you know it—there is yet another thing we don't see eye to eye on . . . Mary always adds 1/2 cup shredded coconut to this cookie recipe, while Sara stays the purist. Play around with this recipe—create *your* own favorite cookies.

1	*CUP PLUS 2 TABLESPOONS ALL-PURPOSE FLOUR*
1/2	*TEASPOON BAKING SODA*
1/2	*TEASPOON KOSHER SALT*
1	*EGG*
1	*TEASPOON VANILLA EXTRACT*
1/2	*CUP (1 STICK) UNSALTED BUTTER OR MARGARINE (SEE NOTE), AT ROOM TEMPERATURE*
1/2	*CUP FIRMLY PACKED LIGHT BROWN SUGAR*
1/2	*CUP GRANULATED SUGAR*
1	*CUP SEMISWEET CHOCOLATE CHIPS OR CHUNKS*
3/4	*CUP (2 1/2 OUNCES) WALNUTS, TOASTED AND CHOPPED (OPTIONAL; SEE PAGE 188)*
1/2	*CUP SWEETENED SHREDDED COCONUT (OPTIONAL)*

Stir together the flour, baking soda, and kosher salt in a small bowl. Set aside.

Stir together the egg and vanilla in a small bowl. In the bowl of a stand mixer fitted with the paddle attachment, beat the butter, brown sugar, and granulated sugar on medium speed until just mixed, about 20 seconds. Scrape down the sides of the bowl. Alternatively, use an electric hand mixer. Add the egg mixture to the butter mixture and beat well, about 10 seconds. Reduce the speed to low, slowly add the dry ingredients, and beat until just incorporated. Stir in the chocolate chips, and walnuts and coconut, if desired.

Position the rack in the center of the oven and preheat to 375 degrees F. Spray 2 baking sheets with vegetable-oil cooking spray or line with parchment paper.

Drop rounded tablespoonfuls of dough 2 inches apart onto the prepared baking sheets. Bake until the cookies are golden brown, 10 to 12 minutes (they will seem underdone). Let the cookies cool on the baking sheets for 2 to 3 minutes, then transfer the cookies to wire racks and let cool completely.

Note: Use unsalted margarine, if you can find it. If not, delete the kosher salt from the recipe.

Ooey-Gooey CARAMEL CANDY BROWNIES

A great brownie recipe is a must-have in every household. These brownies are ooey-gooey, chocolaty wonders, laden with caramel. We use Snickers bars for the caramel, but soft, chewy caramel squares work just fine. To transform the brownies into mile-high sundaes, heat the brownies up, top them with your favorite ice cream (we like pralines and cream or French vanilla), and drown them with homemade Chocolate Sauce (recipe below). SIN CITY!

1 1/2 CUPS SEMISWEET CHOCOLATE CHIPS

3/4 CUP (1 1/2 STICKS) UNSALTED BUTTER, CUT INTO SMALL PIECES

3 EGGS

3/4 CUP SUGAR

1/4 TEASPOON KOSHER SALT

1 1/2 TEASPOONS VANILLA EXTRACT

2/3 CUP ALL-PURPOSE FLOUR

3/4 CUP COARSELY CHOPPED CARAMEL CANDY

Position the rack in the center of the oven and preheat to 350 degrees F. Butter and flour an 8-inch square metal baking dish.

Combine the chocolate chips and butter in the top pan of a double boiler or in a medium metal bowl. Set over a saucepan filled with 2 inches of simmering water over medium heat. Melt the chocolate, stirring occasionally, until smooth, about 2 minutes. Remove from the heat and let cool until lukewarm.

Combine the eggs, sugar, and kosher salt in a small heavy-bottomed saucepan over low heat. Whisk constantly until the sugar melts and the mixture is frothy, about 2 minutes (it should be slightly warm at this point). Pour the egg mixture into the chocolate mixture, add the vanilla, and stir until well mixed. Whisk in the flour until just incorporated.

Spread the batter evenly in the prepared baking dish. Sprinkle the caramel candy evenly over the batter. Bake until a toothpick inserted into the center of the brownies comes out with some moist crumbs attached, 25 to 35 minutes. Do not overcook. Transfer the pan to a wire rack and let the brownies cool completely in the pan before cutting into squares.

Tip: To ensure that the brownies bake evenly, use a metal baking dish rather than a glass one. The brownies will cool faster and will not harden around the edges.

CHOCOLATE SAUCE

Heat 3/4 cup heavy cream in a small saucepan over medium heat. Bring to a simmer, then remove from the heat. Whisk in 1 1/2 cups semisweet chocolate chips. Stir in 1/4 cup light corn syrup, 1 tablespoon unsalted butter, 1 teaspoon vanilla extract, and a pinch of kosher salt. The chocolate sauce will keep, covered and refrigerated for 1 week.
Makes 1 1/2 cups

RASPBERRY-ALMOND DREAM CREAM

Serves 4

Inspired by Italian panna cotta, one of the world's greatest desserts, this foolproof recipe is for you nonbakers out there! Assembled in less than 15 minutes and chilled until serving time, it has a lighter texture than traditional panna cotta and includes less gelatin. There's no tricky unmolding involved, either. Simply chill in decorative glasses (we love to use martini glasses), then garnish with fresh mint sprigs. The result is a dessert so delicate, airy, and dreamy, you'll be on cloud nine. | If you're not an almond lover, omit the almond extract and substitute with the same amount of vanilla extract.

$1\frac{1}{4}$ TEASPOONS UNFLAVORED GELATIN

1   CUP MILK

1   CUP HEAVY CREAM

$\frac{1}{2}$ VANILLA BEAN (3-INCH PIECE) OR 1/4 TEASPOON VANILLA EXTRACT

$\frac{1}{3}$ CUP SUGAR

       PINCH OF KOSHER SALT

$\frac{1}{4}$ TEASPOON ALMOND EXTRACT

$\frac{3}{4}$ CUP FRESH RASPBERRIES

       FRESH MINT SPRIGS FOR GARNISHING

Whisk together the gelatin and milk in a medium bowl. Set aside until the gelatin softens, about 5 minutes.

Combine the cream, vanilla bean (if using), sugar, and kosher salt in a small saucepan over medium-high heat. Bring just to a boil, whisking frequently. Remove the pan from the heat. If using a vanilla bean, transfer the softened bean to a cutting board and let cool slightly. Meanwhile, add the hot cream mixture to the softened gelatin mixture, then add the almond extract (and vanilla extract, if using) and whisk until incorporated.

Using a sharp knife, split the vanilla bean lengthwise, scrape out the small seeds, and add to the cream mixture. Discard the pod. Whisk until the mixture is smooth and the gelatin is dissolved.

Strain the mixture into a bowl and pour about $\frac{1}{2}$ cup into each of 4 martini glasses, juice cups, or ramekins. Drop 6 to 8 raspberries into each glass. Let cool slightly, cover with plastic wrap, and refrigerate until set, about $2\frac{1}{2}$ hours. (When set, they should still be slightly loose in the center.) Garnish with mint sprigs just before serving.

Puckery LEMON PARFAITS WITH SUMMER BERRIES

Serves 6

This puckery lemon parfait is as good as a first kiss! Fresh, beautiful, and a cinch to make in advance, these classy little parfaits can be served straight out of the refrigerator when entertaining. Presented in your favorite glassware (look for fun, old-fashioned parfait glasses in antique stores), they are oh-so-pleasing to the eye. Using a double boiler is a foolproof way to prepare lemon curd with minimal risk of curdling. If you don't own a double boiler, nestle a stainless-steel mixing bowl snugly on top of a medium heavy-bottomed saucepan filled with a couple of inches of simmering water.

LEMON CURD

5	EGGS
3	EGG YOLKS
1	CUP GRANULATED SUGAR
3/4	CUP FRESH LEMON JUICE
	PINCH OF KOSHER SALT
1/2	CUP (1 STICK) COLD UNSALTED BUTTER, CUT INTO 1/2-INCH CUBES
1	CUP COLD HEAVY CREAM
3	TABLESPOONS POWDERED SUGAR

BERRIES

2 1/2	CUPS FRESH BLUEBERRIES, PICKED OVER
2 1/2	CUPS FRESH RASPBERRIES
3 TO 4	TABLESPOONS GRANULATED SUGAR
6	MINT LEAVES

TO MAKE THE LEMON CURD: Whisk together the eggs, egg yolks, and granulated sugar in the top pan of a double boiler or in a medium metal bowl until well mixed. Set over a saucepan filled with 2 inches of simmering water over medium heat. Add the lemon juice and kosher salt. Cook, whisking constantly, until thickened, 7 to 10 minutes. Remove from the heat and whisk in the butter until smooth.

Using a rubber spatula, scrape the mixture into a medium-mesh sieve set over a bowl. Strain the mixture into the bowl, pressing with the back of the spatula. Cool slightly at room temperature, then refrigerate until firm, at least 1 hour.

Combine the cream and powdered sugar in the bowl of a stand mixer fitted with the whisk attachment. Beat on high speed until soft peaks form, about 1 minute. The cream should slowly fall forward when lifted with a whisk. Alternatively, use an electric hand mixer. Fold half of the whipped cream into the chilled lemon curd, then fold in the remaining cream. Refrigerate until ready to assemble.

TO PREPARE THE BERRIES: Just before assembling the parfaits, gently toss the blueberries, raspberries, and 3 tablespoons of the granulated sugar in a medium bowl. Add the remaining tablespoon sugar if necessary, depending on the sweetness of the berries.

CONTINUED

TO ASSEMBLE THE PARFAITS: **Fill six 8- to 10-ounce parfait glasses, wineglasses, or other decorative glasses with 1/4 cup of the berries, followed by a heaping 1/3 cup of the lemon mousse. Repeat the layering process. Distribute the remaining berries on top of the parfaits. Garnish each with a mint leaf just before serving.**

Do-Ahead: **The lemon curd can be prepared in advance (without the addition of whipped cream) and refrigerated for up to 1 week. Parfaits can be assembled 3 to 5 hours ahead of time, covered with plastic wrap, and refrigerated.**

"Hidden-Treasure" BREAD PUDDING

Serves 4

Soft, sweet bread pudding is one of the most comforting desserts we know of, but what makes ours extra special is its hidden treasure. Buried underneath the velvety-smooth pudding lies a rich, molten chocolate surprise. Prepared with croissants, this bread pudding has a soufflélike texture that is ultralight and out of this world. We promise this will be a treasure in your chest of recipes.

2   EGGS

3   EGG YOLKS

1 1/2 CUPS HALF-AND-HALF

1/2   CUP PLUS 2 TABLESPOONS GRANULATED SUGAR

1   TABLESPOON RUM

2   TEASPOONS VANILLA EXTRACT

1/4   TEASPOON KOSHER SALT

1   CUP SEMISWEET CHOCOLATE CHIPS OR CHUNKS

2   CUPS FIRMLY PACKED STALE 1/2-INCH CROISSANT CUBES
     (ABOUT 2 MEDIUM CROISSANTS) (SEE NOTE)
     POWDERED SUGAR FOR DUSTING

Position the rack in the center of the oven and preheat to 350 degrees F.

Whisk together the eggs, egg yolks, half-and-half, granulated sugar, rum, vanilla, and kosher salt in a medium bowl. Set aside. Put 1/4 cup of the chocolate chips in each of four 8-ounce ramekins. Divide the croissant cubes evenly among the ramekins. Pour 3/4 cup of the egg mixture into each ramekin. Let stand for 20 minutes.

Fill a baking pan with 1 inch of boiling water and set the ramekins in the pan. Cover the pan with aluminum foil. Make a few holes in the foil so steam can escape. Bake for about 20 minutes. Carefully remove the foil and bake until the custard is set, about 20 minutes more. A knife inserted into the center should not come out clean but be slightly coated with thick custard that is half set. Remove the ramekins from the baking pan and transfer to a wire rack to cool slightly. Dust with powdered sugar just before serving.

Do-Ahead: The bread pudding can be assembled and baked as directed up to 8 hours in advance. Let stand at room temperature (do not refrigerate). Just before serving, cover the ramekins with aluminum foil, and heat in a 375-degree F oven until very warm, 15 to 20 minutes. When reheating the pudding, it is not necessary to put the ramekins in a pan of boiling water.

Note: All recipes for bread pudding call for stale bread. If there is time, let the croissants sit out exposed to the air for 2 to 3 days. If not, toast fresh croissant cubes in a 275-degree F oven for 15 minutes. Let cool and proceed as directed.

CHAPTER 11

THE GLOBAL BAR

COCKTAIL CULTURE IS ALIVE AND WELL. There's nothing quite like a cocktail to get a party rolling. We put our personal stamp on parties by always featuring one inspired cocktail. In fact, we give our cocktails as much thought as we do our appetizers. Snazzy cocktails add a "buzz" to parties, creating energy and effervescence. For nondrinkers, simply leave out the alcohol—most drinks will taste nearly as fabulous as the "real thing."

We'll never forget the first time we tasted a mojito, at a friend's Cuban-inspired dinner party. We were so wowed by this refreshing, power-packed cocktail that we practically assaulted the bartender for the recipe. It was the mintiest, coolest drink we've ever sipped— it even inspired us to try a cigar with the fellas out back. Moral of that story? Never underestimate the power of a killer cocktail.

When it comes to concocting cocktails, we'll have you pouring, stirring, and whirring like a pro. This chapter offers ten "rock 'em, sock 'em" recipes along with serving suggestions for daiquiris, martinis, mojitos, sangria, Cosmopolitans, and more. Once you've sipped a homemade margarita, prepared with fresh-squeezed lime juice and served in a salt-rimmed glass, you'll never go back to using a mix. In a few easy steps, you'll master old-time favorites like Great Robert's Whiskey Sour Slush (page 227) and fearlessly whip up fabulous new tastes like our Vodka-Spiked Lemonade with Red Rocks (page 226). Cheers! *Long live the cocktail hour!*

P.S. In Kitchen Basics, we offer suggestions on glassware and bar accessories (page 27). You'll find a list of our favorite bar staples in The Global Pantry (page 19).

SAUZA MARGARITAS

Serves 4

Bright, crisp, moderately priced Sauza tequila and fresh lime juice are the secrets to our supremely sippable margarita. And yes, we do add a touch of water, but don't be fooled—our cocktail remains every bit as bold as it should be. Kick those tired margarita mixers to the curb!

4   OUNCES GOOD-QUALITY TEQUILA, PREFERABLY SAUZA
4   OUNCES TRIPLE SEC
1/4 CUP FRESH LIME JUICE
6   OUNCES THAWED FROZEN LIMEADE CONCENTRATE (3/4 CUP)
1/2 CUP WATER
    COARSE SALT FOR RIMS OF GLASSES
    LIME WEDGES FOR SALTING RIMS

Combine the tequila, Triple Sec, lime juice, limeade concentrate, and water in a small pitcher. Stir well. Put the coarse salt in a shallow bowl.

Rub the rim of each glass with a lime wedge and dip the rims into the salt. Fill the glasses with ice, pour in the margarita mixture, and serve.

RASPBERRY CHAMPAGNE SPARKLERS

Serves 4

One of our special-occasion favorites, this sparkler offers sublime sophistication with a playful touch of fruit. Serve this bubbling beauty in tall, svelte flutes from a silver platter sprinkled with a few mint leaves and flower petals.

1   BOTTLE (750ML) CHAMPAGNE OR SPARKLING WINE
    FRESH RASPBERRIES FOR GARNISHING (OPTIONAL)
2   OUNCES RASPBERRY LIQUEUR

Pour about 5 ounces of the Champagne into each of 4 flutes. Drop 3 or 4 raspberries into each flute, if desired. Pour 1/2 ounce of the raspberry liqueur into each glass.

Variations: REPLACE THE RASPBERRY LIQUEUR WITH . . .
1. Blackberry schnapps for a blackberry sparkler
2. Grand Marnier for an orange sparkler
3. Peach schnapps for a peach sparkler
4. Cassis for a kir royale

STRAWBERRY DAIQUIRIS

Serves 2

We love a frosty daiquiri because, no matter where or when it's served, it feels like a vacation. Make the daiquiris 6 to 8 hours before your guests arrive, and pop the daiquiris in the freezer in a sealable plastic bag. Thaw 15 to 20 minutes before serving, then join your guests for cocktails instead of blending away in the kitchen. For a whimsical garnish, moisten the rims of the glasses with a lime wedge, then dip the rims in a shallow bowl of colored sugar crystals (flavored, if you can find them).

1   CUP FRESH STRAWBERRIES, HULLED AND QUARTERED

$^1/_2$ CUP FROZEN STRAWBERRY DAIQUIRI MIX, SUCH AS BACARDI

3   OUNCES LIGHT RUM

2   TABLESPOONS SUGAR, PLUS MORE AS NEEDED

1   TEASPOON FRESH LIME JUICE, PLUS MORE AS NEEDED

3   CUPS SMALL ICE CUBES

2   WHOLE STRAWBERRIES OR LIME SLICES

Combine the quartered strawberries, daiquiri mix, rum, the 2 tablespoons sugar, the 1 teaspoon lime juice, and the ice cubes in a blender. Blend on high speed until smooth, about 10 seconds. Add more sugar or lime juice if necessary. Pour into chilled glasses. If garnishing with strawberries, cut each one about $^3/_4$ inch up from the bottom towards the stem end, taking care not to cut the berry in half. Garnish the daiquiris with the berries or lime slices.

MOJITOS

Serves 2

This cocktail is hot, hot, hot! And cool, cool, cool. The exotic Cuban mojito offers a breathtaking kiss of mint on the heels of rum's sweet embrace. Clean and crisp, the mojito has become one of our warmweather favorites. Traditional mojitos can be a labor of love, especially when the mint is mashed in a mortar and pestle. We recommend you use a blender for ease and efficiency. Garnish with a fresh mint sprig before serving.

¹/₄ CUP THAWED FROZEN LIMEADE CONCENTRATE
2   TABLESPOONS FRESH LIME JUICE
2   TEASPOONS SUGAR
4   OUNCES WHITE RUM
1   CUP CLUB SODA
12 MEDIUM MINT LEAVES
2   MINT SPRIGS

Combine the limeade concentrate, lime juice, sugar, rum, club soda, and mint leaves in a blender. Blend on high speed until the mint is reduced to tiny flecks, about 10 seconds. Pour into ice-filled glasses and garnish each with a mint sprig.

COSMOPOLITANS

Serves 4

The name says it all. Sleek, urbane, and cool, the Cosmopolitan is *the* cocktail for high-spirited sophisticates. Give it added flair by garnishing with a sugar-coated cranberry speared on a beverage pick. To sugarcoat cranberries, moisten them in frothy egg white and then dip in sugar.

6   OUNCES VODKA
4   OUNCES CRANBERRY JUICE
2   OUNCES TRIPLE SEC
2   TEASPOONS FRESH LIME JUICE
4   LIME SLICES

Pour the vodka, cranberry juice, Triple Sec, and lime juice into a large shaker. Fill with ice, cover, and shake. Strain into chilled martini glasses and garnish each with a lime slice.

Variation: For pineapple Cosmopolitans, infuse ³/₄ cup vodka with ³/₄ cup coarsely chopped ripe pineapple. Cover and let stand at room temperature until the vodka is well flavored with the pineapple, about 3 days. Then proceed as directed.

VODKA-SPIKED LEMONADE *with Red Rocks*

Serves 4

Lemonade grows up with a feisty splash of vodka poured over a show-stopping jumble of red "rocks." This cocktail was created in memory of all the great concerts we've attended at Red Rocks, Colorado (Erik's home state). When these bright ice cubes melt, they create an irresistible sweet slush that will have everyone saying, "bottoms up!" We raise a glass to icy, cool lemonade on a Colorado summer night.

1 3/4 CUPS TROPICAL FRUIT PUNCH

3   CUPS WATER

1/2   CUP FRESH LEMON JUICE

1/2   CUP SUGAR

6   OUNCES VODKA OR LEMON-INFUSED VODKA

4   THIN LEMON SLICES

To make the flavored ice cubes, pour the fruit punch into an ice cube tray and freeze.

Combine the water, lemon juice, and sugar in a small pitcher. Stir until the sugar dissolves. Add the vodka. Refrigerate the lemonade if time permits. Fill each glass with 3 or 4 flavored ice cubes and pour in the lemonade. Garnish each with a lemon slice and serve.

Classic MARTINIS

Serves 4

We love a good martini for its timelessness, potency, and power. This seductive star of the cocktail hour entices with its paradox of simplicity and sophistication. It's *the* beverage of choice for the scintillating and swaggering. Chilled glasses are a must when entertaining over martinis. For the purest, freshest-tasting martini, use ice cubes made with bottled water.

8   OUNCES GIN OR VODKA

SPLASH OF VERMOUTH

GREEN OLIVES, PICKLED ONIONS, OR LEMON TWISTS FOR GARNISHING (SEE NOTE)

Pour the gin into a shaker filled with ice. Add the vermouth, cover, and shake. Strain into chilled martini glasses and garnish each with olives, pickled onions, or a lemon twist.

Note: The market is exploding with all kinds of exciting olives . . . blue-cheese stuffed, jalapeño stuffed, you name it. Also look for specialty bottled martini onions—they will catapult your martini into the stratosphere.

Great Robert's WHISKEY SOUR SLUSH

Serves 2

This drink launched our love affair with the definitive Southern spirit, bourbon. We've never been bourbon lovers (though you'd think we would be, coming from the South), but we tell you, the combo of lemon, sugar, and bourbon is seductive. This is one of the all-time great drinks. The legendary concoction of our friend Martha Chamberlin's grandfather, Robert Whitenbeck, will most definitely "cure what ails ya"! We got downright woozy testing this recipe.

5   *OUNCES BOURBON*

2   *TABLESPOONS FRESH LEMON JUICE*

3   *HEAPING TABLESPOONS SUGAR*

2   *CUPS SMALL ICE CUBES*

Combine the bourbon, lemon juice, and sugar in a blender. Blend on medium speed until the sugar dissolves, about 1 minute. Add the ice and blend on high speed until smooth, about 10 seconds. Pour into glasses and serve.

Do-Ahead: Make the Whiskey Sours 6 to 8 hours before your guests arrive, and pop them in the freezer in a sealable plastic bag. Thaw about 15 minutes before serving, then join your guests for cocktails instead of blending away in the kitchen.

Citrusy SANGRIA

Sangria transforms an ordinary bottle of red wine into a celebration! Begin with a young, fruity Beaujolais or Pinot Noir, then scour your market for the season's ripest fruit. Cherries, plums, and blackberries, when purchased at their peak, make great additions. Sangria impresses with its beauty, and with one sip, it transports you to Spain faster than anything we know of. Showcase this gorgeous drink in a big, beautiful pitcher, punch bowl, or wide-rimmed vase.

1	BOTTLE (750ML) FRUITY RED WINE, SUCH AS BEAUJOLAIS OR PINOT NOIR
1/4	CUP THAWED FROZEN ORANGE JUICE CONCENTRATE
1	BOTTLE (12 OUNCES) UNSWEETENED, STRONG BREWED TEA, SUCH AS TEJAVA
2	TABLESPOONS SUGAR
2	LARGE ORANGES, UNPEELED, CUT INTO 1/4-INCH ROUNDS
3/4	CUP SEEDLESS RED GRAPES
3/4	CUP CHOPPED RED APPLE
	CHILLED CLUB SODA AS NEEDED (OPTIONAL)

Combine the wine, orange juice concentrate, tea, and sugar in a medium pitcher. Stir until the sugar dissolves. Add the oranges, grapes, and apple. Refrigerate until ready to serve. Add club soda, if desired. Using a slotted spoon, put 1/4 cup of the fruit in each glass and pour in the wine mixture.

Tip: Sangria tastes best when made 6 to 8 hours in advance so the flavors can marry.

Mary's BLOODY MARYS

Serves 4

The tried-and-true brunch standard gets a new twist when your favorite Bloody Mary mix meets the dashing Clamato, a zesty tomato juice lightly infused with clam broth. (Don't be scared off. . . this stuff is the kicker!) If you like, trade in the classic celery stalk for a tart dill pickle spear, a flirtatious pickled green bean or two, or a proud stalk of pickled asparagus. When we're feeling really racy, we freeze spiced tomato juice in an ice tray and fill the glasses with these flavor-packed cubes instead of ordinary ice.

2	CUPS BLOODY MARY MIX
1 1/2	CUPS CLAMATO JUICE
2	TABLESPOONS FRESH LIME JUICE
2	TEASPOONS WORCESTERSHIRE SAUCE
	FRESHLY GROUND PEPPER
2	TEASPOONS CELERY SALT
	LIME WEDGES FOR SALTING RIMS
8	OUNCES VODKA
4	CELERY STALKS WITH LEAVES

Combine the Bloody Mary mix, Clamato juice, lime juice, and Worcestershire sauce in a medium pitcher. Season with pepper to taste. Refrigerate if time permits. Put the celery salt in a shallow bowl. Rub the rim of each of 4 glasses with a lime wedge and dip the rims into the celery salt. Fill each glass with ice and 2 ounces vodka. Pour in the Bloody Mary mixture, and garnish each with a leafy celery stalk.

CHAPTER 12

COOKING
SIDE-BY-SIDE

LIKE A CHALLENGING BIKE RIDE, a hike up a mountain, or a relaxing vacation, cooking in tandem can be a bonding experience for you and your mate. Try divvying up the kitchen tasks based on what is most comfortable for each of you. Maybe your spouse finds an escape in chopping, dicing, and slicing, while you prefer to stand and stir or to set the table artfully. Creating a great meal with our husbands always gives us a shared feeling of accomplishment.

Breakfast in bed? The ideal day as a duo starts by rolling out of bed, sauntering into the kitchen in your pj's, and putting on a pot of coffee. Now get crackin'! It's just a few eggs, some pots and pans, and a little bit of blender magic. Before you know it, you'll be back in the sack, savoring your perfectly elegant Eggs Benedict (page 175). (By the way, breakfast-in-bed trays are a great item to add to your registry list.)

Romantic picnics? Each year, Mary and Jack pack a picnic lunch and revisit the spot where they got engaged—a breathtakingly beautiful nook in the Marin Headlands, overlooking the Golden Gate Bridge. Jack likes to make "his" pimiento cheese sandwiches (actually our recipe), while Mary prepares their favorite Lemony-Tarragon Crab Dip (page 55), packs it on ice, and picks up a bag of salt-and-vinegar potato chips, some French bread, and a medley of seasonal fruit. Add one large blanket, a chilled bottle of bubbly, and something sweet, and you've got their recipe for romance. What's yours?

Nothing feeds love's fire better than an elegant supper for two. Cooking and dining together bring the focus back to your relationship—it's an opportunity to reconnect and recap the happenings of the day. In no time, you'll be carrying on over your earthy Wild Mushroom Risotto (page 121) and a plate of beautifully dressed mixed greens. To cap off the evening, melt some chocolate (and your loved one's heart) by whipping up our sinfully delicious Chocolate Fondue (page 258).

Whether it's just the two of you, or you're in the kitchen with friends, pour some wine, turn on some tunes, add a generous dose of conversation, and get cooking.

BREAKFAST IN BED

EGGS BENEDICT

BRIDE
GRAB FROM PANTRY:
> *WHITE WINE VINEGAR*
> *CAYENNE PEPPER*
> *SUGAR*

GROOM
GRAB FROM FRIDGE:
> *EGGS*
> *LEMON*
> *BUTTER*

BRIDE AND GROOM
SHOPPING LIST (PLUS ANYTHING FROM
PANTRY/FRIDGE YOU MIGHT BE MISSING):
> *CANADIAN BACON*
> *CREAM*
> *ENGLISH MUFFINS*
> *FRESH TARRAGON OR DILL*
> *FRESHLY SQUEEZED ORANGE JUICE*
> *COFFEE*

BREAKFAST GAME PLAN

1. Get the list and go shopping (preferably the night before).
2. Back at home, assemble pantry items, and pull eggs, lemon, and butter from fridge (let stand at room temperature overnight).
3. In the morning, put on some tunes and sip O.J. together. Put 2 plates in a 200-degree F oven.
4. He gets the coffee brewing.
5. She is in charge of the hollandaise. She begins by heating the butter until bubbling.
6. He gets the water simmering for the poached eggs in a medium nonstick skillet.
7. She adds room-temperature egg yolks and cream plus kosher salt and cayenne to the blender.
8. He puts English muffin halves in the toaster.
9. She drizzles the hot butter into egg mixture, then seasons with lemon juice, white wine vinegar, and a pinch of sugar.
10. He breaks an egg into a small cup and gently places it into the simmering water (or into the individual cups of an egg poacher), then repeats the process with 3 more eggs.
11. She warms the Canadian bacon in a large nonstick skillet.
12. He places 2 toasted English muffins halves on each of 2 warmed plates.
13. She puts the Canadian bacon on the muffin halves.
14. He adds the poached eggs on top.
15. She spoons a generous dollop of hollandaise onto and around the eggs. (She may need to warm the sauce briefly in the microwave, as it is best served very warm.)
16. He garnishes each plate with chopped tarragon or dill.
17. Off they go to enjoy breakfast in bed!

ELEGANT SUPPER FOR TWO

WILD MUSHROOM RISOTTO

MIXED GREEN SALAD

CHOCOLATE FONDUE

BRIDE

GRAB FROM PANTRY:

CAN OF LOW-SODIUM CHICKEN BROTH

OLIVE OIL

ARBORIO RICE

BALSAMIC VINEGAR

BAG OF SEMISWEET CHOCOLATE CHIPS

BRANDY OR GRAND MARNIER

GROOM

GRAB FROM FRIDGE:

BUTTER

BAG OF MIXED GREENS

BRIDE AND GROOM

SHOPPING LIST (PLUS ANYTHING FROM
PANTRY/FRIDGE YOU MIGHT BE MISSING):

1 SMALL YELLOW ONION

8 OUNCES SHIITAKE MUSHROOMS

1 HEAD OF GARLIC

BOTTLE OF DRY WHITE WINE

*CHUNK OF PARMESAN CHEESE, PREFERABLY
    PARMIGIANO-REGGIANO*

FRESH THYME

TRUFFLE OIL (OPTIONAL)

FRESH CHIVES OR FLAT-LEAF PARSLEY

1 PINT HEAVY CREAM

1 PINT STRAWBERRIES

DINNER GAME PLAN

1. Get the list and go shopping.
2. Back at home, assemble pantry items.
3. Pour 2 glasses of white wine (the wine being used for the risotto).
4. Pop in a favorite CD.
5. She brings the chicken broth to a simmer in a small saucepan.
6. He chops the onion and garlic and puts the onion in a large saucepan with hot oil.
7. She slices the mushrooms and adds them to the large pan, then adds the garlic.
8. He adds the rice and begins stirring.
9. She adds the wine and takes a turn at stirring.
10. He adds some broth and takes over stirring.
11. She adds some broth and stirs . . . and so on and so on . . . until all the broth has been used and the risotto is done.

ALTERNATE REMAINING RESPONSIBILITIES

12. Grate the Parmesan cheese.
13. Chop the herbs.
14. Place the salad greens on small plates.
15. Whisk together the balsamic vinegar and olive oil to taste, season with kosher salt and pepper to taste (1 part vinegar to 4 parts oil), and pour over the greens.
16. Add the cheese, thyme, and butter to the risotto, season with kosher salt and pepper, and divide between 2 bowls. Garnish with truffle oil, if desired, cheese and chives, then sit down to dinner for two!
17. After dinner, he heats the cream in a small saucepan.
18. She removes the saucepan from the heat, adds the chocolate chips, a pinch of kosher salt, and a dash of brandy.
19. He pours the warm chocolate mixture into a small bowl and puts the strawberries in a bowl.
20. They share chocolate fondue for two.

ROMANTIC PICNIC

PIMIENTO CHEESE MINI-SANDWICHES

LEMONY-TARRAGON CRAB DIP WITH SALT-AND-VINEGAR POTATO CHIPS

SEASONAL FRESH FRUIT

BRIDE

GRAB FROM PANTRY:

JAR OF PIMIENTOS

PICANTE SAUCE

JAR OF GREEN OLIVES (OPTIONAL)

SUGAR

GROOM

GRAB FROM FRIDGE:

MAYONNAISE

LEMON

BRIDE AND GROOM

SHOPPING LIST (PLUS ANYTHING FROM
PANTRY/FRIDGE YOU MIGHT BE MISSING):

8 OUNCES EXTRA-SHARP WHITE CHEDDAR CHEESE

8 OUNCES EXTRA-SHARP YELLOW CHEDDAR CHEESE

1 YELLOW ONION

FRESH PARSLEY

SMALL DINNER ROLLS OR MINI FRENCH BREADS

ASSORTMENT OF SEASONAL FRUIT

CREAM CHEESE

1 RED ONION

FRESH TARRAGON

FRESH DILL

8 OUNCES FRESH CRABMEAT

1 CUCUMBER

SALT-AND-VINEGAR POTATO CHIPS

LUNCH GAME PLAN

1. Get the list and go shopping.
2. Back at home, assemble pantry items.
3. Pop in a favorite CD.
4. Each grabs a medium bowl and a cutting board.
5. She grates the Cheddar cheeses into her bowl.
6. He chops the red onion and fresh herbs.
7. She chops the pimientos, parsley, and olives, if desired, and grates the yellow onion.
8. He combines the cream cheese, red onion, mayonnaise, lemon juice and zest, and chopped herbs in his bowl.
9. She adds the mayonnaise, pimientos, onion, sugar, pepper, picante sauce, parsley, and olives, if desired, to the cheeses in her bowl and blends well.
10. He picks over the crab, removing any bits of shell, and adds it to his bowl.
11. She refrigerates the pimiento cheese, slices the rolls or bread, and cuts the fresh fruit, if necessary.
12. He chops the cucumber and adds it to his bowl with some kosher salt, pepper, and additional lemon juice.
13. She gets out the picnic basket and fills it with bread, fruit, and beverage of choice.
14. He refrigerates the crab dip and adds the chips to the picnic basket.
15. They pick a picnic spot, pull the spread and dip out of the fridge, transfer them to sealed plastic containers (taking only what is needed), and go!

CHAPTER 13

INSPIRATIONAL MENUS
FOR HOLIDAYS
&
SPECIAL OCCASIONS

WE THINK HOLIDAYS TAKE ON AN EXTRA-SPECIAL DIMENSION during the first years of marriage. At no other time of year were we as inspired to get into the kitchen and nurture our loved ones. Offering great-tasting, homemade food enhanced the occasion, whether we were making Filets Mignon with Green Peppercorns and Brandy-Cream Sauce (page 149) for our first anniversaries, or Sausage and Roasted Garlic Stuffing (page 161) as part of a Thanksgiving feast for our spouses' extended family.

During the holidays, the pressure is on to serve incredible meals. Many years ago, our mom severely overcooked the Christmas prime rib. We remember the tension and disappointment around the table when the well-done meat was presented. So for years, we were nervous about cooking a large, expensive cut of meat, lest we repeat our mother's Christmas catastrophe. We've worked harder than ever to perfect our prime rib recipe so that you won't have to follow in her footsteps.

We encourage you to create your own food traditions. Every Sunday during football season is an "occasion" at the Whiteford house. Sara's husband, Erik, is a die-hard Denver Broncos fan. On game days, Sara does everything she can to compete with the television, often plying him with food to win his attention. She first made the Texas Chili with All the Fixin's (page 114) on Super Bowl Sunday in 1998, the first year the Broncos won the Super Bowl. Erik has insisted that she repeat the menu whenever the Broncos are playing a crucial game—it's become his good-luck charm (not to mention good eats)!

You and your spouse may have very different ideas about what constitutes a traditional Thanksgiving dinner or the perfect Fourth of July picnic. Holidays present the ideal time for launching a lifetime of your own family food traditions. We've included some of our holiday favorites so you can add to the recipes already beloved in your family. We serve Prime Rib with Red Wine Gravy (page 139) for Christmas dinner, Lamb Chops with Mint-Mustard Sauce (page 142) on Valentine's Day, Sauza Margaritas (page 222) to kick off every Fourth of July, and Quick-and-Easy Drop Biscuits (page 185) for any festive seated dinner.

SUPER BOWL PARTY

Set out the Herbed Buttermilk Popcorn and the 1-2-3 Mexican Dip, and your party has begun well before the coin toss! Rowdy game days are a given in our homes, considering we both married sports fanatics. Kick off your party with raucous Whiskey Sour Slushes in place of the expected six-packs of beer. With the do-ahead ease of our Texas Chili with All the Fixin's, you won't miss a single play. And if anyone has room by the end of the 4th quarter, pass around some store-bought ice cream sandwiches before the clock runs out.

GREAT ROBERT'S WHISKEY SOUR SLUSH

1-2-3 MEXICAN DIP

HERBED BUTTERMILK POPCORN

PARTY PECANS

TEXAS CHILI WITH ALL THE FIXIN'S

CAESAR SALAD WITH LEMON-PEPPER SHRIMP

SUPER BOWL PARTY TO-DO LIST

1 WEEK AHEAD

review recipes and make grocery list

3 DAYS AHEAD

shop for groceries (except shrimp)

make Caesar dressing and refrigerate

make croutons for Caesar salad and store in sealable plastic bag

make popcorn seasoning and refrigerate

make party pecans

2 DAYS AHEAD

make chili and refrigerate

1 DAY AHEAD

buy, peel, and skewer shrimp and refrigerate

assemble Mexican dip and refrigerate

wash and dry salad greens (chop romaine)

8 HOURS AHEAD

prepare fixin's for chili, place in small bowls, and refrigerate if necessary

prepare whiskey sour slush and freeze as directed

30 MINUTES AHEAD

make popcorn and toss with seasoning

preheat grill

remove whiskey sour slush from freezer and put in pitcher

remove the fixin's from the refrigerator

warm chili over very low heat

remove Mexican dip from refrigerator and set out with chips

15 MINUTES AHEAD

place salad greens in a large bowl

grill shrimp

JUST BEFORE SERVING

toss salad with dressing

VALENTINE'S DAY

On the ultimate lovers' holiday, we romance our husbands with homemade cards and baked gifts from the heart. Most importantly, we love to show our affection by creating an elegant dinner for two. We always begin with a flute of bubbly and end on a sweet note, in this case, our appropriately red and white Raspberry Almond Dream Cream paired with Shortbread Sweethearts. Irresistible. Don't forget to uncork a special bottle of wine—choose a vintage from the year you were married—and light plenty of candles. We're firm believers in the seductive power of candlelight!

KIR ROYALES (SEE RASPBERRY CHAMPAGNE SPARKLERS)
LAMB CHOPS WITH MINT-MUSTARD SAUCE
COUSCOUS WITH MELTED LEEKS AND THYME
ROASTED ASPARAGUS
RASPBERRY-ALMOND DREAM CREAM
SHORTBREAD SWEETHEARTS

VALENTINE'S DAY TO-DO LIST

3 TO 5 DAYS AHEAD
review recipes and make grocery list

make shortbread dough and refrigerate (cookies can be baked and placed in a sealed container)

2 DAYS AHEAD
shop for groceries

refrigerate Champagne

1 DAY AHEAD
make almond dream cream

8 HOURS AHEAD
clean and slice leeks

2 HOURS AHEAD
trim and peel the asparagus

cook leeks for couscous

chop fresh thyme for couscous and cover with damp paper towel

1 HOUR AHEAD
assemble kir royales (make a toast to your valentine and sip while you cook)

remove lamb chops from refrigerator

30 MINUTES AHEAD
pour boiling chicken stock over couscous and cover

measure ingredients for mint sauce

preheat oven to 450 degrees F

15 MINUTES AHEAD
cook lamb chops

roast the asparagus

while lamb chops are cooking, warm leeks and add them to couscous along with the thyme (keep covered)

while lamb is resting, make mint-mustard sauce

EASTER BRUNCH

Spring is officially in the air with the arrival of Easter. And love is more in the air than ever in the Whiteford household, as Sara and Erik's wedding anniversary typically falls on or around Easter Sunday. Weather permitting, we usually celebrate with an alfresco brunch and enhance the pastels in our table decorations. Splurge on beautiful spring tulips for a centerpiece, and make an egg-dyeing date with your mate before the party. Your colorful homespun Easter eggs will bring childlike delight to everyone's eyes.

MARY'S BLOODY MARYS
SMOKED SALMON PLATTER
SAUSAGE AND CHEDDAR CHEESE STRATA
BUTTER LETTUCE WITH MANGO, GOAT CHEESE, AND MIGHTY MINT VINAIGRETTE
ROASTED ASPARAGUS
PUCKERY LEMON PARFAITS WITH SUMMER BERRIES

EASTER BRUNCH TO-DO LIST

1 WEEK AHEAD
review recipes and make grocery list

make mayonnaise (if homemade) and refrigerate

3 DAYS AHEAD
shop for groceries

2 DAYS AHEAD
make lemon curd and refrigerate

make mint vinaigrette and refrigerate

make Bloody Marys and refrigerate

1 DAY AHEAD
wash and dry salad greens and refrigerate

assemble salmon platter (excluding garnishes and bread), cover with plastic wrap, and refrigerate

prepare asparagus for roasting, wrap in a damp paper towel, and refrigerate

chop macadamia nuts

cook sausage for strata and refrigerate

grate cheese for strata

8 HOURS AHEAD
chop mango and refrigerate

chop green onions and refrigerate

assemble parfaits and refrigerate

1 1/2 HOURS AHEAD
remove goat cheese from refrigerator

preheat oven to 350 degrees F

1 HOUR AHEAD
add bread and garnishes to salmon platter and set out

assemble and bake strata; let cool for 10 to 15 minutes before covering with foil

30 MINUTES AHEAD
increase oven to 450 degrees F

combine salad in large bowl (excluding vinaigrette)

15 MINUTES AHEAD
roast asparagus

toss salad with vinaigrette

serve strata

FOURTH OF JULY

This star-spangled holiday is a great time to raise a festive Sauza margarita and count our lucky stars. Nothing marks summer quite like fresh white corn, finger-lickin' baby back ribs, and cool coleslaw. Gather 'round the picnic table for some good old-fashioned backyard eats with just the right kick of added spice. For a patriotic touch, wrap a sparkler in each guest's napkin and, after the brownies have been devoured, let the fireworks begin!

SAUZA MARGARITAS
"OH-BABY!" BABY BACK RIBS
SWEET CORN WITH JALAPEÑO ESSENCE
SPICY CHIPOTLE BLACK BEANS
CONFETTI COLESLAW
QUICK-AND-EASY DROP BISCUITS
OOEY-GOOEY CARAMEL CANDY BROWNIES

FOURTH OF JULY TO-DO LIST

1 WEEK AHEAD
review recipes and make grocery list

3 DAYS AHEAD
shop for groceries
make dry rub for ribs
make biscuit dough and freeze

2 DAYS AHEAD
shuck corn and refrigerate

1 DAY AHEAD
put dry rub on ribs
shave corn and refrigerate
assemble black beans and refrigerate
shred cabbage, salt, rinse and refrigerate
prepare boiled dressing for coleslaw and refrigerate
bake brownies

8 HOURS AHEAD
squeeze lime juice, assemble margaritas (don't pour over ice), and refrigerate
assemble coleslaw and refrigerate

3 HOURS AHEAD
remove ribs from refrigerator
preheat oven to 300 degrees F

2 HOURS AHEAD
pour margaritas over ice (when guests arrive)
cook ribs

30 MINUTES AHEAD
remove ribs from oven and cover tightly with foil
increase oven temperature to 400 degrees F

15 MINUTES AHEAD
bake biscuits
cook corn
warm black beans

THANKSGIVING

We love, love, love Thanksgiving. No lavish decorating—just a celebration of family, friends, and fabulous food. What could be better? Ask your friends and family to prepare the side dishes to lighten your load. And our detailed timetable will guarantee a stress-free holiday.

ORANGE CHAMPAGNE SPARKLERS (SEE RASPBERRY CHAMPAGNE SPARKLERS)

HOLIDAY TURKEY

SAUSAGE AND ROASTED GARLIC STUFFING

CRANBERRY RELISH

SPINACH WITH RAISINS AND PINE NUTS

SWEET POTATOES WITH PRALINE TOPPING

CREAMY-DREAMY MASHED POTATOES

QUICK-AND-EASY DROP BISCUITS

PUMPKIN PIE WITH BOURBON-SPIKED WHIPPED CREAM

THANKSGIVING TO-DO LIST

1 TO 2 WEEKS AHEAD

order fresh turkey

review recipes and make grocery list

shop for any essential tools and serving pieces

if friends and family will be helping with the meal, assign responsibilities

3 TO 4 DAYS AHEAD

purchase turkey if buying a frozen one and place in refrigerator to thaw (it takes several days)

shop for groceries

make piecrust (if homemade) and freeze

make cranberry relish and refrigerate

roast garlic for stuffing and refrigerate

make biscuit dough and freeze

1 DAY AHEAD

sauté onion, celery, and sausage for stuffing and refrigerate

brine turkey, see Turkey Tips, page 138

let turkey air-dry, uncovered, in refrigerator

make sweet potatoes (do not add topping) and refrigerate

assemble stuffing and refrigerate

5 HOURS AHEAD

roll out piecrust (if homemade) and blind bake

assemble pumpkin pie ingredients and bake

roast turkey

cook spinach, assemble (excluding nuts), and refrigerate; toast pine nuts

3 HOURS AHEAD

make gravy

make mashed potatoes (do not refrigerate)

1 HOUR AHEAD

bring to room temperature and bake stuffing

put topping on sweet potatoes and bake

whip cream and refrigerate

set out ingredients for Orange Champange Sparklers

JUST BEFORE DINNER

bake biscuits

make gravy and warm spinach with raisins and add pine nuts

warm mashed potatoes

HANUKKAH

This menu is such a bright light that you may want to make it all 8 days in a row! The richness and joy of Hanukkah, the Festival of Lights, is matched by the decadence of our Creamy Mushroom Soup with Brie Crostini and tangy Sweet-and-Sour Brisket—our twists on the classic versions. And what Hanukkah menu would be complete without latkes? Our Potato Pancakes with Sour Cream and Chives offer a crispy, sumptuous celebration of tastes. Once you've tried our "Hidden-Treasure" Bread Pudding, you'll feel as if "a great miracle happened here." Those who keep kosher will need to modify some recipes.

COSMOPOLITANS
CREAMY MUSHROOM SOUP WITH BRIE CROSTINI
SWEET-AND-SOUR BRISKET
MAPLE-GLAZED SPICED CARROTS
POTATO PANCAKES WITH SOUR CREAM AND CHIVES
"HIDDEN-TREASURE" BREAD PUDDING

HANUKKAH TO-DO LIST

1 WEEK AHEAD

review recipes and make grocery list

3 DAYS AHEAD

shop for groceries

cut up croissants for bread pudding into cubes and let stand to dry out

2 DAYS AHEAD

make mushroom soup (except the crostini) and refrigerate

make brisket and refrigerate

1 DAY AHEAD

peel and cut carrots and refrigerate

8 HOURS AHEAD

make potato pancakes (if time is limited, these may be frozen at least 1 week in advance and reheated as directed)

assemble and refrigerate ingredients for Cosmopolitans

6 HOURS AHEAD

preheat oven to 350 degrees F

assemble bread pudding and bake (cover and leave at room temperature until ready to reheat)

make maple-glazed carrots and refrigerate

1 HOUR AHEAD

preheat oven to 350 degrees F

warm brisket for about 30 minutes, remove from oven, and cover with foil

assemble Brie crostinis and cover with plastic wrap

30 MINUTES AHEAD

increase oven temperature to 375 degrees F

15 MINUTES AHEAD

set out ingredients for Cosmopolitans

warm crostini in oven

warm potato pancakes

warm mushroom soup

warm carrots

JUST BEFORE DINNER

cover bread pudding with foil and warm in 375-degree F oven

CHRISTMAS

This is our family's traditional Christmas menu. Our tongues wag in anticipation of carving the perfectly pink-all-the-way-through prime rib, while our Creamy-Dreamy Mashed Potatoes lend a satiny-smooth touch. To heck with figgy pudding; our Silken Chocolate Tart with "whip du jour" is downright ethereal.

CLASSIC MARTINIS
PRIME RIB WITH RED WINE GRAVY
CREAMY-DREAMY MASHED POTATOES
MAPLE-GLAZED SPICED CARROTS
BROCCOLI WITH SUN-DRIED TOMATOES AND PARMESAN
SILKEN CHOCOLATE TART

CHRISTMAS TO-DO LIST

1 WEEK AHEAD

review recipes and make list

call butcher and reserve a prime rib for Dec. 23 (ask butcher to remove chine bone and tie it back on)

make piecrust (if homemade) and freeze

2 DAYS AHEAD

shop for groceries and pick up prime rib

1 DAY AHEAD

cut broccoli into florets

peel potatoes, cover with water, and refrigerate

peel and cut carrots and refrigerate

grate Parmesan cheese

set up martini bar (cocktail napkins, glasses, tablecloth, gin, vodka, vermouth, shaker, ice bucket, and bowls for garnishes)

8 HOURS AHEAD

remove prime rib from refrigerator and let stand at room temperature for 2¹/₂ hours

roll out piecrust (if homemade), place in tart pan, and refrigerate

6 HOURS AHEAD

preheat oven for blind baking piecrust

blind bake piecrust

adjust oven to 350 degrees F

make filling for chocolate tart and bake

4¹/₂ TO 5 HOURS AHEAD

reduce oven to 200 degrees F

cook prime rib

3 HOURS AHEAD

make mashed potatoes (do not refrigerate)

make maple-glazed carrots

steam broccoli and prepare remaining ingredients

1 HOUR AHEAD

make red wine gravy

whip cream and refrigerate

30 MINUTES AHEAD

preheat oven to 200 degrees F

15 MINUTES AHEAD

warm mashed potatoes over very low heat, stirring frequently (thin with milk or cream if necessary)

warm broccoli and stir in remaining ingredients

warm carrots

carve prime rib

JUST BEFORE DINNER

place chocolate tart in warm oven and turn off the heat

JUST BEFORE DESSERT

whip cream further by hand if necessary

PICNIC LUNCH

We'll take any opportunity to spend time outdoors—nothing beats a delicious lunch savored on a picnic blanket while the sunshine spreads its warmth. Buy some attractive napkins, some fanciful paper plates and colorful utensils and a pair of portable wine glasses and you've turned a Tupperware-type meal into a special occasion. We love to laze around and ply our husbands with bits of assorted fresh fruit . . . even better when they feed *us*.

CITRUSY SANGRIA

PIMIENTO CHEESE SANDWICHES

ORZO SALAD WITH LEMON, FETA, AND PINE NUTS

CRUDITÉS WITH CAESAR DRESSING

ASSORTED FRESH FRUIT

OUR FAVORITE CHOCOLATE CHIP COOKIES

PICNIC LUNCH TO-DO LIST

3 TO 5 DAYS AHEAD

review recipes and make grocery list

2 DAYS AHEAD

shop for groceries

make pimiento cheese and refrigerate

make Caesar salad dressing and refrigerate

1 DAY AHEAD

toast pine nuts

prepare carrots, broccoli, and asparagus and refrigerate (do not blanch)

make cookies and store at room temperature in a sealable plastic container

8 HOURS AHEAD

assemble and refrigerate sangria

blanch carrots, broccoli, and asparagus and refrigerate

cut red bell peppers and cucumber and refrigerate

make orzo salad and refrigerate

assemble sandwiches, cover tightly, and refrigerate

2 HOURS AHEAD

cut fresh fruit

remove sandwiches, salad, and vegetables from refrigerator, put into sealable plastic containers, and pack picnic basket

COCKTAIL PARTY

Cocktail-party food is all about finger foods with attitude. A cinch to make, these appetizers get appetites going (consider them foreplay to a great meal). Our menu is perfect for casual grazing or sophisticated soirees—blue jeans on a Friday or black tie on a Saturday night. These taste-teasers are so sumptuous and satisfying, they're even enough for a whole dinner, if you so desire.

PINEAPPLE COSMOPOLITANS (SEE COSMOPOLITANS)
MARINATED OLIVES AND FETA CHEESE
WARM ARTICHOKE AND GREEN ONION DIP
SMOKED SALMON PLATTER
CRUDITÉS WITH GREEN ONION–MINT DIP
CHICKEN SATAY

COCKTAIL PARTY TO-DO LIST

5 DAYS AHEAD

review recipes and make grocery list

3 DAYS AHEAD

shop for groceries (except breads)

make pineapple vodka

select serving platters; clean or polish if necessary

2 DAYS AHEAD

marinate olives and refrigerate

make mayonnaise (if homemade) and refrigerate

make green onion–mint dip and refrigerate

make peanut sauce and refrigerate

1 DAY AHEAD

set up bar for Cosmopolitans (cocktail napkins, glasses, tablecloth, pineapple vodka, Triple Sec, cranberry juice, shaker, and ice bucket)

assemble artichoke and green onion dip and refrigerate

assemble smoked salmon platter (excluding garnishes and bread), cover with plastic wrap, and refrigerate

prepare carrots, broccoli, and asparagus and refrigerate (do not blanch)

marinate chicken

8 HOURS AHEAD

blanch broccoli, carrots, and asparagus

cut red bell peppers and cucumber

assemble vegetables on platter with bowl or cup for dip, cover with damp paper towels, and refrigerate

buy fresh bread for olive platter

assemble Cosmopolitan mixture and refrigerate

1 HOUR AHEAD

cut limes to garnish Cosmopolitans

strain olives into serving bowl and pour marinade over feta; let stand at room temperature

slice bread for olive platter, arrange in basket, and cover with cloth

add bread and garnishes to salmon platter and set out

preheat oven to 400 degrees F

30 MINUTES AHEAD

bake artichoke dip

preheat grill and grill chicken

SUMMER SEATED DINNER

We're warm weather–lovin' Southern girls at heart, but we live in temperate San Francisco now where summer is, oddly enough, the coolest time of year. Whatever your geography, whether summer brings balmy or foggy days, we've created the perfect, elegant, easy-to-prepare summer supper for you. Dazzling with a rich array of colors and tastes, this menu has become the favored celebratory meal for our Bastille Day birthdays.

MOJITOS

PORK TENDERLOIN WITH MANGO SALSA AND BLACKBERRY SYRUP

ROASTED ASPARAGUS

COCONUT RICE

SPICED CARROT CAKE WITH FLUFFY CREAM CHEESE ICING

SUMMER SEATED DINNER TO-DO LIST

3 TO 5 DAYS AHEAD

review recipes and make grocery list

2 DAYS AHEAD

shop for groceries

make carrot cake, cool (do not frost), and cover tightly with plastic wrap and refrigerate

1 DAY AHEAD

make icing, frost cake and refrigerate

prepare asparagus for roasting, wrap in a damp paper towel, and refrigerate

6 TO 8 HOURS AHEAD

squeeze lime juice for mojitos

make mango salsa

remove cake from refrigerator

1 HOUR AHEAD

make mojitos

assemble ingredients for coconut rice

30 MINUTES AHEAD

preheat oven to 450 degrees F

cook rice

make blackberry syrup

sauté pork tenderloins, finish cooking in oven, cover with foil, and let rest

15 MINUTES AHEAD

roast asparagus

slice tenderloins

FIRESIDE GATHERING

Warm, cozy, and undeniably romantic, the fireside is one of our favorite places to entertain our husbands or a couple of close friends. Kick off your evening in high style by serving martinis, then coast into the comforting and fun-to-eat Brie and Champagne Fondue. Relish our Butterflied Leg of Lamb with Grilled Lemon and Rosemary, and cap off the evening with a rustic Harvest Apple Crisp.

CLASSIC MARTINIS

GRILLED BUTTERFLIED LEG OF LAMB WITH LEMON AND ROSEMARY

BRIE AND CHAMPAGNE FONDUE

ARUGULA WITH CRANBERRIES, CAMBOZOLA, WALNUTS, AND RASPBERRY VINAIGRETTE

HARVEST APPLE CRISP

FIRESIDE GATHERING TO-DO LIST

3 TO 5 DAYS AHEAD
review recipes and make grocery list

2 DAYS AHEAD
shop for groceries (except fresh breads for fondue)

1 DAY AHEAD
marinate lamb and refrigerate

grate cheese for fondue

remove rind from Brie and cut cheese into pieces

toast walnuts for salad

make raspberry vinaigrette

set up martini bar (cocktail napkins, glasses, tablecloth, gin, vodka, vermouth, shaker, ice bucket, and olives, pickled onions, or lemon twists)

8 HOURS AHEAD
buy fresh breads for fondue

4 HOURS AHEAD
assemble fruit filling

make topping for apple crisp (do not place on filling)

2 1/2 HOURS AHEAD
preheat oven to 350 degrees F

2 HOURS AHEAD
place topping on apple crisp and bake

1 HOUR AHEAD
preheat the grill

grill lamb

measure ingredients for fondue

15 MINUTES AHEAD
make fondue

assemble salad and dress just before serving

FIRST ANNIVERSARY

This is it! You have so much to celebrate. We have created a tradition of eating in on our anniversaries—it's so much easier to savor each other in the comfort of our own homes. This menu has all the flavor and appeal of a restaurant meal. Make it your gift to each other. We think the nectarine tarts are a delightful ending to this meal. But if nectarines aren't at the height of their season, check below for seasonal variations.

BLACKBERRY CHAMPAGNE SPARKLERS (SEE RASPBERRY CHAMPAGNE SPARKLERS)

RED LEAF LETTUCE WITH GRAPES, BLUE CHEESE, PECANS, AND BALSAMIC VINAIGRETTE

FILETS MIGNON WITH GREEN PEPPERCORNS AND BRANDY-CREAM SAUCE

KILLER ROASTED POTATOES

NECTARINE TARTS FOR TWO

FIRST ANNIVERSARY TO-DO LIST

3 TO 5 DAYS AHEAD

review recipes and make grocery list

refrigerate champagne

2 DAYS AHEAD

shop for groceries

make balsamic vinaigrette and refrigerate

toast pecans

1 DAY AHEAD

wash and dry salad greens and refrigerate

make green peppercorns and brandy-cream sauce and refrigerate

3 TO 5 HOURS AHEAD

preheat oven to 400 degrees F

assemble nectarine tarts and bake

2 HOURS AHEAD

increase oven to 450 degrees F

1 1/2 HOURS AHEAD

prepare potatoes and cook

30 MINUTES AHEAD

make champagne sparklers and enjoy while preparing rest of meal

remove filets from refrigerator

assemble salad (do not toss with vinaigrette)

15 MINUTES AHEAD

cook steaks and let rest for a few minutes

warm green peppercorns and brandy-cream sauce

toss salad with vinaigrette

reduce oven to 200 degrees F

JUST BEFORE DINNER

warm nectarine tarts in oven

SEASONAL VARIATIONS

SPRING: Strawberries with lemon shortbread cookies and strawberry preserves

SUMMER: Cherries with amarette cookies and red currant jelly

FALL: Pear and dried cranberries with gingersnaps and apricot jelly

WINTER: Apples with oatmeal cookies and apple jelly

CHAPTER 14

DINNERS & DESSERTS
IN A DASH

DO YOU EVER FEEL LIKE GOING TO BED WITHOUT SUPPER because you just can't muster up the energy to pull *anything* together for dinner? (We do sometimes, and it's not for lack of hunger!) The recipes in this chapter are designed for those nights. While you may be exhausted, a delicious, home-cooked meal is easily within your reach. The key to these great-tasting entrées and desserts is that they rely on items already stocked in your pantry, and they come together lightning quick.

These meals skimp on time, not on flavor. The punch comes from one or a few specialty items, such as sun-dried tomatoes, green curry paste, marinated artichokes, or hoisin sauce—all easily found in your grocery store. While you'll have most of the ingredients for these no-brainer recipes on hand, you will need a few fresh items to round out the dishes.

Don't be afraid to experiment! This is truly how we cook during the week. It's not as much about entertaining as it is about everyday living, yet *all* of these recipes impress. If you're like us, you'll turn to this chapter more often than not, creating masterpieces in minutes.

Even our husbands, who leave most of the culinary responsibilities to us, cook at least one meal a week using these recipes. Jack's mainstays are Pasta with Roasted Red Bell Pepper Sauce (page 254) and Cumin-Crusted Halibut with Salsa Verde (page 253), while Erik's specialties are Chicken, Chipotle, and Tortilla Soup (page 254) and Chicken with Tarragon Mustard and Pretzels (page 257). We're both gluttons for Rum-Spiked Coconut Tapioca (page 260), and we're downright obsessed with the Cherry Potpies (page 261)— never hurts to make them à la mode.

We love this chapter so much because we find it gratifying to cook meals that taste this good in such a short amount of time. All of the recipes—and the philosophy behind them—really speak to us. Big-bang flavors created in 15 to 30 minutes, tops!

LINGUINE ALFREDO WITH CLAMS *Serves* 2

KEY INGREDIENTS

ONION

WHITE WINE

ALFREDO SAUCE

CLAMS

LEMON JUICE

PARSLEY

LINGUINE

PARMESAN CHEESE

Sauté a small sliced onion in olive oil until soft. Add about $1/4$ cup white wine and cook for 1 to 2 minutes. Add about 1 cup of Alfredo sauce, one 6.5-ounce can clams with juices, and juice of $1/2$ lemon. Bring to a simmer. Toss in a handful of chopped fresh parsley. Toss sauce with cooked linguine and season with pepper. Serve in pasta bowls and garnish with grated Parmesan cheese.

STUFFED CHICKEN PARMESAN *Serves* 2

KEY INGREDIENTS

SPINACH

RICOTTA CHEESE

ALFREDO SAUCE

LEMON

NUTMEG

CHICKEN BREASTS

PROSCIUTTO

SWISS CHEESE

*SEASONED BREAD
  CRUMBS (OPTIONAL)*

Preheat oven to 425 degrees F. Squeeze the excess liquid from one 10-ounce package thawed frozen spinach. Combine with $1/2$ cup ricotta cheese, a generous $1/4$ cup Alfredo sauce, squeeze of lemon, pinch of nutmeg, kosher salt, and freshly ground pepper. Place 2 skinless, boneless chicken breast halves between 2 pieces of plastic wrap. Whack with the back of a wooden spoon until the surface area nearly doubles. Place in a baking dish. Season with kosher salt and freshly ground pepper. Slather some additional Alfredo sauce over each breast followed by prosciutto, the spinach mixture, and Swiss cheese. Top with seasoned bread crumbs if you have them on hand. Bake for about 15 minutes.

TUNA WITH WHITE BEANS, ARTICHOKES, AND BLACK OLIVE TAPENADE *Serves 2*

KEY INGREDIENTS

TUNA STEAKS

CANNELLINI BEANS

CHICKEN BROTH

BLACK OLIVE TAPENADE

SUN-DRIED TOMATOES

DRIED OREGANO

MARINATED ARTICHOKES

BALSAMIC VINEGAR

ARUGULA OR BASIL

Brush 2 tuna steaks with olive oil. Season with kosher salt and freshly ground pepper. Grill to desired doneness. Meanwhile, combine one 15^1/$_4$-ounce can drained cannellini beans and ^{1}/$_2$ cup chicken broth in a skillet over medium heat. Stir in a dollop of tapenade, a handful of chopped sun-dried tomatoes, a pinch or two of oregano, one 6.5-ounce jar drained marinated artichokes and a splash of balsamic vinegar. Toss and season to taste. Place tuna on a plate and top with bean and artichoke medley. Garnish with arugula leaves or fresh basil.

CUMIN-CRUSTED HALIBUT WITH SALSA VERDE *Serves 2*

KEY INGREDIENTS

ONION

HALIBUT FILLETS

CUMIN

CHICKEN OR VEGETABLE BROTH

SALSA VERDE

SOUR CREAM

BLACK BEANS

CILANTRO

Sauté a small sliced onion in a little olive oil over medium heat. Reduce heat and add 2 skinless halibut fillets seasoned with kosher salt and ground cumin. Add a splash of chicken or vegetable broth and cook until fish is opaque in the center. Transfer fish to a platter. Add about ^{1}/$_2$ cup salsa verde and a dollop of sour cream to the pan. Warm sauce. Warm one 15-ounce can black beans in a saucepan. Pour sauce over fish and garnish with fresh cilantro leaves. Serve with black beans.

PASTA WITH ROASTED RED BELL PEPPER SAUCE *Serves* 2

KEY INGREDIENTS

*ROASTED RED BELL
  PEPPERS*

CREAM

BALSAMIC VINEGAR

GARLIC

TABASCO SAUCE

PASTA

*DRY-CURED BLACK
  OLIVES*

BASIL

PARMESAN CHEESE

Purée one 8-ounce jar drained roasted red bell peppers with about $1/2$ cup cream, a splash or two of balsamic vinegar, a small garlic clove, dash of Tabasco, and pinch of kosher salt. Pour over cooked pasta tossed with extra-virgin olive oil. Garnish with chopped dry-cured black olives, chopped fresh basil, and Parmesan cheese.

CHICKEN, CHIPOTLE, AND TORTILLA SOUP *Serves* 2

KEY INGREDIENTS

CHICKEN BROTH

*MEXICAN-STYLE
  STEWED TOMATOES*

CHIPOTLE CHILES

DELI-ROASTED CHICKEN

MONTEREY JACK CHEESE

AVOCADO

LIME

TORTILLA CHIPS

CILANTRO

Combine one 14-ounce can chicken broth, 1 ($14^{1}/2$ ounce) can stewed tomatoes, and a dab of chopped chipotle chiles in a small saucepan. Simmer over medium heat for about 5 minutes. Shred chicken and put about $1/2$ cup in each of 2 bowls along with a handful of grated Monterey Jack cheese and diced avocado. Pour broth mixture into bowls and season with fresh lime juice. Top with tortilla chips and chopped fresh cilantro. Garnish with a lime wedge.

PORK, BELL PEPPER, AND SNOW PEA STIR-FRY *Serves 2*

KEY INGREDIENTS

ONION

RED BELL PEPPER

PORK TENDERLOIN

SOY SAUCE (OPTIONAL)

GINGER

SHERRY

HOISIN SAUCE

SNOW PEAS

RICE

ASIAN SESAME OIL

SALTED PEANUTS (OPTIONAL)

Sauté a small sliced onion and a small sliced bell pepper in a little olive oil in a large skillet over high heat until softened. Season a thinly sliced pork tenderloin (about 8 ounces) with kosher salt or soy sauce, if desired. Add pork and about 1 teaspoon chopped fresh ginger to the skillet. Cook for about 1 minute. Add about $1/4$ cup each sherry, hoisin sauce, and water. Add a large handful of snow peas. Simmer for 1 minute and serve over cooked rice. Drizzle with sesame oil and garnish with a handful of peanuts if you have them on hand.

GREEN CURRY WITH SHRIMP *Serves 2*

KEY INGREDIENTS

ONION

GARLIC

UNSWEETENED COCONUT MILK

CHICKEN BROTH

GREEN CURRY PASTE

OODLES OF NOODLES (SHRIMP FLAVORED)

LIME JUICE

ROCK SHRIMP OR PEELED SHRIMP

FROZEN PEAS

BASIL OR CILANTRO (OPTIONAL)

Sauté a small chopped onion and a large chopped garlic clove in a little olive oil. Sprinkle with 2 teaspoons flour. Cook for 1 minute. Whisk in about 1 cup coconut milk, 1 cup chicken broth, 1 teaspoon green curry paste, 1 heaping teaspoon sugar, the flavor packet from Oodles of Noodles, and 1 generous tablespoon fresh lime juice. Bring to a boil and add the noodles. Simmer for 2 to 3 minutes. Season about 8 ounces peeled shrimp with kosher salt and add to the pan. Stir in 2 handfuls of peas. Simmer until the shrimp is opaque, about 2 minutes. Stir and season to taste with kosher salt. Garnish with chopped fresh basil or cilantro if you have it on hand.

CHINESE CHICKEN SALAD *Serves* 2

KEY INGREDIENTS

CHICKEN BREASTS

NAPA CABBAGE

GREEN ONIONS

SALTED PEANUTS

CHOW MEIN NOODLES

CILANTRO

PEANUT SAUCE

*SEASONED RICE
  VINEGAR*

Brush 2 skinless, boneless chicken breast halves with a little olive oil. Season with kosher salt and pepper. Grill until opaque in the center. Put about 4 cups sliced cabbage in a bowl with a handful *each* of chopped green onions, peanuts, chow mein noodles, and chopped fresh cilantro. Add warm sliced chicken. Dress with about $1/2$ cup peanut sauce and a splash of seasoned rice vinegar.

CHICKEN WITH TARRAGON MUSTARD AND PRETZELS *Serves* 2

KEY INGREDIENTS

CHICKEN BREASTS

DRIED DILL WEED

TARRAGON MUSTARD

SOUR CREAM

*HONEY-MUSTARD
  PRETZELS*

ASPARAGUS

LEMON WEDGES

Preheat oven to 425 degrees F. Place 2 skinless, boneless chicken breast halves between 2 pieces of plastic wrap. Whack with the back of a wooden spoon until the surface area nearly doubles. Place on a foil-lined baking sheet. Season both sides of chicken breasts with kosher salt, pepper, and dill. Mix about 2 heaping tablespoons mustard with about 2 heaping tablespoons sour cream. Slather on chicken breasts. Top with crushed pretzels. Place asparagus on baking sheet next to chicken and toss asparagus with extra-virgin olive oil, kosher salt, and pepper. Bake for about 15 minutes. Serve with lemon wedges.

CHOCOLATE FONDUE *Serves* 2

KEY INGREDIENTS

CREAM

SEMISWEET CHOCOLATE CHIPS

BRANDY OR GRAND MARNIER

STRAWBERRIES

Heat about $^1/_3$ cup cream in a small saucepan over medium heat until bubbling around the edges. Remove from heat and add about $^3/_4$ cup chocolate chips. Let stand until softened, 1 to 2 minutes. Season with a pinch of kosher salt and dash of brandy. Whisk until smooth. Pour into a small bowl and serve with strawberries for dipping. Alternatively, serve with sliced bananas, fresh cherries, bite-sized pieces of pound cake, or assorted Italian cookies.

TRIPLE-DECKER POUND CAKE WITH RASPBERRIES AND LEMON GLAZE *Serves* 2

KEY INGREDIENTS

PURCHASED POUND CAKE

RASPBERRY PRESERVES

LEMON

POWDERED SUGAR

FRESH RASPBERRIES

Cut a frozen pound cake (such as Sara Lee) in half crosswise. Wrap and freeze the remaining half. Trim off the brown top and the end, wasting as little as possible. Place cake on its side and slice twice lengthwise, creating three $^1/_2$-inch-thick rectangular pieces. Spread a thin layer of raspberry preserves, about 1 tablespoon, on each of 2 layers. Sandwich them together, creating a "triple deck." Cut in half and place each piece upright on a small plate. Zest lemon and roughly chop zest. Put in a small bowl with 1 generous tablespoon lemon juice. Stir in enough powdered sugar, about $^1/_2$ cup, to create a glaze. Add a pinch of kosher salt. Spread glaze on top of both pieces of cake, allowing glaze to drizzle down the sides. Top with a few raspberries and scatter a few on the plate.

HAZELNUT HOT CHOCOLATE *Serves 2*

KEY INGREDIENTS

MILK

CREAM

CHOCOLATE HAZELNUT SPREAD, SUCH AS NUTELLA

FRANGELICO OR VANILLA EXTRACT

Heat about 2 cups milk and a dash of cream in a saucepan over medium heat until almost simmering. Add about 1/4 cup chocolate hazelnut spread and a pinch of kosher salt. Whisk vigorously until frothy. Divide among 2 small mugs and cap off with a shot of Frangelico liqueur or a nip of vanilla.

RUM-SPIKED COCONUT TAPIOCA *Serves 2*

KEY INGREDIENTS

EGG

UNSWEETENED COCONUT MILK

SUGAR

MILK

TAPIOCA

RUM

COCONUT EXTRACT

Whisk 1 egg in a small saucepan. Add half of a 14-ounce can unsweetened coconut milk, 1 heaping cup sugar, 1/4 cup milk, 2 heaping tablespoons quick-cooking tapioca, and a pinch of kosher salt. Whisk and let stand for 5 minutes. Bring to a boil over medium-high heat, whisking constantly. Remove from heat and add a splash of rum and 2 drops coconut extract. Divide between 2 bowls. Serve warm or chilled. If serving chilled, place plastic wrap on surface and refrigerate.

CHERRY POTPIES *Serves 2*

KEY INGREDIENTS

FROZEN PUFF PASTRY

CANNED CHERRIES (IN WATER)

SUGAR

CORNSTARCH

CHERRY PRESERVES

UNSALTED BUTTER

ALMOND EXTRACT

GROUND CINNAMON

EGG

Preheat oven to 425 degrees F. Remove 1 sheet of puff pastry from the freezer. Using a heavy knife, cut the pastry in half crosswise and return the remaining half to the freezer for later use. Let thaw briefly, unfold the pastry, and cut in half again crosswise, creating two 5-inch squares. Strain one 14^1/2-ounce can cherries, reserving the juice. Combine a heaping ^{1}/2 cup sugar, 2 table-spoons cornstarch, the reserved cherry juice, 2 tablespoons cherry preserves, and a pinch of kosher salt in a small saucepan. Stirring with a whisk, bring the mixture to a boil for about 1 minute. Remove from heat.

Add ^{1}/4 cup sugar, the cherries, a dollop of butter, dash of almond extract, and pinch of cinnamon to the pan and stir. Divide between two 8-ounce ramekins. Transfer to a foil-lined baking sheet and cover each ramekin with a puff pastry square. Press gently on the rim of the ramekin so the pastry will adhere. Pierce 3 small holes in the center of the pies. Whisk the egg with 1 table-spoon water. Brush pies with lightly beaten egg and bake for 20 minutes in the upper third of the oven. Let stand for at least 20 minutes before serving. Potpies can be assembled several hours ahead, refrigerated, and baked just before serving.

DEFINITIONS OF COMMONLY USED COOKING TERMS

AL DENTE: An Italian term meaning "to the tooth." Pasta or vegetables cooked al dente should offer a slight resistance when bitten.

AU GRATIN: A bread crumb and butter or cheese topping for creamed foods or casseroles that is baked or broiled until browned.

BAKE: To cook in an oven.

BASTE: To moisten foods, primarily meats, while cooking using pan juices or reserved liquids.

BLANCH: To cook foods briefly in boiling salted water.

BOIL: To cook in a liquid over high heat so that bubbles constantly rise and break on the surface.

BRAISE: To cook slowly over low heat in a small amount of liquid, either in the oven or on the stovetop.

BROIL: To cook directly under heat, generally by placing foods in an oven or toaster-rack set at its highest possible point.

CARAMELIZE: To cook vegetables or fruits slowly over low heat until they release their natural sugars and take on a deep amber or caramel-brown appearance. Or, to melt sugar until it turns golden brown.

CHOP: To cut into small pieces.

CREAM: To blend a fat (butter, oil, shortening) with a dry ingredient until it reaches a light, airy consistency.

DICE: To cut into small, uniform cubes.

DREDGE: To drag foods in seasoned flour, dried herbs, or sugar to coat.

FOLD: To incorporate a light, beaten ingredient into another, heavier ingredient using a delicate folding motion, which retains the texture of the lighter ingredient.

FRY: To cook in hot fat.

GRATE: To rub on a grater and shred into small slivers.

GRILL: To cook over an open flame on a grill or over high, dry heat in a grill pan.

JULIENNE: To cut into thin, matchstick-like strips.

KNEAD: To work dough by pressing and folding it with the hands.

MARINATE: To soak food in a seasoned liquid in order to tenderize and infuse flavor.

MINCE: To cut into fine bits.

PARBOIL: To boil foods until partially cooked.

PEEL: To remove the tough outer skin of fruits or vegetables.

PURÉE: To pass fruits or vegetables through a ricer or sieve, or process in a blender or food processor to achieve a smooth, velvety consistency.

REDUCE: To cook sauces until their volume has decreased in order to concentrate flavor and thicken the sauce.

REFRESH: To plunge foods into ice water to stop the cooking.

ROAST: To cook, uncovered, in an oven.

SAUTÉ: To cook briefly over high heat in a skillet in a small amount of hot oil or butter.

SEAR: To brown the outer surface of meats or fish by turning them in a very hot skillet.

SHRED: To cut or grate into small slivers.

SIFT: To pass dry ingredients through a sifter or sieve to lighten, remove lumps, and evenly distribute the ingredients.

SIMMER: To cook in a liquid kept just below a boil so that tiny bubbles occasionally rise to the surface.

SKEWER: To pierce foods for cooking or serving with a wooden or metal stick.

STEAM: To cook, covered, in the vapor created by boiling water.

STEW: To cook slowly in liquid over a long period of time.

STIR-FRY: To cook quickly in little or no fat over high heat in a wok or skillet, stirring constantly.

WHIP: To beat ingredients rapidly in order to aerate and increase volume.

ZEST: To remove the flavor-packed outer skin of citrus fruits with the aid of a microplane, zester, or peeler, avoiding removal of the bitter white pith underneath the skin.

GUIDE TO SEASONAL FRUITS
& VEGETABLES

As our friend Michael Chiarello says, "Wait one or two weeks into a vegetable's season, eat it twice a week during the height of the season, and then give it up." We couldn't agree more.

There is absolutely nothing better than cooking with fruits and vegetables at the peak of their ripeness. Seasonal ingredients require minimal preparation because they taste great when allowed to shine naturally. We feel so fortunate to live in the San Francisco Bay Area and to have access to many farmers' markets year-round. California abounds with the freshest produce in the world, from artichokes and asparagus to almonds and garlic.

Our favorite Saturday-morning activity is to take a family outing to the farmers' market for a heavenly breakfast and coffee, followed by a leisurely stroll past the friendly vendors' stands. We chat with the local organic growers, sampling deep-fried asparagus in the spring, picking out the juiciest tomatoes in summertime, and tasting crisp apples in the fall. There are fresh-pressed juices, farmstead cheeses, lavender and clover honeys, dried fruits and berries, plants and flowers, smoked fish and meats, bottled ethnic foods, and so much more. With its colorful array of fruits, veggies, and flowers, the farmers' market inspires us every week. We dash home with a brimming market basket, stocked for the week with the freshest produce to be found. The farmers' market feeds our souls, motivating us to create meals around whatever is in season that week.

For the season's finest produce, it's best to buy directly from local farmers' markets. If you don't have access to a farmers' market, contact your Chamber of Commerce for a listing of area farm stands. It will be well worth the time. Our parents drive 45 minutes to Winston-Salem to visit their local farmers' market. Besides the opportunity to enjoy the freshest produce, visiting the markets is great fun and gives you a glimpse into the farming community.

Don't be discouraged if you can't find a farmers' market near you—many supermarkets maintain relationships with local growers, offering you fresh produce year-round. Look for signs indicating that produce is seasonal and locally grown.

Whether shopping at the farmers' market or your local supermarket, follow our general produce calendar that follows. Keep in mind that growing seasons vary from state to state and region to region.

SPRING

When spring has sprung, those lush green delicacies like sweet English peas, plump artichokes, pencil-thin asparagus, and fava beans are plentiful at the market.

You'll find sweet, juicy strawberries and shiny red cherries, ripe for the pickin'! Our advice is to take advantage of these heavenly vegetables and fruits while they last.

VEGETABLES:

Artichokes
Asparagus
Avocados
Beets
Carrots
English peas
Fava beans
Green beans
Green garlic
New potatoes
Radishes
Rhubarb
Snow peas
Spinach
Spring salad mix (bitter greens such as arugula, Belgian endive, escarole, and frisée)
Sugar snap peas
Vidalia onions
Zucchini

FRUIT:

Apricots
Cherries
Strawberries

SUMMER

When we think summer, we think succulent, sugary, white corn on the cob and perfectly ripe red tomatoes. We can't get enough of either! Tomatoes are so sweet during the summer that we love to eat them just like apples. In California, we have access to a great variety of tomatoes—multicolored heirlooms, Green Zebras, Sweet 100s, Marvel Stripes, Early Girls, and Brandywines—a galaxy of flavors. Then there's the exciting and colorful array of berries, juicy peaches, and aromatic melons. Summer is the best time of year to showcase vegetables and fruits "in the raw."

VEGETABLES:

Beets
Corn
Cucumbers
Eggplant
Fresh herbs
Garlic
Green beans
Okra
Onions
Potatoes
Summer squash
Tomatoes

FRUIT:

Blackberries
Blueberries
Figs
Grapes
Limes
Mangoes
Melons
Nectarines
Peaches
Plums
Raspberries

FALL

Fall is a season of transition, when produce is particularly plentiful. In many warmer climates, summer produce (the last of the cucumbers, tomatoes, and peppers) is still available. In cooler regions, early winter produce (root vegetables and winter squashes) makes an entrance.

When the weather gets cooler, we race to the farmers' market to pick up rich, sweet butternut squash; crispy apples; and seductive, fleshy figs. The fall market is brimming with leafy chard, bold, red cranberries, and pumpkins in every shape and size.

Fall inspires us to roast just about anything—parsnips, squash, beets, Brussels sprouts, rutabagas, turnips, and sweet potatoes. We relish all the warmth and richness the season offers.

VEGETABLES:

Arugula
Bell peppers
Broccoli
Brussels sprouts
Cabbages
    (green, napa, red, savoy)
Celery
Fennel
Garlic

Greens
    (beet, chard, kale, turnip)
Green tomatoes
Leeks
Mushrooms
Parsnips
Pumpkins

Radishes
Rutabagas
Shallots
Shelling beans
Spinach
Sweet potatoes
Turnips
Winter squashes
    (acorn, butternut, spaghetti)

FRUIT:

Apples
Citrus
    (lemon, orange, tangerine)
Cranberries
Figs
Grapes
Kiwifruit
Pears
Persimmons
Pomegranates

WINTER

Winter is the perfect season to bundle up for a date to your local farmers' market. Buy root vegetables and greens for a warming stew, then stop off for a hot chocolate on the way home.

Our farmers' market is decidedly smaller in the wintertime, as some local growers' produce can't withstand the cold or frost. But there are still plenty of great things to be found—hearty cabbages, earthy Brussels sprouts, spicy turnips, and sturdy greens.

Winter cooking is about long-simmered soups and robust stews—those comfort foods that we crave when the weather turns cold. Cozy up to the fire while you braise, stew, and roast to your heart's content.

VEGETABLES:

Avocados
Broccoli
Brussels sprouts
Cabbage
    (green, napa, red, savoy)
Carrots
Cauliflower

Fennel
Green onions
Greens
    (beet, chard, collard, kale, turnip)
Leeks
Parsnips
Sweet potatoes

Turnips
Wild mushrooms
Winter squash
    (acorn, butternut, spaghetti)
Yams

FRUIT:

Citrus
    (grapefruit, lemon, orange, tangerine)
Dates
Pears

INDEX

A

Alfredo sauce, 20
Apples
  Harvest Apple Crisp, 208
  Pan-Fried Pork Chops with Glazed
    Apples, 107
Appliances, 16
Artichokes, 20
  Artichokes with Lemon-Garlic
    Butter, 60
  eating, 60
  Tuna with White Beans, Artichokes,
    and Black Olive Tapenade, 253
  Warm Artichoke and Green Onion
    Dip, 54
Arugula with Cranberries, Cambozola,
  Walnuts, and Raspberry Vinaigrette, 89
Asian Spinach Salad with Hoisin-
  Glazed Salmon, 93
Asparagus
  Bow Tie Pasta with Asparagus, Sun-
    Dried Tomatoes, and Boursin, 122
  Roasted Asparagus, 152
  trimming and peeling, 152
Avocados
  Guacamole, 58

B

Bacon, Linguine with Scallops,
  Spinach, and, 124–25
Baking equipment, 15
Baking powder, 20
Baking soda, 20
Balsamic Vinaigrette, 45
Balsamic vinegar, 20
Bananas
  Peanut Butter Toast with Icy-Cold
    Banana Milk, 181
  Rise-and-Shine Smoothie, 189
  Unbelievable Banana Bread, 188
  Yogurt-Granola Parfaits, 186
Bar, 17, 27. See also Cocktail parties
Barbecue sauce, 20
Basil
  chiffonade, 160
  Pesto, 48
Beans, 20
  Green Beans, Beets, and Goat
    Cheese with Sherry Vinaigrette, 88

Mexican Chicken Salad with Taco-
  Ranch Dressing, 97
Mrs. Birdsong's Cabbage Soup,
  76–77
1-2-3 Mexican Dip, 59
Spicy Chipotle Black Beans, 162
Texas Chili with All the Fixin's, 114
Tuna with White Beans, Artichokes,
  and Black Olive Tapenade, 253
Beef
  Beef Burgundy, 111
  Better Than Grandma's Meat Loaf, 117
  Classic Lasagna, 103
  Filets Mignons with Green
    Peppercorns and Brandy-Cream
    Sauce, 149
  Grilled London Broil Fajitas, 147–48
  Mrs. Birdsong's Cabbage Soup,
    76–77
  Prime Rib with Red Wine Gravy, 139
  Stuffed Bell Peppers, 117
  Sweet-and-Sour Brisket, 113
  Texas Chili with All the Fixin's, 114
Beets, Green Beans, and Goat
  Cheese with Sherry Vinaigrette, 88
Bell peppers
  Pasta with Roasted Red Bell Pepper
    Sauce, 254
  Pork, Bell Pepper, and Snow Pea
    Stir-Fry, 256
  roasted, 24, 135
  Roasted Red Pepper Salsa, 135
  Stuffed Bell Peppers, 117
Berries. See also individual berries
  Mom's "Flyaway" Pancakes with
    Melted Berries, 183–84
  Puckery Lemon Parfaits with
    Summer Berries, 217–18
Better Than Grandma's Meat Loaf, 117
Beverages, 222–29, 260
Biscuits, Quick-and-Easy Drop, 185
Blackberry Syrup, 141
Bloody Marys, Mary's, 229
Bouillon, 20
Bourbon
  Bourbon-Spiked Whipped Cream,
    204–5
  Great Robert's Whiskey Sour Slush,
    227

Bow Tie Pasta with Asparagus, Sun-
  Dried Tomatoes, and Boursin, 122
Bread
  Brie and Champagne Fondue, 101
  Brie Crostini, 73
  Croutons, 43
  crumbs, 117
  French Toast with Hot Buttered
    Rum–Maple Syrup, 180
  "Hidden-Treasure" Bread Pudding, 219
  Peanut Butter Toast with Icy-Cold
    Banana Milk, 181
  Sausage and Cheddar Cheese
    Strata, 178
  Sausage and Roasted Garlic
    Stuffing, 161
  sticks, 20
  Unbelievable Banana Bread, 188
Breakfast in Bed menu, 232
Brie
  Brie and Champagne Fondue, 101
  Brie Crostini, 73
Broccoli
  Broccoli with Sun-Dried Tomatoes
    and Parmesan, 156
  Chicken "Divine," 133
Broth, 20
Brownies, Ooooey-Gooey Caramel
  Candy, 214
Butter Lettuce with Mango, Goat Cheese,
  and Mighty Mint Vinaigrette, 83
Buttermilk, powdered, 20–21, 65

C

Cabbage
  Chinese Chicken Salad, 257
  Confetti Coleslaw, 92
  Mrs. Birdsong's Cabbage Soup, 76–77
Caesar Dressing, 44
Caesar Salad with Lemon-Pepper
  Shrimp, 96
Cakes
  mixes, 21
  Shhh, Don't Tell—Chocolate Fudge
    Birthday Cake!, 195–96
  Spiced Carrot Cake with Fluffy
    Cream Cheese Icing, 193–94
  Triple-Decker Pound Cake with
    Raspberries and Lemon Glaze, 258

Canola oil, 21
Capers, 21
Carrots
　Maple-Glazed Spiced Carrots, 157
　Spiced Carrot Cake, 193–94
Champagne
　Brie and Champagne Fondue, 101
　Champagne-Cream Sauce, 124–25
　Raspberry Champagne Sparklers, 222
Cheddar cheese
　Cheddar Cheese–Dill Biscuits, 185
　1-2-3 Mexican Dip, 59
　Pimiento Cheese Spread, 51
　Sausage and Cheddar Cheese
　　Strata, 178
　Stovetop Macaroni and Cheese, 116
Cheese. See also individual cheeses
　Arugula with Cranberries,
　　Cambozola, Walnuts, and Raspberry
　　Vinaigrette, 89
　Bow Tie Pasta with Asparagus, Sun-
　　Dried Tomatoes, and Boursin, 122
　Chicken "Divine," 133
　Chicken with Prosciutto, Fontina,
　　and Mushroom Sauce, 132
　Classic Lasagna, 103
　Individual Four-Cheese Pizzas, 102
　Red Leaf Lettuce with Grapes, Blue
　　Cheese, Pecans, and Balsamic
　　Vinaigrette, 86
　Roasted Tomato Pie, 160
　in salads, 85
　Stuffed Chicken Parmesan, 252
　Summer Tomato Stacks, 91
Cheesecake, Very Vanilla, 200–201
　Cherry Potpies, 261
Chicken
　carving, 106
　Chicken, Chipotle, and Tortilla Soup,
　　254
　Chicken "Divine," 133
　Chicken Satay, 64
　Chicken Soup for Your Soul Mate, 72
　Chicken Stock, 30
　Chicken with Prosciutto, Fontina,
　　and Mushroom Sauce, 132
　Chicken with Tarragon Mustard and
　　Pretzels, 257

Chinese Chicken Salad, 257
　Grilled Chicken with Roasted Red
　　Pepper Salsa, 135
　Mexican Chicken Salad with Taco-
　　Ranch Dressing, 97
　Personalized Chicken Potpies,
　　109–10
　Roast Chicken and Vegetables for
　　Two, 105–6
　Stuffed Chicken Parmesan, 252
Chili, Texas, with All the Fixin's, 114
Chinese Chicken Salad, 257
Chocolate
　cake mix, 21
　Chocolate Fondue, 258
　Chocolate Sauce, 214
　Hazelnut Hot Chocolate, 260
　"Hidden-Treasure" Bread Pudding,
　　219
　morsels, 21
　Ooooey-Gooey Caramel Candy
　　Brownies, 214
　Our Favorite Chocolate Chip
　　Cookies, 212
　Peanut Butter Pie Sealed with
　　Kisses, 202
　Shhh, Don't Tell—Chocolate Fudge
　　Birthday Cake!, 195–96
　Silken Chocolate Tart, 203
Christmas menu, 244
Citrusy Sangria, 228
Clams, Linguine Alfredo with, 252
Cocktail parties
　menu, 246
　recipes, 222–29
Cocoa, 21
Coconut extract, 21
Coconut milk, 21
　Coconut Rice, 170
　Green Curry with Shrimp, 256
　Rum-Spiked Coconut Tapioca, 260
　Thai-Style Corn Soup with Shrimp
　　and Green Curry, 81
Confetti Coleslaw, 92
Cookies
　Daddy's Oatmeal Cookies, 211
　Ooooey-Gooey Caramel Candy
　　Brownies, 214

Our Favorite Chocolate Chip
　　Cookies, 212
　Shortbread Sweethearts, 210
Cooking terms, 262
Corn
　Sweet Corn with Jalapeño Essence,
　　155
　Thai-Style Corn Soup with Shrimp
　　and Green Curry, 81
Cornbread mix, 21
Corn Chip–Crusted Halibut with
　　Creamy Salsa and Cilantro, 129
Cornstarch, 21
Cosmopolitans, 225
Couscous
　about, 21–22
　Couscous with Melted Leeks and
　　Thyme, 171
Crab Dip, Lemony-Tarragon, 55
Crackers, 22
Cranberries
　Arugula with Cranberries,
　　Cambozola, Walnuts, and
　　Raspberry Vinaigrette, 89
　Cosmopolitans, 225
　Cranberry Relish, 49
　Wild Rice with Dried Cranberries,
　　Green Onions, and Pecans, 169
Cream cheese
　Fluffy Cream Cheese Icing, 193–94
　Frittata with Sun-Dried Tomatoes,
　　Cream Cheese, and Basil, 177
　Goat Cheese, Sun-Dried Tomato,
　　and Pesto Torta, 62
　Lemony-Tarragon Crab Dip, 55
　Very Vanilla Cheesecake, 200–201
Creamy-Dreamy Mashed Potatoes, 163
Creamy Mushroom Soup with Brie
　　Crostini, 73
Crème fraîche, 128
Crostini, Brie, 73
Croutons, 43
Crudités with Green Onion–Mint Dip, 57
Cucumbers, Pickled, 131
Cumin-Crusted Halibut with Salsa
　　Verde, 253
Curry, Green, with Shrimp, 256
Curry paste, green, 22
Cutlery, 14

D

Daddy's Oatmeal Cookies, 211
Daiquiris, Strawberry, 223
Desserts. *See also* Cakes; Cookies;
    Pies; Tarts
  Cherry Potpies, 261
  Chocolate Fondue, 258
  Harvest Apple Crisp, 208
  "Hidden-Treasure" Bread Pudding,
    219
  Puckery Lemon Parfaits with
    Summer Berries, 217–18
  Raspberry-Almond Dream Cream, 215
  Rum-Spiked Coconut Tapioca, 260
  Strawberry Shortcakes d'Amour,
    197–98
  Very Vanilla Cheesecake, 200–201
Dips, 54–59

E

Easter Brunch menu, 240
Eggs
  Eggs Benedict, 175–76
  Frittata with Sun-Dried Tomatoes,
    Cream Cheese, and Basil, 177
  Sausage and Cheddar Cheese
    Strata, 178
Elegant Supper for Two menu, 233
Equipment, 13–17

F

Fajitas, Grilled London Broil, 147–48
Feta cheese
  Marinated Olives and Feta Cheese, 68
  Orzo Salad with Lemon, Feta, and
    Pine Nuts, 94
Filets Mignons with Green Peppercorns
  and Brandy-Cream Sauce, 149
Fireside Gathering menu, 248
First Anniversary menu, 249
Fish
  Asian Spinach Salad with Hoisin-
    Glazed Salmon, 93
  Corn Chip–Crusted Halibut with
    Creamy Salsa, 129
  Grilled Tuna with Soy-Ginger Glaze,
    131
  Salmon with Honey-Mustard Glaze,
    128

Smoked Salmon Platter, 66
  Tuna with White Beans, Artichokes,
    and Black Olive Tapenade, 253
Flaky Piecrust, 39–40
Flour, 22
Fondue
  Brie and Champagne Fondue, 101
  Chocolate Fondue, 258
Fourth of July menu, 241
French Toast with Hot Buttered
  Rum–Maple Syrup, 180
Frittata with Sun-Dried Tomatoes,
  Cream Cheese, and Basil, 177
Fruits. *See also individual fruits*
  Citrusy Sangria, 228
  dried, 22
  in salads, 85
  seasonal, 263–65

G

Garlic, roasted, 34
Gazpacho, Summer Garden, 74
Gin
  Classic Martinis, 226
Glassware, 17
Goat cheese
  Butter Lettuce with Mango, Goat
    Cheese, and Mighty Mint
    Vinaigrette, 83
  Goat Cheese, Sun-Dried Tomato,
    and Pesto Torta, 62
  Green Beans, Beets, and Goat
    Cheese with Sherry Vinaigrette, 88
Granola Parfaits, Yogurt-, 186
Grapes, Red Leaf Lettuce with Blue
  Cheese, Pecans, Balsamic
  Vinaigrette, and, 86
Great Robert's Whiskey Sour Slush, 227
Green Beans, Beets, and Goat Cheese
  with Sherry Vinaigrette, 88
Green Curry with Shrimp, 256
Green Onion–Mint Dip, 57
Gruyère cheese
  Caramelized Onion, Gruyère, and
    Olive Tarts, 61
  Sherry-Spiked French Onion Soup, 82
Guacamole, 58
"Gussied-Up" Marinara Sauce, 36

H

Halibut
  Corn Chip–Crusted Halibut with
    Creamy Salsa, 129
  Cumin-Crusted Halibut with Salsa
    Verde, 253
Hanukkah menu, 243
Harvest Apple Crisp, 208
Hazelnut Hot Chocolate, 260
Herbed Buttermilk Popcorn, 65
Herbs, 26
"Hidden-Treasure" Bread Pudding, 219
Hoisin sauce, 22
Holiday Turkey, 137–38
Hollandaise Sauce, 175–76
Honey, 22
Horseradish, 22

I

Individual Four-Cheese Pizzas, 102

J

Jam, 22

K

Ketchup, 22
Killer Roasted Potatoes, 166
Knives, 14

L

Lamb
  Grilled Butterflied Leg of Lamb, 145
  Lamb Chops with Mint-Mustard
    Sauce, 142
Lasagna, Classic, 103
Leeks, Melted, Couscous with Thyme
  and, 171
Lemons
  Lemony-Tarragon Crab Dip, 55
  Puckery Lemon Parfaits with
    Summer Berries, 217–18
  Vodka-Spiked Lemonade with Red
    Rocks, 226
Linguine
  Linguine Alfredo with Clams, 252
  Linguine with Scallops, Spinach, and
    Bacon, 124–25

M

Macaroni and Cheese, Stovetop, 116
Mangoes
  Butter Lettuce with Mango, Goat
    Cheese, and Mighty Mint
    Vinaigrette, 83
  Mango Salsa, 141
Maple-Glazed Spiced Carrots, 157
Maple syrup, 22
Margaritas, Sauza, 222
Marinade, Our "Can't-Do-Without," 33
Marinara sauce, 22
  "Gussied-Up" Marinara Sauce, 36
  Summertime Marinara Sauce, 37
Martinis, Classic, 226
Mary's Bloody Marys, 229
Matzo, 164
Mayonnaise, 23, 32
Meat Loaf, Better Than Grandma's, 117
Menus, 231–49
Mexican Chicken Salad with Taco-
  Ranch Dressing, 97
Mighty Mint Vinaigrette, 45
Mojitos, 225
Mom's "Flyaway" Pancakes with
  Melted Berries, 183–84
Mrs. Birdsong's Cabbage Soup, 76–77
Mushrooms
  Chicken with Prosciutto, Fontina,
    and Mushroom Sauce, 132
  Creamy Mushroom Soup with Brie
    Crostini, 73
  Wild Mushroom Risotto, 121
Mustard, 23

N

Nectarine Tarts for Two, 207
Noodles. See Pasta and noodles
Nutella, 23
Nuts, 23. See also individual nuts

O

Oatmeal
  about, 23
  Daddy's Oatmeal Cookies, 211
  "Oh-Baby!" Baby Back Ribs, 112
Oils, 21, 23
Olives, 23
  Marinated Olives and Feta Cheese, 68
  oil, 23

tapenade, 20
1-2-3 Mexican Dip, 59
Onions
  Caramelized Onion, Gruyère, and
    Olive Tarts, 61
  Caramelized Onions, 50
  Sherry-Spiked French Onion Soup, 82
Oooey-Gooey Caramel Candy
  Brownies, 214
Orzo Salad with Lemon, Feta, and Pine
  Nuts, 94
Our "Can't-Do-Without" Marinade, 33
Our Favorite Chocolate Chip Cookies, 212

P

Pancakes
  mixes, 23
  Mom's "Flyaway" Pancakes with
    Melted Berries, 183–84
  Potato Pancakes with Sour Cream
    and Chives, 164
Pans, 14–15
Pantry items, 19–27
Parfaits
  Puckery Lemon Parfaits with
    Summer Berries, 217–18
  Yogurt-Granola Parfaits, 186
  Party Pecans, 69
Pasta and noodles, 23. See also
    Couscous
  Bow Tie Pasta with Asparagus, Sun-
    Dried Tomatoes, and Boursin, 122
  Chicken "Divine," 133
  Chicken Soup for Your Soul Mate, 72
  Chinese Chicken Salad, 257
  Classic Lasagna, 103
  Linguine Alfredo with Clams, 252
  Linguine with Scallops, Spinach, and
    Bacon, 124–25
  Orzo Salad with Lemon, Feta, and
    Pine Nuts, 94
  Pasta with Pesto, Shrimp, and Sweet
    100s, 126
  Pasta with Roasted Red Bell Pepper
    Sauce, 254
  Stovetop Macaroni and Cheese, 116
Peanuts and peanut butter, 23
  Peanut Butter Pie Sealed with
    Kisses, 202

Peanut Butter Toast with Icy-Cold
    Banana Milk, 181
  Peanut Sauce, 24, 46
Peas, Sweet, with Red Onion and
  Mint, 158
Pecans
  Party Pecans, 69
  Red Leaf Lettuce with Grapes, Blue
    Cheese, Pecans, and Balsamic
    Vinaigrette, 86
  Sweet Potatoes with Praline
    Topping, 167
  Wild Rice with Dried Cranberries,
    Green Onions, and Pecans, 169
Peppercorns, 24
Personalized Chicken Potpies, 109–10
Pesto, 48
Pickled Cucumbers, 131
Pickles, 24
Picnic menus, 234, 245
Pies. See also Potpies
  Flaky Piecrust, 39–40
  Peanut Butter Pie Sealed with
    Kisses, 202
  Pumpkin Pie with Bourbon-Spiked
    Whipped Cream, 204–5
  Roasted Tomato Pie, 160
Pimiento Cheese Spread, 51
Pizzas
  Individual Four-Cheese Pizzas, 102
  Pizza Dough, 41–42
Popcorn, Herbed Buttermilk, 65
Pork
  "Oh-Baby!" Baby Back Ribs, 112
  Pan-Fried Pork Chops with Glazed
    Apples, 107
  Pork, Bell Pepper, and Snow Pea
    Stir-Fry, 256
  Pork Tenderloin with Mango Salsa
    and Blackberry Syrup, 141
Potato Chips, Salt-and-Vinegar,
  Lemony-Tarragon Crab Dip with, 55
Potatoes
  Creamy-Dreamy Mashed Potatoes, 163
  Killer Roasted Potatoes, 166
  Potato Pancakes with Sour Cream
    and Chives, 164
Potpies
  Cherry Potpies, 261

Personalized Chicken Potpies, 109–10
Pots, 14–15
Pretzels, Chicken with Tarragon Mustard and, 257
Prime Rib with Red Wine Gravy, 139
Puckery Lemon Parfaits with Summer Berries, 217–18
Pudding, "Hidden-Treasure" Bread, 219
Pumpkin Pie with Bourbon-Spiked Whipped Cream, 204–5

Q

Quick-and-Easy Drop Biscuits, 185

R

Raspberries
  Raspberry-Almond Dream Cream, 215
  Raspberry Champagne Sparklers, 222
  Raspberry Vinaigrette, 89
  Triple-Decker Pound Cake with Raspberries and Lemon Glaze, 258
Red Leaf Lettuce with Grapes, Blue Cheese, Pecans, and Balsamic Vinaigrette, 86
Relish, Cranberry, 49
Ribs, "Oh-Baby!" Baby Back, 112
Rice, 24
  Coconut Rice, 170
  Wild Mushroom Risotto, 121
Rise-and-Shine Smoothie, 189
Romantic Picnic menu, 234
Rum
  Mojitos, 225
  Rum-Spiked Coconut Tapioca, 260
  Strawberry Daiquiris, 223

S

Salad dressings. *See also* Vinaigrettes
  Caesar Dressing, 44
  Taco-Ranch Dressing, 97
  tips for, 84
Salads
  Arugula with Cranberries, Cambozola, Walnuts, and Raspberry Vinaigrette, 89
  Asian Spinach Salad with Hoisin-Glazed Salmon, 93

Butter Lettuce with Mango, Goat Cheese, and Mighty Mint Vinaigrette, 83
Caesar Salad with Lemon-Pepper Shrimp, 96
Chinese Chicken Salad, 257
combinations for, 85
Confetti Coleslaw, 92
Green Beans, Beets, and Goat Cheese with Sherry Vinaigrette, 88
Mexican Chicken Salad with Taco-Ranch Dressing, 97
Orzo Salad with Lemon, Feta, and Pine Nuts, 94
Red Leaf Lettuce with Grapes, Blue Cheese, Pecans, and Balsamic Vinaigrette, 86
Summer Tomato Stacks, 91
tips for, 84
Salmon
  Asian Spinach Salad with Hoisin-Glazed Salmon, 93
  Salmon with Honey-Mustard Glaze, 128
  Smoked Salmon Platter, 66
Salsa, 24
  Mango Salsa, 141
  Roasted Red Pepper Salsa, 135
Salt, 24
Sangria, Citrusy, 228
Satay, Chicken, 64
Sauces
  Alfredo, 20
  barbecue, 20
  Champagne-Cream Sauce, 124–25
  Chocolate Sauce, 214
  "Gussied-Up" Marinara Sauce, 36
  hoisin, 22
  Hollandaise Sauce, 175–76
  marinara, 22
  Peanut Sauce, 24, 46
  Pesto, 48
  soy, 24
  Summertime Marinara Sauce, 37
  Sweet-and-Sour Sauce, 113
  Tabasco, 25
  Tahini-Ginger Dipping Sauce, 47
  Worcestershire, 25
Sausage
  Better Than Grandma's Meat Loaf, 117

Classic Lasagna, 103
Sausage and Cheddar Cheese Strata, 178
Sausage and Roasted Garlic Stuffing, 161
Stuffed Bell Peppers, 117
Texas Chili with All the Fixin's, 114
Sauza Margaritas, 222
Scallops, Linguine with Spinach, Bacon, and, 124–25
Sherry-Spiked French Onion Soup, 82
Shhh, Don't Tell—Chocolate Fudge Birthday Cake!, 195–96
Shortbread Sweethearts, 210
Shortcakes d'Amour, Strawberry, 197–98
Shrimp
  Caesar Salad with Lemon-Pepper Shrimp, 96
  Green Curry with Shrimp, 256
  Pasta with Pesto, Shrimp, and Sweet 100s, 126
  Thai-Style Corn Soup with Shrimp and Green Curry, 81
Silken Chocolate Tart, 203
Smoothie, Rise-and-Shine, 189
Snow Pea, Pork, and Bell Pepper Stir-Fry, 256
Soups
  Chicken, Chipotle, and Tortilla Soup, 254
  Chicken Soup for Your Soul Mate, 72
  Creamy Mushroom Soup with Brie Crostini, 73
  Mrs. Birdsong's Cabbage Soup, 76–77
  Roasted Butternut Squash Soup, 79
  Sherry-Spiked French Onion Soup, 82
  Summer Garden Gazpacho, 74
  Thai-Style Corn Soup with Shrimp and Green Curry, 81
Soy sauce, 24
Spices, 26
Spinach
  Asian Spinach Salad with Hoisin-Glazed Salmon, 93
  Linguine with Scallops, Spinach, and Bacon, 124–25
  Spinach with Raisins and Pine Nuts, 153
  Stuffed Chicken Parmesan, 252

Spirits, 24
Squash Soup, Roasted Butternut, 79
Stocks
    Chicken Stock, 30
    Vegetable Stock, 31
Stovetop Macaroni and Cheese, 116
Strata, Sausage and Cheddar
    Cheese, 178
Strawberries
    Chocolate Fondue, 258
    Rise-and-Shine Smoothie, 189
    Strawberry Daiquiris, 223
    Strawberry Shortcakes d'Amour,
        197–98
    Yogurt-Granola Parfaits, 186
Stuffing, Sausage and Roasted Garlic, 161
Sugar, 25
Summer Garden Gazpacho, 74
Summer Seated Dinner menu, 247
Summertime Marinara Sauce, 37
Summer Tomato Stacks, 91
Super Bowl Party menu, 238
Sweet-and-Sour Brisket, 113
Sweet-and-Sour Sauce, 113
Sweet Corn with Jalapeño Essence, 155
Sweet Peas with Red Onion and Mint, 158
Sweet Potatoes with Praline Topping,
    167

T
Tabasco Sauce, 25
Taco-Ranch Dressing, 97
Tahini-Ginger Dipping Sauce, 47
Tapenade, 20
Tapioca
    about, 25
    Rum-Spiked Coconut Tapioca, 260
Tarts
    Caramelized Onion, Gruyère, and
        Olive Tarts, 61
    Nectarine Tarts for Two, 207
    Silken Chocolate Tart, 203
Tequila
    Sauza Margaritas, 222
Texas Chili with All the Fixin's, 114
Thai-Style Corn Soup with Shrimp and
    Green Curry, 81
Thanksgiving menu, 242
Tomatoes

Bow Tie Pasta with Asparagus, Sun-
    Dried Tomatoes, and Boursin, 122
canned, 21
Chicken, Chipotle, and Tortilla Soup,
    254
Frittata with Sun-Dried Tomatoes,
    Cream Cheese, and Basil, 177
Goat Cheese, Sun-Dried Tomato,
    and Pesto Torta, 62
Mrs. Birdsong's Cabbage Soup,
    76–77
Pasta with Pesto, Shrimp, and Sweet
    100s, 126
Roasted Tomato Pie, 160
Summer Garden Gazpacho, 74
Summertime Marinara Sauce, 37
Summer Tomato Stacks, 91
sun-dried, 25
Texas Chili with All the Fixin's, 114
Torta, Goat Cheese, Sun-Dried
Tomato, and Pesto, 62
Tortilla chips
    Chicken, Chipotle, and Tortilla Soup,
        254
    Mexican Chicken Salad with Taco-
        Ranch Dressing, 97
Tortillas
    Grilled London Broil Fajitas, 147–48
    warming, 148
Triple-Decker Pound Cake with
    Raspberries and Lemon Glaze, 258
Tuna, 25
    Grilled Tuna with Soy-Ginger Glaze,
        131
    Tuna with White Beans, Artichokes,
        and Black Olive Tapenade, 253
Turkey
    carving, 106
    Holiday Turkey, 137–38
    tips for, 138

U
Unbelievable Banana Bread, 188
Utensils, 16

V
Valentine's Day menu, 239
Vanilla, 25, 201
Vegetables. See also individual
        vegetables
    Crudités with Green Onion–Mint
        Dip, 57
    Roast Chicken and Vegetables for
        Two, 105–6
    seasonal, 263–65
    Summer Garden Gazpacho, 74
    Vegetable Stock, 31
Very Vanilla Cheesecake, 200–201
Vinaigrettes
    Balsamic Vinaigrette, 45
    Mighty Mint Vinaigrette, 45
    Raspberry Vinaigrette, 89
Vinegar, 20, 25
Vodka
    Classic Martinis, 226
    Cosmopolitans, 225
    Mary's Bloody Marys, 229
    Vodka-Spiked Lemonade with Red
        Rocks, 226

W
Walnuts
    Arugula with Cranberries,
        Cambozola, Walnuts, and
        Raspberry Vinaigrette, 89
    toasted, 188
    Unbelievable Banana Bread, 188
Whiskey Sour Slush, Great Robert's, 227
Wild Mushroom Risotto, 121
Wild Rice with Dried Cranberries,
    Green Onions, and Pecans, 169
Wine. See also Champagne
    Citrusy Sangria, 228
    vinegar, 25
Worcestershire sauce, 25

Y
Yeast, 25
Yogurt
    Rise-and-Shine Smoothie, 189
    Yogurt-Granola Parfaits, 186

TABLE OF EQUIVALENTS

The exact equivalents in the following tables have been rounded for convenience.

LIQUID/DRY MEASURES

U.S.	METRIC
¼ teaspoon	1.25 milliliters
½ teaspoon	2.5 milliliters
1 teaspoon	5 milliliters
1 tablespoon (3 teaspoons)	15 milliliters
1 fluid ounce (2 tablespoons)	30 milliliters
¼ cup	60 milliliters
⅓ cup	80 milliliters
½ cup	120 milliliters
1 cup	240 milliliters
1 pint (2 cups)	480 milliliters
1 quart (4 cups, 32 ounces)	960 milliliters
1 gallon (4 quarts)	3.84 liters
1 ounce (by weight)	28 grams
1 pound	454 grams
2.2 pounds	1 kilogram

LENGTH

U.S.	METRIC
⅛ inch	3 millimeters
¼ inch	6 millimeters
½ inch	12 millimeters
1 inch	2.5 centimeters

OVEN TEMPERATURE

FAHRENHEIT	CELSIUS	GAS
250	120	½
275	140	1
300	150	2
325	160	3
350	180	4
375	190	5
400	200	6
425	220	7
450	230	8
475	240	9
500	260	10